Mass Media
and the Popular Arts

Fredric Rissover
Assistant Professor of English
Meramec Community College

David C. Birch
Instructor in English
Formerly of Meramec Community College

MASS MEDIA AND THE POPULAR ARTS

McGRAW-HILL BOOK COMPANY

New York   St. Louis   San Francisco   Düsseldorf   Kuala Lumpur   London
Mexico   Montreal   New Delhi   Panama   Rio de Janeiro   Singapore   Sydney   Toronto

Mass Media
and the Popular Arts

           90 MAMB 798765

This book was set in Alphavers Book by University Graph-
ics, Inc., and printed on permanent paper and bound by
The Maple Press Company. The designer was Paula Tuerk.
The editing supervisor was Ellen Simon. Stuart Levine
supervised production.
Cover photograph by Paula Tuerk.

Acknowledgments

Edward Arthur, "The *Other* Side of the Mountain," *St. Louis Post-Dispatch,* April 18, 1969.
     By permission of the author.
Associated Press Newsfeatures, "Seek Smut? It Won't Motivate You, Headshrinkers Say."
     Copyright 1969 by The Associated Press Newsfeatures. Reprinted by permission.
James Baldwin, "Everybody's Protest Novel," from *Notes of a Native Son.* Copyright
     © 1949, 1955, by James Baldwin.
Betty Beale, column in the Washington, D.C., *Evening Star,* September 24, 1968. Copy-
     right 1968 by The Evening Star–The Sunday Star, Washington, D.C. Reprinted by
     permission.
Duane Bradley, "What Is News?" from *The Newspaper: Its Place in a Democracy* by
     Duane Bradley. Copyright © 1965 by Duane Bradley, by permission of Van Nostrand
     Reinhold Company.
Robert Christgau, "Soul Is Selling," from "Secular Music." *Esquire,* October 1967. © 1967
     by Esquire, Inc. Reprinted by permission of Esquire magazine.
Larry Cohen, "The New Film Audience," from "The New Film Audience: From Andy Hardy
     to Arlo Guthrie," in *Saturday Review,* December 27, 1969. Copyright 1969 by Satur-
     day Review, Inc. Reprinted by permission.
Norman Cousins, "Science, Education and the Enjoyment of Living," from "Art, Adrenalin,
     and the Enjoyment of Living," in *Saturday Review,* April 20, 1968. Copyright 1968
     by Saturday Review, Inc. Reprinted by permission.
Harvey Cox, "The Playboy and Miss America," from *The Secular City.* Copyright © by
     Harvey Cox, 1965. Reprinted with the permission of The Macmillan Co.
Robert E. Dallos, "Growing Influence of Black Radio," from "Black Radio Stations Send
     Soul and Service to Millions." *The New York Times,* November 11, 1968. Copyright
     © 1968 by The New York Times Company. Reprinted by permission.

Contents by Media and Art Forms

P87
Rs

Selections which concern more than one of the mass media and popular arts are listed here in the additional units to which they relate.

Contents by Media Art Forms

Contents by Social Themes

Mass Appeal and the Consumer Economy

Politics and Campaigning

Propaganda and News Slanting

Sex and Sexual Identity

The purpose of *Mass Media and the Popular Arts* is to encourage freshmen and sophomores to investigate, evaluate, and appreciate more fully the workings of the mass media and the popular arts and to recognize how these media and art forms daily influence them and their society. These studies, which clearly have great relevance to students, have been too long neglected in our schools, or have been touched upon only lightly, or have been relegated to upper division college courses and graduate seminars.

When we began to teach a new course in mass communication at Meramec Community College a few years ago, we discovered as we looked for a textbook that no anthology in print particularly suited the needs of our students. The few volumes we could find dealt with the subject, or parts of it, on a level of sophistication suited only for college upperclassmen or graduate students. Therefore, we set about compiling an anthology geared to the interests and abilities of students at the junior college level. We made special efforts to serve these students.

First, we compiled a wide variety of selections which we thought would interest students and whose style and arguments students can readily follow. A few more sophisticated selections—such as James Baldwin's "Everybody's Protest Novel"—are included for the more advanced students who might like to read them or for the instructor to present in class. And we employed many ads, cartoons, and photographs which illustrate and underline important points in the written selections.

Second, we chose selections which are current or which have application to current culture. Old radio programs, silent movies, or popular music from Tin Pan Alley, for example, are not included.

Third, we arranged our selections clearly by media and art forms, facilitating their study in generic units. However, we have also included an additional thematic contents to encourage consideration of significant social and cultural issues related to mass media and popular arts.

Fourth, we followed each selection with a list of specific points to help the student locate and analyze important ideas and details and to provide the bases for class discussions or short writing assignments. Following each unit within the anthology we also provide a list of broader topics for investigation, discussion, and writing. A selected bibliography to encourage further investigation appears at the end of the book.

We hope that this anthology will prove useful in the many new courses in communication and mass media which are appearing in schools in increasing numbers. For such courses we expect this book to supplement class examination of the media and the popular art forms themselves and not substitute for it. This book should help to explain how the media and art forms have developed, how they function, and how they reflect and affect society. It should also help to raise questions and encourage students to do their own investigating. We hope that *Mass Media and the Popular Arts* may offer interesting reading in other courses, too—composition, journalism, and sociology, for example—where it can suggest topics for discussion and writing, writing models, and insights into an important area of our culture.

However this anthology may be used, in whatever courses, we hope that both students and teachers will find it stimulating and enjoyable.

We want to express our appreciation to our colleagues and students at Meramec Community College for their encouragement and their help. Special thanks go to Mrs. Diane Birch and to our colleagues and friends Dennis L. Focht, C. J. Zander, Mrs. Jean Zander, and Dale Dufer for their suggestions and contributions. Thanks are due also to Mrs. Virginia Hagebush, Mrs. Martha Newman, and Mrs. Margaret Peterson of the Meramec library staff for their help in locating selections and tracking down sources, and to Mrs. Delores Lenger, Miss Jenny Lee, and Miss Kristina Wehrle for their help in typing manuscript and correspondence. We dedicate this book to all our friends, colleagues, and students who have contributed so generously to our education in this exciting subject.

Fredric Rissover

David C. Birch

We have only to imagine life without newspapers, magazines, paperback books, phonograph records, radio, television, or movies to recognize how the mass media and popular art forms have become a necessary part of our lives. Obviously, anything so important to us as this ever-present source of information, stimulation, and sometimes hypnotism should be understood as thoroughly as possible. Therefore, we owe it to ourselves to examine how the mass media and the popular arts work and how they affect us, rather than simply assimilating them in a semiconscious trance.

Mass media and popular arts are both concerned with communication—transmitting information, ideas, or experiences—from one or more senders to one or more receivers. Communications media are the tools, instruments, or materials which people use to transmit information or experience.

Mass communication involves the transmission of information to many receivers simultaneously, although the definition of "many" changes with the times. When a politician a hundred years ago addressed a public meeting of five hundred voters, he felt that he was engaging in mass communication. When a politican nowadays speaks to a group of the same size, he considers it personal contact because a public address system would allow him to communicate with thousands of voters and with a spot on television he would reach millions simultaneously.

Mass communication media, usually called simply "mass media," are the tools, instruments, or materials which allow the sender of information to contact large numbers of receivers simultaneously. For American Indians of a hundred years ago, a signal drum or a signal fire was a mass medium. When we speak of mass media now, we refer to mechanical and electronic devices such as printing presses, cameras, projectors, transmitters, record players, radios, television sets, and audio- and videotape machines which enable communications with thousands or millions of people at a time. The mass media discussed in this anthology include print, photography, film, sound recording, radio, and television.

On the other hand, art involves a kind of communication which has form and beauty and which is intended to evoke pleasure. Instead of existing primarily to achieve a practical result, art is designed to be a meaningful experience in itself. By "popular art" usually we mean art which appeals to large groups of people within a culture simultaneously. In this age of mass media, "large groups of people" often means "millions of people." The popular arts make their widespread appeal because they usually involve subjects of wide interest which can be understood readily by the majority of people. Rock music with its clear beat and its easy-to-follow melodies, is a good example. Nearly everyone, even those who would prefer to hear something else, can easily understand it. A symphonic work by Copland or Stravinsky, on the other hand, appreciated by only a fraction of the general public, cannot be considered popular art. It is difficult, however, to make a precise distinction between what is popular art and what is not. Some works of art which were popular when originally produced, such as Shakespeare's plays and Dickens's novels, have passed the test of time and are now considered "fine art." Conversely, much of Tschaikovsky's music, once enjoyed by a relatively small segment of society, has become through the media of radio, phonograph records, and movie sound tracks as popular as some hit songs. The popular arts considered in this anthology include advertising, journalism, cartoons, radio and television shows, photographs and motion pictures, popular fiction, and popular music.

With regard to any mass medium or popular art form, two principal considerations must be kept in mind. First, how does the medium transmit its information or the art form achieve its effects? Second, how do the media and art forms, separately or in various combinations, influence or reflect the ideas and taste of the public?

In examining and evaluating the popular arts, we should be aware of the influences which the mass media have upon them. Radio, for example, has tended to encourage popular music that is homogenized and easy to swallow, whereas the record player, and particularly long playing records, has tended to stimulate an appreciation for more subtle and complex popular music that can be listened to pleasurably many times. Similarly, a certain news event reported in a newspaper article sometimes appears quite differently in a magazine feature and quite differently again on a television news broadcast. In this respect, the mass media operate like different camera lenses with different combinations of clear focus and distortion. To evaluate what we see through these lenses, we must understand how they affect the images they transmit to us.

We should also be aware of the ways that the popular arts are influenced by the attempts of writers, speakers, sponsors, and others to reach as large an audience as they can in as brief a time as possible. The political candidate speaking to small groups with particular interests will present speeches which treat these interests in detail and which avoid subjects that might be boring or offensive. But the political candidate speaking to a mass audience on radio or television must try to interest everyone and offend no one. Consequently, he will praise freedom, law and order, and equal opportunity while condemning communism, crime in the streets, and discrimination—in other words, he will say practically nothing. Similarly, television sponsors whose main concern is to reach millions of viewers whom they see as potential customers will usually back the programs aimed at the lowest common level of public understanding and interest. If we do not recognize these facts, we can be led to believe we are being informed when we are being merely patronized or pacified.

For examining or evaluating mass media and popular arts, some questions such as these can serve as a kind of critical checklist:

1. To what audience does the communication or work of art seem to appeal? How well does it succeed?

2. What seems to be the apparent purpose of the work? What immediate effect does it achieve?

3. What basic human needs or desires are appealed to? What image is appealed to? Is any fixed response called for?

4. What persuasion or propaganda devices are employed? How well?

5. What attitudes toward the subject and the audience are expressed openly or implied?

6. What social, moral, or artistic value does the work have?

7. What is the relationship between the form or style and the subject? What is the relationship between the medium and the subject? How effective are these relationships?

The selections in this anthology can help us in several ways to ask and to answer questions such as these.

First, some of the selections serve as a guide to the ways in which particular media transmit their information and the ways in which particular art forms achieve their effects. These selections should be read in preparation for or along with an examination of the medium or art form itself. The selections in this volume are intended to supplement examinations of the media and art forms, not to supplant them. In some cases, of course, as with the song lyrics, ads, photographs, and cartoons, this volume provides some examples of the art forms.

Second, some of the selections provide information on the ways the various mass media and popular arts affect the ideas and tastes and even the morality, politics, and economy of our society. These selections may be read while the media are being examined or after.

Third, the Points to Consider following each selection, the Topics for Investigation, Discussion, and Writing at the end of each unit, and the thematic table of contents at the beginning of the volume suggest ways that the interrelationships of the mass media and popular arts can be observed and ways in which the study of these influential elements of our society can lay the groundwork for considerations of stereotypes and images, pornography and violence, protest and criticism, and other such socially significant issues.

Most of the art forms and commentary presented in this volume are relatively recent—written, drawn, or photographed within the last ten years or so—because popular art tends to change rapidly in some respects, and some popular art loses its meaning or effectiveness with the passage of time. Still, a few older articles have been included to show that while certain qualities of popular art change, others remain surprisingly constant and that no matter how much popular art forms change, they continue to reflect society and to affect society in similar ways. The heroes of "grade B" movies—both in movie houses and on TV—still act and are reacted to like the hero of Saroyan's "Love, Death, Sacrifice, and So Forth" (p. 195) first published in 1934. The California dream generated by the mass media existed in 1939 when Nathanael West examined it in *The Day of the Locust* (p. 199), and it remains with us today. The heroine of the melodramatic best seller that Edmund Wilson ambushed in 1946 (p. 225) is still around—with various names and in or out of various costumes—in current best sellers, women's magazines, and movies. "Everybody's Protest Novel," written by James Baldwin in 1949 (p. 239), could easily be expanded today to include everybody's protest song or everybody's protest film.

The study of mass media and popular arts in high schools and colleges is relatively new, and a few conservatives still doubt its appropriateness in a general liberal arts curriculum. Yet more and more schools are recognizing its value as a study in itself and as a key to other studies relevant to contemporary culture. In time, courses in films, cartoons, or popular music may be as common as courses in literature, art, or music appreciation. If such courses are not permitted to grow stagnant or overly abstract, they will surely become some of our most useful and enjoyable studies.

Personality Packages

Erich Fromm
The Art of Loving, 1956

. . . Modern capitalism needs men who co-operate smoothly and in large numbers; who want to consume more and more; and whose tastes are standardized and can be easily influenced and anticipated. It needs men who feel free and independent, not subject to any authority or principle or conscience—yet willing to be commanded, to do what is expected of them, to fit into the social machine without friction; who can be guided without force, led without leaders, prompted without aim—except the one to make good, to be on the move, to function, to go ahead.

What is the outcome? Modern man is alienated from himself, from his fellow men, and from nature. He has been transformed into a commodity, experiences his life forces as an investment which must bring him the maximum profit obtainable under existing market conditions. Human relations are essentially those of alienated automatons, each basing his security on staying close to the herd, and not being different in thought, feeling or action. While everybody tries to be as close as possible to the rest, everybody remains utterly alone, pervaded by the deep sense of insecurity, anxiety and guilt which always results when human separateness cannot be overcome. Our civilization offers many palliatives[1] which help people to be consciously unaware of this aloneness: first of all the strict routine of bureaucratized, mechanical work, which helps people to remain unaware of their most fundamental human desires, of the longing for transcendence and unity. Inasmuch as the routine alone does not succeed in this, man overcomes his unconscious despair by the routine of amusement, the passive consumption of sounds and sights offered by the amusement industry; furthermore by the satisfaction of buying ever new things, and soon exchanging them for others. Modern man is actually close to the picture Huxley describes in his *Brave New World:* well fed, well clad, satisfied sexually, yet without self, without any except the most superficial contact with his fellow men, guided by the slogans which Huxley formulated so succinctly, such as: "When the individual feels, the community reels"; or "Never put off till tomorrow the fun you can have today," or, as the crowning statement: "Everybody is happy nowadays." Man's happiness today consists in "having fun." Having fun lies in the satisfaction of consuming and "taking in" commodities, sights, food, drinks, cigarettes, people, lectures, books, movies—all are consumed, swallowed. The world is one great object for our appetite, a big apple, a big bottle, a big breast; we are the sucklers, the eternally expectant ones, the hopeful ones—and the eternally disappointed ones.

---

[1] Palliatives are ways of reducing the painful consequences of a problem without really solving the problem.

Our character is geared to exchange and to receive, to barter and to consume; everything, spiritual as well as material objects, becomes an object of exchange and of consumption.

The situation as far as love is concerned corresponds, as it has to by necessity, to this social character of modern man. Automatons cannot love; they can only exchange their "personality packages" and hope for a fair bargain. . . .

POINTS TO CONSIDER

Erich Fromm: Personality Packages

1. Why does modern man often feel alienated from himself and from other men as well as from nature and from society as a whole?

2. In what kind of behavior does modern man engage to help him feel more secure? What kinds of security are offered by society?

3. What is the difference between "having fun" and "being happy"?

4. What are "personality packages"? Consider as you read the selections in this book on various mass media and popular art forms how they often tend to fill up personality packages rather than communicate to individual personalities. Why do you think this is so? Do you note any exceptions? What are they?

PART ONE

ADVERTISING

Advertising is one of the most insistently present, most complex, most sophisticated, and most influential of popular art forms because, of course, it has become such an important part of our economy. Advertising surrounds us, inside our homes as well as outside: it appeals to us from signs and billboards, magazines and newspapers, radio and television, labels and packages. The media of print, photography, electric lights, radio and television broadcasting, and even, unfortunately, the telephone, transmit it. It employs nearly every art form conceivable. The sophistication of modern advertising enables it to appeal to almost all of our basic physical and emotional needs and weaknesses—those we recognize and those we don't—on conscious and unconscious levels. It reflects and affects our attitudes and our values concerning love and sex, family life, health, business, society, politics, and practically every other aspect of our lives. Its methods have helped to shape modern journalism, broadcasting, and education, as well as business and politics. Advertising is an appropriate subject, therefore, with which to begin an examination of mass media and the popular arts and the ways in which they mirror and influence our society.

The Ad and the Id

Vance Packard

Harper's Bazaar, August 1957

The early nineteen fifties witnessed the beginnings of a revolution in American advertising: Madison Avenue became conscious of the *unconscious.* Evidence had piled up that the responses of consumers to the questions of market researchers were frequently unreliable—in other words, that people often don't want what they say they want. Some years ago, for instance, a great automobile company committed one of the costliest blunders in automobile history through reliance on the old-style "nose counting" methods. Direct consumer surveys indicated that people wanted a sensible car in tune with the times—without frills, maneuverable and easy to park. A glance at today's cars—elongated, fish-finned and in riotous technicolor—shows how misleading were the results of the survey. Errors of this sort convinced manufacturers and advertisers that they must take into account the irrationality of consumer behavior—that they must carry their surveys into the submerged areas of the human mind. The result is a strange and rather exotic phenomenon entirely new to the market place—the use of a kind of mass psychoanalysis to guide campaigns of persuasion. The ad is being tailored to meet the needs of the id.[1]

The so-called "depth approach" to selling problems is known as motivational research, or simply M.R. Social scientists by the hundreds have been recruited for this massive exploration of the consumer's psyche, and hundreds of millions of dollars are being spent on it. Two-thirds of the nation's leading advertising agencies have been using the depth approach (along with the more conventional methods), and one major agency resorts to it for every single product it handles, to detect possible hidden appeals and resistances.

A number of factors have contributed to the rapid growth of motivational research. By the mid-nineteen fifties, American producers were achieving a fabulous output. This meant that we must be persuaded to buy more and more to keep the wheels of the economy turning. As the president of National Sales Executives exclaimed: "Capitalism is dead—consumerism is king!" Another formidable obstacle that faced the merchandisers in our advanced technology was the increasing similarity of competing products. While it might still be possible for people of discrimination to distinguish between brands of cigarettes, whiskey, detergent, and so on, it became increasingly difficult to teach them to do so on any rational basis. Still, loyalty to a particular brand had to be created, and it was

---

[1] The id in Freudian psychology is the part of our mind which generates our most basic animal urges and impulses.

done in many instances by "building a personality"—playful, conservative or showy—into the brand. In this way, Procter and Gamble's image makers have projected a living personification for each of their brands of soap (Ivory is mother and daughter on a sort of pedestal of purity; Camay a glamorous woman), and a Chicago chain of food stores decided that the image which would give it the edge over its competitors should have "the traits we like in our friends"—generosity, cleanliness, etc.

What the depth researchers are looking for, of course, are the hidden *whys* of our behavior—why many people are intimidated by banks, why men are drawn into showrooms by convertibles but emerge with sedans, why women go into a trance-like state at the supermarket and why junior likes noisy cereal. The principal tools of M.R. are the techniques of psychiatry—interviews "in depth" (but without the couch, which might make the consumer guinea pig wary); Rorschach (ink blot) tests; stress tests, in which the rate at which you blink your eyes is recorded by hidden cameras; lie detectors; word association tests; and finally the group interview, which, surprisingly, has the effect of breaking down inhibitions. (One candid statement prompts another and presently a roomful of people are freely discussing laxatives, deodorants, weight reducers and athlete's foot.)

The efforts of the persuaders to probe our everyday habits for hidden meanings are often fascinating purely for the revelations—some amusing, some rather appalling—which they offer us about ourselves. The average American likes to think of himself as a rugged individualist and, above all, a thoughtful, hard-headed consumer of the products of American enterprise. But in the findings of the motivational researchers, we are apt to emerge as comic actors in a genial if twitchy Thurberian world—bundles of daydreams, secret yearnings and curious emotional quirks.

In learning to sell to our subconscious, the persuaders soon discovered unsuspected areas of tension and guilt. Self-indulgent and easy-does-it products are a significant sector of the total American market, yet Americans, it seems, have in them a larger streak of Puritanism than is generally recognized. For instance, the hidden attitude of women toward labor-saving devices is decidedly surprising. Working wives can accept them, but the full-time housewife is liable to feel that they threaten her importance and creativity. The research director of an ad agency sadly explained the situation as follows: "If you tell the housewife that by using your washing machine, drier or dishwasher she can be free to play bridge, you're dead!—the housewife today already feels guilty about the fact that she is not working as hard as her mother. Instead, you should emphasize that appliances free her to have more time with her children." Makers of ready-mixes and foods with "built in maid service" ran into the same sort of problem. In the early days, the packages promised to take over all the work, but wives were not grateful for this boon. A leading motivational analyst, James Vicary, has stated the reason. Cake-making, he finds, is steeped in creative symbolism for women—it is, in fact, "a traditional acting out of the birth of a child." This feeling shows up in our folklore in such jokes as the one which says that brides whose cakes fall obviously can't produce a baby yet. (A Chicago analyst has noted that gardening, too, is a symbolic "pregnancy activity" and thus is particularly popular with women past the child-bearing age who need creative outlets.)

Subconscious tensions about food also rose to plague the makers of Jello a few years ago. Jello had become known to millions of households as a quick dessert, simple and shirt-sleeved in character. Then the ad-men, trying to make it more captivating, started showing it in beautiful, layered, lavishly decorated concoctions. The ads were not a success, and the Institute for Motivational Research was able to tell why. Many women, looking at these feats of fussy preparation, wondered if they could duplicate them, and often concluded that if they had to go to all that work, they would much rather make their own dessert without someone standing over their shoulder telling them how to do it. The Jello people, alerted, went back to showing simple mounds of the stuff, and added to their attraction largely by such simple devices as fairy-tale drawings.

The whole area of food, in fact, would seem to be booby-trapped with hidden problems for women. Mr. Vicary noticed, for instance, that young wives in particular tended to avoid the smaller, clerk-manned grocery stores in favor of the supermarket. He was able to isolate the explanation: newly married women are more ignorant about food than older women and are afraid the clerk will find them out. A Midwestern grocery chain found that this state of fearfulness centered around butcher clerks in particular. Faced with a discussion of cuts of meat, where their lack of knowledge is often profound, many women feel anxiety. After "depth-probing" the situation, the chain began training its butchers to exhibit extraordinary patience and garrulity[2] with younger women, and the strategy has paid off by turning the chain into a haven for innocents.

Supermarkets, on the other hand, are so tension-free as to make many women fall into a state bordering on hypnotic trance. Anxious to trace the reasons for the enormous rise in so-called impulse buying in American supermarkets (today seven out of ten purchases in supermarkets are made on impulse—the shopping list of old is becoming obsolete), Mr. James Vicary made a remarkable test. He had assumed that some special psychology must be at work to put women in an impulsive state when they got into supermarkets, possibly the tension of confronting so many products and having to make rapid decisions. Since our blink rate is one rough index of our inner tension, Mr. Vicary installed hidden cameras to record the blink rate of women shoppers. Normally, we blink about thirty-two times a minute, and he expected to see the rate go up as the ladies faced their decisions. Nothing of the sort occurred. The rate went down, down, down to a subnormal fourteen blinks a minute for the average woman—a condition of hypnoidal trance. Many of the women collided with boxes or passed the whirring

[2] Garrulity is the practice of talking freely.

cameras without noticing them. But when they approached the checkout counters with their loaded carts, their blink rate would start rising back toward normal; and when they heard the bell of the cash register, the rate shot up to the abnormal figure of forty-five a minute, a symptom of acute anxiety. Mr. Vicary's explanation of the trance: the woman feels herself a queen in a fairyland filled with lovely, accessible objects, unimaginable in former years and all whispering "buy me, buy me."

The calorie consciousness which swept the country, beginning a few years ago, created other psychological troubles for foodmakers. A number of brewing companies, who had thought to capitalize on the phenomenon, tried to outdo one another in plugging low-caloried beer, and for a time sales did go up. But M.R. hoisted warning flags. Dr. Ernest Dichter, head of the Institute for Motivational Research, warned that calorie consciousness is a sort of psychological penance. People go on diets because they are trying to punish themselves for past indulgence. Hence, low-calorie diets are not supposed to be pleasant. What the brewers were conveying in effect, was that real beer must be fattening and that low-calorie beer was somehow denatured. "Thus," said the Institute, "when a beer advertises itself as low in calories, the consumer reacts by feeling the beer has a poor taste." Perhaps this cautionary note was responsible for one brewer's recent clarion call: "Made by people who like beer for people who drink beer, and plenty of it!"

Another product which found its market temporarily constricted because of too much harping on calories was Ry-Krisp, which ran advertisements containing calorie tables and showing very slim people nibbling the wafers. Motivational analysts found that Ry-Krisp had developed for itself a self-punishment image as a food that was "good" for people—an image which drove away people not in a self-punishing mood. Corrective action was taken: in advertisements, Ry-Krisp began appearing with tempting foods and was described as delicious and festive. This more permissive approach nearly doubled sales in test areas.

Even in travel we have hidden anxieties which marketers find it profitable to take into account. A number of years ago, an airline became disturbed by the fact that so many passengers flew only when pressed for time, and it hired a conventional research firm to find out why. The simple answer came back that they didn't fly because they were afraid of being killed, but an intensive advertising campaign emphasizing safety yielded disappointing results. At last Dr. Dichter was called in. His answer, based on picture tests which encouraged potential travelers to imagine themselves involved in airline crashes, was different and astonishing. What the traveler feared was not death but a sort of posthumous embarrassment. The husband pictured his wife receiving the news and saying, "The damned fool, he should have gone by train." The obvious answer was to convince wives of the common sense of flying, which would bring their husbands home faster from business trips, and to get them in the air (to get their feet wet, as it were) with tempting family flying plans.

Still other subconscious fears, and not always the obvious ones, relate to money. Motivational studies have proved, for example, that it is not guilt about owing money which makes people hesitate to approach the bank for a loan. The fear is of the bank itself, which is seen as an angry father-figure who will disapprove of our untidy financial affairs. Many people would rather go to a loan company, in spite of the higher interest rate, simply because the moral tone associated with it is lower; in fact, there is a complete shift in moral dominance in which the borrower becomes a righteous fellow, temporarily forced into low company, and the higher cost of the loan is a small price to pay for such a changed view of ourselves. It is worth noting that a good many banks today are trying to mellow the stern image of themselves by removing the bars on teller windows, making wider use of glass fronts and staging folksy little exhibits which depict them—at worst—as rather crusty but charming old gentlemen in Scotch hats.

It will surprise nobody to learn that sex plays an enormously important part in selling. But how it works *is* frequently surprising. Sex images have, of course, long been cherished by ad-makers, but in the depth approach sex takes on some extraordinary ramifications and subtleties. A classic example is the study of automobiles made by Dr. Dichter which became known as "Mistress Versus Wife"—a study responsible for the invention of the most successful new car style introduced to the American market for several years. Dealers had long been aware that a convertible in the window drew the male customer into the showroom. They also knew that he usually ended by choosing a four-door sedan. The convertible, said Dr. Dichter, had associations of youth and adventure—it was symbolic of the mistress. But the sedan was the girl one married because she would make a good wife and mother. How could an automobile symbolically combine the appeals of mistress and wife? The answer was the celebrated hardtop, which Dr. Dichter's organization takes full credit for inspiring.

A company advertising a home permanent wave ran into another sexual problem, which was solved by M.R. They had thought it would be a brilliant idea to picture a mother and daughter with identical hairdos captioned: "A Double Header Hit with Dad." Wives, interviewed at the conscious level, said they didn't object at all to the implied idea of competition for the husband-father's admiration, but the company was still apprehensive—rightly, as it turned out. Depth interviews revealed that women would indeed deeply resent the "hit with dad" theme, and it was hastily dropped.

As for the American male, he stands in equal need of sexual reassurance, particularly as women continue to invade the traditional strongholds. The fact that cigar makers have been enjoying their greatest prosperity in twenty years has been credited by many to the man-at-bay, and at least one ad agency disagrees with the efforts of the Cigar Institute of America to draw women into the picture. This agency, puzzled by the failure of a campaign which had pictured a smiling woman offering cigars to a group of men, ordered a depth survey to uncover the reason. The conclusion was that men enjoy cigars precisely because they are objectionable to women; nor is the man sincere who politely asks if the ladies mind his lighting up. As the head of the agency put it: "He knows . . . he is going to stink up the room."

Motivational analysis has even discovered certain products to be sexually "maladjusted," and it is responsible for several spectacular cases of planned transvestitism.[3] When the cancer scare drove millions of men to try filter tips, the makers of Marlboro cigarettes decided to cash in by changing the sex of a cigarette originally designed for women. The ads began to show a series of rugged males, engaged in virile occupations and all of them, by an extraordinary coincidence, tattooed. The tattoo motif puzzled a good many people, since the tattoo is a common phenomenon among delinquents in reformatories. Marlboro, however, decided it was exactly what was needed to give its men a virile and "interesting past" look—the same look arrived at, by other means, in the one-eyed man in the Hathaway shirt.

When Lloyd Warner published his book, *Social Class in America,* in 1948, it created a respectful stir in academic circles; but in later years it was to create an even greater one among merchandisers. Like David Riesman in his classic, *The Lonely Crowd,* or Russell Lynes, whose famous dissection of high-, middle- and low-brows charted the social significance of such items as tossed salad and rye whiskey, Warner defined social classes less in terms of wealth and power than criteria of status, and merchandisers have begun to give considerable thought to his conclusions. Burleigh Gardener, for example, founder of the M.R. firm of Social Research, Inc., has taken Warner's concepts as his guiding thesis. Social Research has put a class label on many sorts of house-furnishings: the solid color carpet, it appears, is upper class; the "knickknack" shelf lower class; Venetian blinds are upper middle class.

Chicago's Color Research Institute (a psychoanalytically minded group) ran into some of the intricacies of class structure when it was asked to design two candy boxes, one intended to sell to lower class buyers at $1.95, the other to an upper class clientele at $3.50. The Institute's researches led it to a curious recommendation: the box for the cheaper candy would be in vermilion metal tied with a bright blue ribbon, and it would have to cost fifty cents; the box for the expensive candy could be made of pale pink pasteboard at a cost of no more than nine cents. The reason? Candy-giving is an important rite in the lower class, and the girl is likely to treasure the box, whereas the upper class girl will ignore the box (the candy is what counts) and will probably throw it away.

Many advertising men have filled the air above their Madison Avenue rookeries with arguments over the validity and potency of M.R. And the researchers themselves have added to the confusion by disagreeing with each other's meth-

---

[3] Transvestitism is the wearing of clothes considered appropriate only for the opposite sex.

ods and results. Of more concern, however, to the average citizen are the possibilities for mass manipulation opened up by motivational research. Disturbing examples of such manipulation have, unfortunately, appeared in politics, industrial relations (a California engineering school boasts that its graduates are "custom-built men") and even in the church, where ministers are being advised how they can more effectively control their congregations. The manipulative approach to politics is not, of course, new—Machiavelli[4] was perfectly familiar with it. But the manipulation of the people by a tyrant is an infinitely simpler problem than that of dealing with the citizens of a free society, who can spurn your solicitations if they want to. Now, however, mass persuasion in this kind of situation has been greatly reinforced by the techniques of the symbol manipulators, who have drawn on Pavlov and his conditioned reflexes, Freud and his father images, Riesman and his concept of modern American voters as spectator-consumers of politics. In the 1956 election, both parties tried to "merchandise" their candidates by commercial marketing methods, using on billboards slogans of scientifically tested appeal, hammering out key messages until the public was saturation-bombed, and grooming their candidates to look "sincere" in front of the TV camera. As one advertising man put it: "I think of a man in a voting booth who hesitates between the two levers as if he were pausing between competing tubes of tooth paste in a drugstore. The brand that has made the highest penetration in his brain will win his choice."

What are the implications of all this persuasion in terms of morality? The social scientists and psychiatrists have a workable rationale for explaining their co-operation with, say, the merchandisers. They are broadening the world's knowledge of human behavior; and knowledge, as Alfred Whitehead has said, keeps no better than fish. But there remains the disturbing fact that by scientifically catering to the irrational, the persuaders are working toward a progressively less rational society. We may wonder if, in a few decades when it becomes technically feasible, we will be ripe for biocontrol, a brand new science for controlling mental processes, emotional reactions and sense perceptions by bio-electrical signals. Already, rats with full bellies have been made to feel ravenously hungry, and to feel fear when they had nothing to be afraid of. As one electronic engineer has said: "The ultimate achievement of biocontrol may be the control of man himself. . . . The controlled subjects would never be permitted to think as individuals. A few months after birth, a surgeon would equip each child with a socket mounted under the scalp and electrodes reaching selected areas of brain tissue. . . . The child's sensory perceptions and muscular activity could either be modified or completely controlled by bioelectric signals radiating from state-controlled transmitters." He added that the electrodes would cause no discomfort.

[4] Niccolo Machiavelli (1469–1527) was an Italian statesman and writer who advocated the elimination of morality from politics. A politician who is cunning or unscrupulous in his efforts to attain political objectives is often called machiavellian.

I'm sure the persuaders of 1957 would be appalled by such a prospect. Most of them are likeable, earnest men who just want to control us a little bit, to maneuver us into buying something that we may actually need. But when you start manipulating people, where exactly do you stop?

◪ POINTS TO CONSIDER ◪

Vance Packard: The Ad and the Id

1. What is motivational research or the "depth approach"? What needs was MR developed to fulfill?
2. What factors have contributed to the rapid growth of MR?
3. What are some of the investigative techniques which MR employs?
4. What interesting discoveries about consumer fears and motivations have the MR men made? For example:

    Why mustn't products be made to seem too easy or pleasant?
    Why do supermarkets play soft music?
    Why won't some people travel by air?
    Why do men like to smoke cigars?
    Why do married men admire convertibles but buy sedans?

5. What is meant by the term "image"? What are some current ads which make strong appeals to an image?
6. What do some men believe is a greater determiner of social status than wealth? How has this observation affected marketing?
7. What are some of the benefits to the public of MR? What are some of the dangers to the public of MR? What are the moral implications in the widespread use of MR?

Ad

Kenneth Fearing

WANTED: Men;
Millions of men are WANTED AT ONCE in a big new field;
NEW, TREMENDOUS, THRILLING, GREAT.

If you've ever been a figure in the chamber of horrors,
If you've ever escaped from the psychiatric ward,
If you thrill at the thought of throwing poison into wells, have heavenly
                    visions of people, by the thousands, dying in flames—

YOU ARE THE VERY MAN WE WANT
We mean business and our business is YOU
WANTED: A race of brand-new men.

Apply: Middle Europe;
No skill needed;
No ambition required; no brains wanted and no character allowed;

TAKE A PERMANENT JOB IN THE COMING PROFESSION
Wages: DEATH.

 POINTS TO CONSIDER

Kenneth Fearing: Ad

1. What is the job for which men are wanted? How do you learn this?
2. What ad techniques does Fearing use?
3. How does Fearing's use of ad techniques reveal his feeling about the subject on which he is commenting?

Pop Poem—2/29¢

Ronald Gross
Pop Poems, 1967

FOR ANDY WARHOL

makes old pans shine like new
burned-on scorch
greasy film
disappears in seconds

A New Utensil   If Product Or
Free If Brillo   Performance
Fails To Clean   Defective

Replacement or refund
to consumer

Contents Counted, Inspected, Mechanically Loaded to Insure Accuracy

On Notice, Any Shortages Promptly Replaced.

```
F   I   S        With pink polishing
O   N   H                               soap
R   S   I        Outdoors, Brillo
    T   N        whitens white
    A   E        walls, gets burned
    N            grease off grills
    T            5 Pads          5 PADS
```

Brilloisthesoappadthat'sreally
madetoshine.Containsenoughpink
polishingsoaptodoaraftofheavy
dutyjobs.Evenoldpanscansparkle
likenew.Ovens,greasybroilersclean
upfastwithBrillo.

TIP!	in Brillo	if you	As long as there's
The	will make the	let the suds	suds—there's
special	pads last	dry on the pad	no room
rust-resister	and last	between usings.	for rust.

Ronald Gross: Pop Poem—2/29¢

1. This poem is dedicated to Andy Warhol, the pop artist who became well known for his paintings of Campbell's soup cans and Brillo boxes. What is the similarity between what Warhol and other pop artists are telling us about society in their pictures and what Gross is telling us about society in his pop poem?

2. In what sense may a Campbell's soup can be considered a "work of art" or may the wording on a Brillo box be considered a "poem"? Do you agree with some critics that such art or poetry is really trivial or phony?

3. Why does Gross arrange the words and phrases on the page as he does?

4. Can you write some pop poems of your own based upon packages, signs, news articles, ad jingles and slogans, official forms, and the like? Do you think that writing a few such poems might make you more aware of any elements of popular culture?

Miltown Place, Or, Life with Sponsors

Marya Mannes
More in Anger, 1958

My family couldn't brush their teeth after every meal, but we had something more precious together. I guess you could call it "togetherness."

My mother and father did everything together, and so did we. I can't remember a single moment when there wasn't a family-size bottle of Coke on the indoor barbecue pit.

So many little scenes flash through my mind as I think of those years in Crestwood: my father, laughing through his smoke rings as he chortled, "Winston tastes good!"; Aunt Birdie, who came from Mobile, chirping roguishly "Lahk a cigarette should!"; my mother seeing my teen-age sister Shirley off to a dance with the heart-warming whisper: "Don't be half-safe!"

My mother was the most unforgetable character I had ever met. I see her now, rubbing her freshly ironed wash against her cheek and murmuring of its whiteness; or rushing to my father as he came home from work and crying, "Darling, have you heard the wonderful news? Professional laundries use *soap,* not detergents!" My mother had that kind of mind.

We children spent many childhood hours browsing through old *Reader's Digests.* "It's the small things that count," my father always used to say. Years later, in the isolation booths of jack-pot shows, we used to thank our stars for the rich background of knowledge those little old *Digests* gave us. Everyone said we sparkled.

Every Sunday we had Dean Pike and Norman Vincent Peale for dinner, and Mother used to make Kraft pizzas for them. They often remarked on her sealed-in goodness and creamy richness. Some people said it was Geritol, but we knew that it was her moral and spiritual values that made her like that.

"Never forget," she used to say when she sipped her calorie-free beer. "This is a friendly, freedom-loving nation."

The only sad note in those unforgettable years concerned my nearest brother, Prelvis. He lived in a dream world of his own. "I wonder," he would say, vacantly, "where the yellow went!" But he had great sweetness in him, and my mother was infinitely patient. Even when he ice-skated over the kitchen floor, she would merely run a mop over the wax and the tracks would disappear. "No rub, no wipe!" she would quip merrily as she rubbed and wiped.

The most unforgettable character I ever knew (next to Mother) was our family doctor, whom we called "Doc." Whenever any of us were sick, no matter what from, "Doc" would draw little pictures of our intestines and show us how fast Bufferin brought relief. (He was the fifth out of four doctors.)

Yet we were not without romance. I will never forget when Shirley married Bob and he gave her a set of flat silver. As she looked up into his eyes, fingering a salad fork, he said, with infinite tenderness, "This Regency pattern is another way of saying 'I love you.'" Putting on my Playtex "living gloves" to help Mother with the dishes, I yearned for a love like that. "With Joy," she comforted me, instinctively, "dishwashing is *almost* nice!"

Part of our togetherness in those days was the sharing of minds as well as hands, and, of course, the spirit. Each of us prayed before our respective tasks: Father before his board meeting, Mother before cooking, us children before exams. Every morning Mother read aloud from Mr. Peale's column in *Look,* and once a week Father read us the *Life* editorial, to set us straight. All of us kept up with Pearl Buck. And on Christmas Eve, we joined our voices to Bing Crosby's as he sang carols from Hollywood.

I will never forget when our world fell apart. It was the year when four out of five doctors said "Anxiety Is Good for You." This marked the end of an era.

My mother no longer rubs her cheek against her wash or lets something golden happen with Fluffo. She plays a bull fiddle and reads Henry Miller.[1]

My father wears hair shirts and corresponds with Simone de Beauvoir;[2] my sister Shirley and Bob got divorced after she put his Ike buttons in the Disposall, and Prelvis is waiting for Godot[3] in a degraded Southern town.

Miltown Place, the temple of togetherness, has been sold to the Society for the Propagation of the Failure.

And I? As I write, I am lying in a stupor from Wolfschmidt,[4] sucking my thumb.

 POINTS TO CONSIDER

Marya Mannes: Miltown Place

1. Where does the title, "Miltown Place," come from? In what ways is it an apt description of the manner in which the "family" lives?

2. How has the family acquired the attitudes and values by which it lives? What are some of these values? Is anything terribly wrong with a life like this? Why?

[1] Henry Miller is the author of books such as *Tropic of Cancer* which describe a style of life free from responsibility and inhibition.

[2] Simone de Beauvoir is a French writer who has examined the psychology and philosophy of feminine identity.

[3] *Waiting for Godot* is a play by Samuel Beckett in which two tramps spend their lives waiting for someone named Godot to arrive and give their lives direction and meaning, but Godot never comes.

[4] Wolfschmidt's is a frequently advertised brand of vodka.

3. What happens to the family in the end? What aspects of their existence remain unchanged? In what sense has nothing really changed for them?

4. Is Miltown Place a pure fantasy, a composite of advertising stereotypes, or is it an exaggeration of reality? Is it possible that many people are like the people in the family without being aware of it?

Love According to Madison Avenue

Morton M. Hunt
Horizon, November 1959

In studying the love life of the ancient Romans, I have been struck by the fact that some of the sharpest and most illuminating evidence comes not from weighty works of history but from wayward and trivial sources. A lustful *graffito* scratched on a marble column, palpitating for the scarred arms of a gladiator;[1] indecorous decorations on the bedroom walls of a seaside villa; a versified book of cosmetic recipes; a sentimental funeral oration carved on a huge tombstone—these are the real voices of the past.

It occurs to me, therefore, that in our own time the sociologists with their ponderous surveys, the psychologists with their dissecting analyses, and the cultural historians with their masses of documentation may be missing the truth and the essence of modern love. Perhaps those who write the contemporary equivalent of *graffiti* come closer. I suggest that the persons who do so are those who scribble on Madison Avenue—not on the building fronts, to be sure, but on typewriter paper, in air-conditioned cubicles in the well-carpeted offices of B. B. D. & O., K. & E., Y. & R., E. W. R. & R., and so on.[2]

Certainly they see a number of truths about American love that have never been reported in the scientific literature. For one thing, the ad men apparently perceive more clearly than anyone else just how deeply love has penetrated and

[1] Graffito is a statement written or scratched on the wall of a public place.
[2] These are the initials of some well-known national advertising agencies.

colored the ordinary routine of American life until a number of formerly nonerotic objects have become associated with the most tender scenes and the most romantic moments. Eating utensils, for example, are not thought by most cultural historians to have any love-value, and even the Freudians see symbolism only in the knife. But the ad men for Oneida silverware are more acute reporters of the local scene. In a recent ad in *Mademoiselle* they recorded the spontaneous love-dialogue of two young people examining a teaspoon at a store counter:

> She: It's a dream come true, Bob. . . . I thought we'd *never* find it. Now we could almost choose blindfolded—just by following our hearts.
> He: Looks as if *both* our hearts are set on "Lasting Spring"—it's a "forever thing," like our marriage!

Paolo and Francesca were moved by a poem, Tristan and Iseult by a potion, but with young lovers in America it is the sight of a four-piece place setting at $18 (plus Federal tax) that unlocks the gates of the heart.[3]

Similarly, it is the writers of fashion copy who see through the shadows and mists of native puritanism and recognize that the shoe, which traditionally has played no recognized part in American lovemaking, has recently acquired an aura of erotic value such as it has not had since Solomon, or whoever wrote the *Song of Solomon,* sang the finest bit of advertising copy yet: "How beautiful are thy feet with shoes, O prince's daughter!" In a comparably rapturous vein, the Wohl Shoe Company of St. Louis offered young women, via the February 15, 1959, issue of *Vogue,* a pump described as a "dream of a shoe," and spelled out the dream visually: a lovely young miss leaned upon the manly chest of a masked *caballero.* No prosaic considerations of arch support or hygienic insole for her; the shoe is no longer a piece of utilitarian clothing, but a *laissez-passer* to the wondrous fantasy world of romance.[4] Underwear, too, according to the testimony of the Madison Avenue confraternity, has an equally transporting effect.[5] A case in point is a message some of them produced for Seamprufe, Inc. in a recent issue of *Seventeen.* In this instance, the journey took place in time as well as in space: the ad showed a medieval knight in chain mail, mounted upon a white charger, in the act of sweeping up with one arm a damsel improbably clad only in a lace-trimmed slip of nylon tricot. If, indeed, lingerie produces such reveries in American women, one can only be struck with admiration at the strength of

---

[3] Paolo and Francesca: young lovers in Dante's *Divine Comedy* who were aroused by a poem and later punished in hell for their lust. Tristan and Iseult: in a medieval legend Tristan was delivering Iseult to be the bride of a man she didn't want to marry. In despair, she attempted to poison both Tristan and herself, but her servant substituted a love potion for the poison and Tristan and Iseult fell in love with each other.

[4] *Laissez-passer* is a permit to enter.

[5] A confraternity is a group of men united in a single profession, in this case advertising.

character they show in getting past the state of deshabille and actually arriving at their jobs or starting their housework.

Like shoes and slips, it would seem that many liquids which formerly were thirst quenchers have also picked up amorous overtones in recent years. Coca-Cola was for decades a drink that made merely for a refreshing pause; nowadays, we learn, it is also an accoutrement of teen-age love-trysts.[6] In the April issue of *Seventeen,* for example, a Coke ad shows lad and lass, carrying a bagful of Coke, looking for a picnic spot; finding it, they shed some outer clothes and open a couple of Cokes; this causes them at once to fall tenderly upon each other's bosom, ecstatically guzzling, preparatory to nuzzling.

Even more noteworthy is the instance of beer. This drink was once the hearty, indelicate, eructative refreshment of the hard-working plebeian male.[7] It has apparently undergone a marvelous metamorphosis in recent years, becoming not only suitable for delicate lips, but acquiring an aura of enchantment and romance. A series of Schlitz advertisements in several major magazines has shown young couples parked by a lakeside at twilight, alone on a snow-capped mountaintop, and so on. Young, attractive, and clearly drawn to each other, they are always drinking beer out of one glass; these lovers, and their circumstances, exemplify the hedonistic exhortation under the picture: "Know the real joy of good living."[8] This, to be sure, could refer either to the romance or the beer; the ad is not explicit. Nor can one be sure whether romance inspired a desire for beer or beer a desire for romance. One thing *is* indisputable: the distinctive odor of hops, now found upon the attractive female, must have been reclassified in the national aesthetic system, becoming a scent rather than a smell.

Other procedures, once gustatory, have likewise become amatory, or so it would seem.[9] The smoking of tobacco, long thought appropriate to manly work or solitary reflection, has become almost obligatory at times of flirtation or intimacy. From the ubiquitous scenes of nubile young people igniting their little white tubes, one gains the impression that drawing in a lungful of soot and carcinogens has an amorous value as great as once did the reading aloud of Byron or the strumming of a banjo.[10] Amatory smoking does present one awkward problem, however, since countless ads (not by cigarette makers) report that love is inconceivable unless the mouth and breath are totally unsullied. Once again the problem is solved by a reshuffling of the national stimulus-response bonds, until smoke, on the breath, becomes exciting; the old proverb should really be altered to read: "Where there is smoke, there will soon be fire." Let

---

[6] An accoutrement is an accessory; a tryst is a meeting in some secretive or private place.

[7] Eructative means causing belching; a plebeian is a member of the lower class.

[8] Hedonistic means believing that life should be lived for pleasure.

[9] Gustatory means pertaining to eating or drinking; amatory means pertaining to love.

[10] Ubiquitous means being everywhere; nubile means available for marriage; carcinogens are irritants which cause cancer.

no one find fault with this or make mock of it. Do not lovers in the Trobriand Islands extract and eat lice from one another's hair, becoming mightily inflamed with love by the procedure? If, in the liberal spirit of cultural relativism, one accepts this and refuses to find it revolting, should he not do the same in the case of the reeking Americans?

Still, Americans themselves have not yet altogether succeeded in eroticizing the by-products of smoking,[11] as Madison Avenue itself admits. A remarkably candid ad for Parliament cigarettes recently came right out about the risk to amorous aesthetics: man and girl were shown, heads thrillingly close together, match lit for their cigarettes, while the copy, drawing attention to the recessed filter, promised in a throaty aside, "No filter feedback on your lips . . . or hers." Love in America in 1959 is evidently not for the oaf, but for the thoughtful practitioner of methodology. Ovid himself, that dedicated professor of tasteful dalliance, would have recognized in the Parliament copy writer a kindred spirit, a fellow toiler in the vineyards of impeccable passion.

Again and again the ad men indicate how easily Americans are aroused to lust or moved to tenderness by formerly nonerotic consumer products. Consider the vitamins offered in *Cosmopolitan* by the Vitasafe Corporation: their effect is plainly amorous, for the middle-aged couple are snuggling happily while the woman confesses, from an overflowing heart, "He made me feel like a bride again." Consider the electric portable offered by Smith-Corona: a book-laden youth passing a pretty girl looks down at her typewriter with a mooncalf expression, but it is clear that the machine has made him tender towards the girl as well. Consider fudge, of all things: Carnation Evaporated Milk shows a lass plastering it on cupcakes, while a crewcut lad eats one out of her hand, the plain implication being that fudge is an important component of her sex appeal.

This point is not spelled out in so many words, but sometimes obscurity is in itself a species of truth. The Marlboro people have been portraying rugged middle-aged sporting types lighting cigarettes for lovely young things; in small type under each such picture is the cryptic text, "The cigarette designed for men that women like." The Delphic Oracle[12] herself might have written it; parse it and puzzle over it as one will, he cannot be sure whether the "that" liked by the young thing is the cigarette designed for men, or the men themselves. But the truth lies not in deciding which one; the answer is that it means *both* of them, for they are blended in her mind and emotions. *That* is the truth the copy writer was conveying—in the prevailing romantic American landscape, the erotic object and the erotic person have become indistinguishable.

Precisely the same conclusion may be drawn from Pan American World Air-

---

[11] To eroticize something is to cause it to be romantically stimulated. Eros was a Greek god of love.

[12] The Delphic Oracle in Greek legend was the priestess of Apollo at Delphi whose prophecies were difficult to interpret and often had more than one meaning.

ways' appeal to businesswomen in *Mademoiselle.* "Look what Jet Clippers can do for your dreams," it reads, and illustrates what it means: the young business-woman is seated on a hillside with a morsel of Roman ruin behind her and a dark-haired handsome man beside her. What is the dream referred to—the man or the *mise-en-scène?* Possibly the text gives a further clue. "The fun of new experi-ences comes faster on Pan Am wings," it says. No help there; that still fits either one. But does it really matter? Not in the least: the trip abroad, the Roman ruin, the handsome man are all inseparable and indivisible. Love and the product are two aspects of a single essence; that is all they know on Madison Avenue, and all they need to know.

Within this general picture of American love, as set down by the creative men in the copy and art departments of the major agencies, no detail is more intriguing than the observation that contemporary Americans, though suppos-edly scornful of occultism, rely upon a variety of philters, amulets, talismans, potions, and brews, without which love is unattainable.[13]

It is, of course, no secret to anyone that the normal exudates of the human body, the wrinkles that come after youth, and such other common characteristics as dull hair, small breasts, plumpness, and blackheads are totally incompatible with affection and sex, and that no person with any of these defects can possibly find happiness in life. Luckily there is available today a splendid armamentari-um[14] of lotions, oils, paddings, pills, cleansers, and paints the use of which ob-viates the fault and admits the user to the arena of love.

But this is only the surface of truth. A closer inspection of advertising art and copy reveals a far subtler message being set down for all to read who are not willfully blind. If I read it rightly, there would appear to be, in modern love, a mysterious disembodiment of emotion: it is not so much the *beautiful person* who is loved, but the *beautifying instrumentality.* Observe the statement made repeatedly in ads for Coty's "L'Aimant": "Nothing makes a woman more feminine to a man. . . ." What exegesis[15] can there be, except that the femininity is in the bottled liquid, and not, basically, in the woman? And the same brand of meta-physics must lie behind the Lanvin ad which shows a small boy kissing a small girl who, though pleased, admits to herself: "He loves me . . . he loves my Mommy's Arpège!" The artful minx knows the truth; only by virtue of the applied balsam is she a nymphet, and he, willy-nilly, a nympholept.[16]

The female of all ages is continually advised that she need only wipe on this unguent, pat on this fragrance, slip on this magical garment, and lo! he sees with

---

[13] Occultism is belief in mysterious or supernatural powers. Philters, amulets, and so forth are objects and drugs with magic powers.

[14] An armamentarium is a collection or an array.

[15] An exegesis is an interpretation or explanation, originally of a Biblical passage.

[16] A minx is an impudent girl; a nymphet is an unusually sexy young girl; and "he, willy-nilly, a nympholept" means he is bewitched by the nymphet whether or not he wants to be.

new eyes, thinks with a different brain, loses his own purpose and becomes a willing slave. "If he can't make up his mind . . . wear Wind Song," whispers Prince Matchabelli. Lanvin slyly peddles the same kind of bottled powers, offering them with the tag, "How to make him lose the first round!" And let a woman but slip into a marvelous checked suit made by Junior Sophisticates, and, she is advised, "What can he do but surrender. . . ."

All this has a disturbingly supernatural sound, yet a hauntingly familiar one. What *is* it all an echo of? What old, well-known, half-forgotten nightmare? So musing, one may recall that there *were* women once who cloaked themselves in borrowed beauty to steal the love of man—sinful women who compacted with Satan to receive unlawful powers, and in return did his vile work for him. Suddenly, certain words and phrases in advertising copy, seemingly harmless, begin to assume an ominous sound. Danskin, Inc., who make a lounging outfit modeled after ballet costumes, use the telltale phrase, "for your 'at home' *bewitching* hours" (my italics). For being bewitching, 30,000 women were burned alive during the fifteenth and sixteenth centuries; let the word not go by unnoticed. And Dawnelle, Inc. frankly (or is it carelessly?) harks back to woman's ancient primal alliance with the Prince of Darkness in both copy and illustration. Says the copy: "You're the temptress who wins him, in Dawnelle's handsewn gloves"; the illustration, meanwhile, shows not one, but four gloved female hands offering a fatuously grinning male four ripe apples. (Has Eve grown more arms, or is the Serpent in an arms race too?)

And now the most damning fact begins to appear more clearly. In distinct defiance of the overtly approved mores, the entrapment or illusion created almost always operates within a context of illicit connection. The ads for a hundred products hint at it, but those of the perfume makers are practically outspoken. The names of perfumes are in themselves an insidious and deadly attack upon Judeo-Christian morality—e.g., "Tabu," "Indiscrète," "Conquête," "Temptation," "Surrender," and "My Sin"—while the copy strengthens the assault in words such as these:

"danger in every drop"
"the 'forbidden' fragrance"
"provocative as a stranger's smile"
"dare to wear it only when you seek to conquer"
"a whispered invitation for a man to be masterful."

One could extract from all this a sinister truth, namely that woman descended of Eve is still borrowing powers and enchantments in order to arouse man's lusts and thereby satisfy her own, and in the process is performing Satan's work of dragging man into mortal sin. Six centuries ago the best-educated men in Europe considered the situation a clear and present danger and spoke of it in terms like these:

In the woman wantonly adorned to capture souls, the garland upon her head is as a firebrand of Hell to kindle men, so too the horned headdress of another, so the brooch upon the breast [of a third]. . . . Each is a spark, breathing hellfire [and] damning the souls God has created and redeemed at such great cost.

Thus spoke John Bromyard, a typical fourteenth-century English preacher and compiler of sermons, and thus had spoken in earlier times Tertullian, Jerome, and Chrysostom. Today none but advertising men link the same factors in a single picture of woman; but whether the ad men are the Bromyards and Tertullians of our era or whether they are agents of the Foul Fiend is not altogether clear.

The seductive female is not the only pattern of womanhood about which Madison Avenue furnishes an abundance of information. The other and sharply contrasting pattern is that of the fiancée-wife-mother. The ancient dichotomy[17] of Woman into Eve and Mary, mistress and mother, witch and lady, apparently did not disappear with the end of feudalism but lives on still, according to the evidence at hand.

For whenever the female in an advertisement is alluring and beguiling, whenever her smile is secretive and mysterious, she represents the ancient spirit of Profane Love and her mystery is, ultimately, nothing but concupiscence.[18] But when woman is portrayed in the role of fiancée, bride, or wife, she possesses none of these qualities; instead she is feminine in a pure and wholesome sense. The American Gem Society, addressing an ad to the girl about to become engaged, portrays her as a dreaming young thing, chin cupped in hands, wide eyes staring off into the roseate future, guileless face almost completely innocent of make-up, mouth smiling trustfully and a little wistfully. She is Everyman's kid sister or girl friend, but never his passionflower. The Kinsey crowd may publish their revolting statistics on the premarital sexual experiences of American girls, but the advertisements tell a different and lovelier version of the truth: the girl who gets a diamond engagement ring has not been besmirched by sexual experiments or known the indecent hunger of desire.

Even in the embrace of her fiance she preserves a high-minded concentration upon nonsexual matters. A dinnerware ad in *Seventeen* shows a young couple who have ridden in a sleigh out to a secluded field through which runs a purling stream. The lad romantically picks up the girl in his arms and carries her across the virgin snow, while she tenderly and practically murmurs to him, "You get the license . . . I'll get the Lenox." His intentions may have been licentious rather than licensable, but this comment at once purifies and clarifies his mind.

Nuptials and honeymoon make no perceptible change in this side of her character; the bride's mood may be yielding, but her blood runs cool. "Isn't this how you want to live?" asks the Fostoria Glass Company, portraying an ideal young marriage: a young wife, holding a piece of crystal stemware near a single

[17] A dichotomy is a division into two parts.
[18] Concupiscence is lust or sexuality.

burning taper, seems lost in admiration of the glass and the candle, and only vaguely aware of the handsome husband hovering beside her. She is smiling at him, more or less, with her neat, childish little mouth firmly closed—and a generation trained by Marilyn Monroe does not miss the significance of *that*. Not long ago a Heublein Cocktails ad in *Life* featured what seems merely an amusing line—"A wife's warmest welcome is well chilled"; like so many other jokes, perhaps it says more than it intends to.

After a suitable time, the wife becomes a mother, but despite this presumptive evidence of sexual activity, she remains thoroughly pure. In a Vigoro ad we see her romping on the lawn with her husband and children; she is tanned, healthy, and essentially *friendly*. In a Johnson outboard motor ad we see her roaring along with her husband and children in a speedboat; she is sunburned, tousled, and essentially a *good sport*. In a G-E ad we see her clapping her hands gleefully as her husband and daughter present her with a dishwasher; she is slim, pretty (in a low-heeled way), and essentially *homey*.

We see her in many other situations—cooking, washing, shopping, playing games—and she is almost invariably clean-looking, hearty, efficient, and brightly lit. Dan River Mills recently devoted a spread in *Life* to the modern American family and showed four typical examples. Every one of the four consisted of a handsome young man, a pretty young woman, and two children (between the ages of four and eight), all dressed in cottons by Dan River. In not one picture is the man touching, holding, or even looking at his wife; in three out of four, he is not even standing beside her, but is separated from her by one of the children. The American wife, it seems reasonable to conclude, is a pal, a helpmeet, a kind of older girl friend; she is emphatically not a lover.

The children have a double function in preserving the mother image: they prove her fecundity, but by their very presence they neutralize or purify the erotic overtones of certain situations. Do she and her husband don Weldon pajamas?—in come the kids, in similar pajamas, making everything sanitary and aboveboard. Does she go off for a ride with her man in a Chrysler product?—she tucks a little girl into her lap, and all is sweet, all is sound. Do she and he park their Chevrolet in a secluded woodland spot?—happily, they brought the dog along, and it is upon the beast that affection is bestowed. Have she and her husband grown cheerfully middle-aged and regained their privacy as the children left home?—the General Motors time-payment plan shows them hugging *two* dogs, one for each. No wonder the dog is called man's best friend—he defends, by his very presence, the purity of the American wife and mother.

Certain other aspects of American love, though not so fully portrayed, are illuminatingly touched upon in magazine advertisements. For it is apparent from any careful scrutiny of the ads that Americans require the stimulus of exotic, remote, or uncomfortable surroundings, in order to experience the real transports of delight. Here is an advertisement showing a couple on a wild, chilly-looking beach at sundown (how *did* they get that automobile down there without making tracks in the sand?); here is another couple deep in the forest primeval, smoking cigarettes and hugging each other; here is a third exploring a wild stream bank in their good clothing, undaunted by steep declivity[19] or tangled underbrush. Oasis Cigarettes render continual reports of lovers cozily nestled on a desert cactus, moodily bussing each other in some dim alley of the Vieux Carré of New Orleans, or perching together in a high window overlooking Monte Carlo. They never wax romantic in Middletown, U.S.A.; they never grow fond in a middle-class living room. Wind-swept Alpine crags, the slippery decks of heeled-over yawls, castles without plumbing, streams in the heart of a jungle—these would seem to be the typical loci of love,[20] rather than the sofa, bed, or park bench. How all this may be possible—since most people are forced to spend their lives at or near home—is a nagging question; perhaps the meaning of it all is that love, in the twentieth century, is an actuality for the wealthy, but still only a dream for the poor and the middle class.

Likewise tantalizing are the occasional hints of restiveness and impending revolt on the part of modern man. Ensnared and bewitched by the minx, captured and domesticated by the wife, does he begin nowadays to stir in his chains, remembering the olden days? Drummond Knitwear, in *The New York Times,* portrays two sturdy upright chaps clad in knitted shirts, with a luscious female supine at their feet. Can it be mere coincidence that the Cigar Institute of America shows a manly stogy-fancier hefting a caveman's club, while a maiden clad in a leopardskin crouches adoringly at heel? No, it is not coincidence, for here again is Chief Apparel, in *Playboy,* showing us a Bikini-clad morsel sprawled pantingly on the floor before a gentleman clad in dashing sports attire. But perhaps the significant clue is that in all three advertisements the gentlemen are ignoring the females. Woman is a toy (the ad men seem to be saying)—a plaything to be enjoyed when man chooses, and to be scorned when he does not.

Finally, and most challenging of all, is the handful of frivolous and irreverent remarks in recent advertisements that may conceivably portend a general devaluation of love in the near future. Hanes Hosiery in *The New Yorker* shows us a cartoon of a depressed chap clutching a bottle of poison and thinking, "I'd better drink it. All she wants from me is seamless stockings by Hanes." One does not get flippant about God or the Flag; perhaps Love, long the peer of both of these, is losing its position. A Lea & Perrins ad shows a man and woman curled up warmly together, just after dinner; it is the best of all possible times for serious talk, but listen to what she says: "Do you love Lea & Perrins more than me?" Is nothing sacred to woman any longer, that she dares to jest at a time like this?

Whatever may be the ultimate meaning of all these things, one must congratulate the cultural historians of the future; a treasure of evidence is awaiting them, if they will but look away from the scientific studies and scholarly theses and pay attention to the scribblings on Madison Avenue.

[19] A declivity is a hillside or slope.
[20] Loci are places or locations.

POINTS TO CONSIDER

Morton M. Hunt: Love According to Madison Avenue

1. Why do you think the writer uses so many uncommon words like ubiquitous, carcinogens, and concupiscence? What does it reveal about his attitude toward the subject?

2. Do you agree with Hunt that our ad writers tell us more about our culture than our historians do?

3. What ads do you know of that try to make their products seem more appealing by relating them to romance or sex appeal?

4. What does Hunt mean when he says about advertising that "the erotic object and the erotic person have become indistinguishable"? What examples can you think of to illustrate this?

5. What kinds of products are sold as "love charms"? What is the point of portraying some products as sinister enchantments?

6. What artificial distinctions do ads make between women as lovers and women as wives and mothers? What kinds of ads illustrate this?

7. What other unreal or fantasy portrayals of love appear commonly in American advertising? How do you think these approaches help to sell products? How do these approaches affect you?

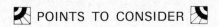 POINTS TO CONSIDER

Ad for Life of Virginia

1. At whom is this ad primarily aimed? How do you know?

2. Why does the first sentence of the ad stress the things that parents *cannot* do for the child? What sort of subconscious anxieties are likely to be touched by this emphasis? Do you see this as a subtle attempt to make parents feel vaguely guilty? How would such guilt feelings relate to the product advertised: "life insurance"?

3. What does the ad mean by the phrase "face reality"? Why does the ad state this so vaguely? Do you think it would be more effective to substitute something like "face the fact that you could die tomorrow"? Explain.

4. Why doesn't the ad describe in detail one or more of its various life insurance plans?

5. What sort of role does the ad suggest that the insurance man will play? Is this similar to the image a bank assumes? Explain.

Courtesy of Cargill, Wilson and Acree, Inc., Richmond, Virginia

You can't face the lost puppy, or the first broken date for her. But you could face reality. It helps to talk about it with a good insurance man.

POINTS TO CONSIDER

Ad for Roi-Tan Cigars

1. To what masculine images does the ad for Roi-Tan cigars appeal?

2. What kind of psychological appeals, other than appeals to masculine images, are employed in this ad?

3. Why do you suppose no women (except for a pearly thumbnail) appear in this ad which attempts to appeal to men?

Courtesy of American Cigar Company and Gardner Advertising Company

If Roi-Tan wasn't the best selling ten cent cigar, you couldn't buy it for ten cents.

There's only one reason you can buy a fine tasting blend of imported and domestic tobacco like Roi-Tan for only a dime. The fact that we make so many of them.

And if we didn't, we'd have to charge more just like lots of other cigar makers do.

So no matter what price you pay for cigars, try a Roi-Tan and find out how much more great taste you can get for a dime. Roi-Tan The Crowd Pleaser.

Stylishly long slender cigars are becoming more and more preferred by today's cigar smoker. Another reason why the Falcons are one of the more popular of the many Roi-Tan shapes and sizes.

Ad for Ambush Perfume

1. Is the girl in the ad a kid-sister-sweetheart or a mistress-seductress or both? Do you see her as pure or evil? Can you think of better words to describe her?

2. Why is "Ambush" a more appropriate word for a woman's perfume than, say, "Attack"?

3. Morton Hunt's article (p. 22) discusses the advertising of 1959. Do this ad and the previous ad suggest that the popular advertising image of woman has changed? Explain.

Courtesy of Dana Perfumes Corp.

Why not wait in Ambush?

Perfume by Dana.
ALSO—COLOGNE · SPRAY COLOGNE · BATH POWDER · SOAP

▨ POINTS TO CONSIDER ▧

Ad for Lenox China

1. Compare the clothes worn by the couple in this ad with those worn by the married couple in the Mercury ad. What do you think accounts for the differences?

2. What is suggested by the fact that the blanket and the umbrella, as well as the couple's clothes, are all white? How is this similar to the 1959 Lenox ad that Hunt describes?

3. What does the tower add to the effect of the scene? What does the umbrella add?

4. What does the food basket tell us? How does it perform a function similar to that performed by the dogs in the ads Morton Hunt describes?

Courtesy Lenox China/Crystal

Love leads to Lenox

POINTS TO CONSIDER

Ad for Mercury Station Wagon

1. If the children in this picture were not shown, what other things might suggest that the man and woman shown are married?

2. Besides assuring us that the couple pictured are indeed married, why are the children appropriate to this ad?

3. Is a station wagon usually thought of as a man's car? (See Vance Packard, "The Ad and the Id," p. 9). Why do you think the ad stresses the idea?

4. Would it seem that the wife pictured here is, as Morton Hunt says, "emphatically not a lover"? How does what we see of the couple's relationship fit in with the main idea of the ad: "The Man's Car"?

Better ideas make a better wagon. A <u>man's</u> wagon.

A man shouldn't have to treat people like baggage, Mercury figures.

So we put a Dual-Action Tailgate on our Mercury wagons. It swings open like a door for people. Down like a platform for easy cargo handling. Crafty.

So are the side panels on the Colony Park, above, that look like yacht deck walnut—but there's the strength of steel underneath.

And the choice of third-seat options, either rear-facing or dual center-facing (see left) so kids get their own built-in playroom and aren't breathing down your neck as you drive.

A man needs man-sized room. The Colony Park takes 4-ft.-wide loads without scraping either side. The 2-seat model hides 11.7 cu. ft. of gear in below-decks storage space that's lockable.

Other man-pampering features power rear window. Power front disc brakes. See your Mercury Man, your Mercury dealer.

Mercury, the Man's Car.

If you guys don't buy
these new Drummond sweaters,
we'll go right back
to male models.

FROM $17 TO $35, IN LOTS OF COLORS: OF PURE WOOL, SUEDE AND WOOL, OR MOHAIR-AND-WOOL BLEND. AT GOOD STORES; OR WRITE DRUMMOND, EMPIRE STATE BUILDING, NEW YORK, N.Y. 10001.

What sportsmen like about Lochlana® shirts by Hathaway

A Lochlana feels like no other shirt in the world. Warm as wool but a lot lighter. Soft as cashmere but much hardier. You can wear a Lochlana shirt next to your skin and never feel the urge to scratch.

In cooler weather, wear *two* — a buttoned Lochlana over a knitted Lochlana (as shown in our picture). This is called the "layered" look. Plenty warm — but still lightweight.

And for the sportsman who wants more — Hathaway designs Lochlanas so they're good *looking*, too.

Lochlana is woven exclusively for Hathaway in Switzerland of 50% wool "tops" blended with 50% cotton. ("Tops" are the long, smooth strands of wool that you get after you've combed out all the short, scratchy hairs.)

Hathaway shirts are still being hand-tailored. So they cost a little more than most. $21 for these button-down shirts in checks — $18 in solids — $15 for the turtle-necks. For store names, write C. F. Hathaway, Dept. F, Waterville, Me.

Hathaway®
THE WARNACO GROUP

Even if he's running for class president there's no need to pay a fancy price for his underwear and shirts...not if they're Fruit of the Loom.

When a man dresses up for something special, he wants to feel special. You can give him that feeling for a lot less than you think. For just 79¢ you can get him long-wearing Fruit of the Loom Sanforized ® wash-and-wear cotton shorts. With extra seat room, extra leg room, extra give and take in the waist. Even new Golden Fruit of the Loom underwear is just 99¢. And it's no-iron Dacron* polyester and

cotton. Same savings go for Fruit of the Loom permanent press shirts. Trim, tapered, fine quality dress and sport shirts, just $2.99 to $4.99. See, there's no need to pay a fancy price for his underwear and shirts. Not if they're Fruit of the Loom. Why not get him some for school.
The price is so low, the value so high . . . you can't afford not to buy Fruit of the Loom.

Men's Underwear-59¢, 79¢ & 99¢/Men's Shirts-$2.99, $3.99 & $4.99/Boys' Underwear-39¢ & 59¢/Infants' Underwear-39¢ to 89¢

*DuPont's reg. T.M.

⬢ POINTS TO CONSIDER ⬢

Three Ads for Shirts

1. At what audience is each of the three ads aimed? How does each ad appeal to that audience and its particular image? How well do the ads reflect the personalities of the magazines in which they appear?

2. What differences do you find between the language and style of the *Good Housekeeping* ad and that of the *Field and Stream* ad? How do these differences reflect the differing appeals of the ads?

3. To what extent do all three of the ads reflect the values and practices discussed by Harvey Cox in "The Playboy and Miss America" (p. 103)?

Courtesy Andrew M. Weiss, Inc. (p. 42)

Courtesy C. S. Hathaway Company, *Field and Stream,* October 12, 1968 (p. 43)

Courtesy of Union Underwear Company, Inc. (p. 44)

For The
Young at Heart —

 POINTS TO CONSIDER

Al Capp: General Bullmoose versus the Coldsmobile

1. What common advertising and propaganda approaches are used to market "The Idiot's Delight" and the "The Coldsmobile"? (See "The Ad and the Id," p. 9, and "How to Detect Propaganda," p. 64.)

2. How many different institutions and kinds of people does Capp manage to poke fun at in this single cartoon sequence? What methods does he use?

Reprinted through the courtesy of the Chicago Tribune-New York News Syndicate, Inc.

Ideas for Investigation, Discussion, and Writing

Advertising

1. **a.** Collect half a dozen or so magazine and newspaper ads for the same kind of product or service. What different techniques or appeals are used? Which do you consider effective and which ineffective? Why?

    b. Observe several television commercials for the same kind of product or service. What different techniques or appeals are used? How do they compare to or differ from those employed in magazine or newspaper ads? Which do you consider effective and which ineffective?

2. **a.** Examine the advertising in several magazines obviously intended for different types of readers (e.g., *Good Housekeeping, Field and Stream, The New Yorker,* and *Saturday Review*). How do the products and services advertised differ to suit the image of each magazine?

    b. Examine the advertising for one kind of product or service in several different types of magazines. How do the ad techniques and appeals differ to suit the image of each magazine?

3. Observe some television commercials broadcast at different times of the day and of the week. How do the subjects and styles of the commercials indicate the different audiences for which they are intended?

4. **a.** Lay out a full-page magazine ad of your own for some original or unusual product or service. Use pictures (you can cut them from magazines or newspapers), headlines, and copy in any proportion you choose. Then write a paragraph explaining the techniques and appeals that you used.

    b. Write a twenty-second television commercial for some original or unusual product or service. Indicate what is seen on the screen and what announcements, dialogue, or music is heard. Then write a paragraph explaining the techniques and appeals that you used.

5. Tour a large supermarket, an all-purpose drugstore, or a large variety store. How many different persuasive techniques can you discover that the store is employing? How effective do you feel that each one is?

6. Write a short paper or prepare a short talk on what you feel are the advantages or disadvantages of large-scale advertising. Or, perhaps you could stage a debate in which some people argued one side and some the other.

7. Of how many different sources of advertising are you aware? Write an essay discussing the importance of advertising to your life. To what extent do you think advertising affects what you buy, what you do, what you think, and what you are?

8. Discuss the idea of advertising as an art. Is it possible for an ad to be something more than simply skillful persuasion or clever attention getting? Is it possible for an ad to transcend its function as a selling device and evoke the kind of emotional response usually associated with pure art? Or are there perhaps only parts of the ad, such as its photography, its music, or its use of language that can be enjoyed as art? Find a number of ads which prove your point.

PART TWO

JOURNALISM

Millions of people who seldom read books are reached by journalism in magazines and newspapers. Magazines feature, individually or in combination, all the subjects that people want to read about. Some magazines concentrate on one subject—news, an art form, or a hobby; others concentrate on reaching a particular readership with a particular image—parents, housewives, or average young men who want to feel like successful men-about-town. Best-selling love story and celebrity scandal magazines supply a steady stream of gossip and romantic fantasy to occupy and comfort women who consider their lives lacking in emotion or adventure. Almost all magazines feature advertising geared to their subject and readership; and some magazines exist primarily to advertise.

Most readers also subscribe to a daily newspaper which informs them of international, national, and local news and provides entertainment features along with a wide range of advertising. Although other media provide popular news coverage, newspaper reporting is generally more timely than that of magazines and more thorough and detailed than that of radio and television. Newspapers not only report events, they help to shape events by uncovering and publicizing social and political issues, by supporting political candidates, and by presenting the opinions of their staff and their readers. Newspapers also have a great effect on the economies of the areas they serve with relatively low-priced and daily advertising for both businesses and individuals.

Like advertising, which is such an important part of it, magazine and newspaper journalism is a composite mass medium and popular art form. It employs the media of print and photography and the arts of writing, photo-journalism, and cartooning to entertain, inform, and influence its readers.

Duane Bradley

The Newspaper: Its Place in Democracy, 1965

What is news? It is the honest and unbiased and complete account of events of interest and concern to the public.

A typical metropolitan daily may receive approximately 8 million words of copy each day from its staff, wire services, feature syndicates, correspondents and special writers. Of this, only about 100,000 can be used in the paper.

Local stories are gathered by staff reporters and correspondents. Each reporter is responsible for certain types of news and some have what are called "beats." One may cover the city offices, another the police court and state police, someone else the society news. Correspondents from neighborhood areas and surrounding towns write or telephone news from their localities.

A reporter on his beat will make notes of various stories he encounters, then return to the office and write them. On a larger paper, or during an emergency when time is precious, he may phone them in to the "desk" where a rewrite man will take them.

Other people also telephone in stories or suggestions for stories. No newspaper has enough reporters to cover every spot where news may break, nor can it possibly keep up with all of the activities in any town. Members of the public and town officials frequently notify a paper when an important issue is coming up in a town meeting, when a deer has wandered into a suburban neighborhood, or when a certain couple is planning to celebrate a golden wedding anniversary.

Public relations and publicity people for all sorts of individuals and organizations regularly send stories to newspapers. Some of these stories are legitimate news, and some are merely designed to keep clients in the spotlight of public attention.

Foreign and out-of-state news stories often carry a set of initials in the dateline which indicates that they were supplied by one of the wire services. AP means Associated Press. UPI means United Press International. Such a story from New York, for instance, was covered by a wire service staff member at the spot where it occurred and phoned in to the New York office. It was handled by a rewrite man, then edited and teletyped to subscribing New York bureaus and to regional bureau offices throughout the country. At each regional office it was again edited before being teletyped to subscribing newspapers in the area. This editing is done to fit the needs of out-of-town papers which will not want as long a story as those near the area where the event happened. At the local paper, a city editor or news editor evaluated the story and decided where it was to be used in his paper. He then passed it to the copy desk where it was again refined, pared to a specific length, and headlined. It was scrutinized by an editorial board before being sent to the composing room. A newspaper which subscribes to a wire service may edit stories to fit its needs but may not change the content or slant them without removing the wire service identification.

All news stories, once written, are edited and designated for particular spots in the paper. Their length, their position and whether or not news photos accompany them will depend on their importance compared to other news in the same issue.

There is a well-known truism about news that defines it as something out of the ordinary. It says that if a dog bites a man it is not news, but that if a man bites a dog, it *is* news. Anyone who reads the average newspaper will realize that this hardly applies to a large per cent of what is presented to him as news. Much space in all newspapers is devoted to ordinary, expected, and not particularly surprising events:

The Elks have a picnic, the PTA holds a reception for new members, the League of Women Voters offers transportation to the polls, the Little League wins a game, ten speeders are fined in police court—these stories, multiplied a thousand-fold, appear daily in newspapers all across America.

Seemingly even less important and exciting than these are what are called "meet-the-train" items. "Mr. and Mrs. Joseph Smith were dinner guests at the home of Mr. and Mrs. Sam Brown on Thursday, March 19." "Miss Jane Brown has returned home from Chatham College, where she has just completed her junior year." Newspapers value these stories more than you might suppose because they are so important to those whose names are mentioned.

The "big" stories, the hurricane that demolishes a town, the child lost in the woods, the bank robbery, the escaped criminal, do not happen so often, and may well be called "man bites dog" stories.

The type of story that is hardest to get and offers the most potential danger to a paper is the one kept hidden from the public. The good reporter and the good editor are never content with routine news and regular "handouts" from official sources, but are always on the alert for what is not easy to see.

A city plans a huge new park in a residential area. It is much needed to provide recreation facilities for large numbers of children. On the other hand, who now owns the land where it will be located, and when did they buy it? (Did the plans leak from certain city officials so that relatives and friends could buy the land at a low price, to resell later at a profit?) How much will be paid for the land, and who decides on its value? How are the contracts for the necessary work to be awarded? Who has written the specifications for construction and will everything be of the best quality? The alert paper seeking this information will have no difficulty if all city officials are honest, but a crooked administration will resent a public scrutiny of its affairs. The paper that battles dishonest public officials is asking for trouble, but many a good paper has brought about great social reforms by doing just that.

News in American newspapers is supposed to be honest, accurate, concise, and easy to understand. It should not be written to serve any special interests, groups, or individuals. Most reporters and editors pride themselves on living up to these standards. It is much more difficult than it might seem to be sure that this is always done.

News which gives a one-sided impression is "slanted." A reporter or editor can, consciously or unconsciously, slant news in many different ways.

The selection of which stories to print may slant the news. Some Southern newspapers have carried almost no news about racial difficulties in their areas, which may have given the impression that such things did not exist there. Some Northern newspapers have ignored stories of racial difficulties in the North, but headlined those in the South, which may have given the impression that it was a purely regional problem. During a presidential campaign, partisan Republican papers may print countless stories about the huge crowds attending speeches made by the Republican candidate and hardly mention the same sort of crowds present to hear the Democratic candidate. Partisan Democratic papers may run stories showing the popularity of their candidate, and select those which show a lack of popularity on the part of his opponent.

When done deliberately, this sort of slanting defeats the purpose of giving the public a clear and balanced picture of current events. It is often done, in a minor way, with no such intention. The editor who is an avid sports fan is apt to have a larger sports section than the one who is uninterested in sports but deeply involved in politics. The reporter who is fascinated by the business growth of the city will see more stories there than in its schools.

Responsible editors are aware that they often "create" news by selecting it for their columns. There are dozens of different departments in any state government, and news is apt to be in the making in all of them most of the time. The highway department is planning new roads, the department of employment is devising new tests for prospective employees, the treasurer has a report on the state's financial condition, the state promotion department is running a contest to choose a state flower, the state police department is reorganizing, the governor is making a speech, the welfare department reports an unusually heavy case load, the state park authority wants to create a new park in land reclaimed by a flood control project. Most of these matters are routine and might ordinarily be handled by routine news treatment.

Suppose that the newspaper editor decides that the matter of reclaimed land is of the utmost importance to the state, either because he thinks it should be a park or because he thinks it should be left untouched and used for a wild life refuge. He can put a good reporter on the story, set him to work digging up background and similar situations in other states, and run a series of front page stories which treat the matter as if it were the only really vital thing going on in the state. He could do the same with any one of the listed stories and give it importance at the expense of other news.

The attempt to make a paper interesting and exciting can slant news. Some newspapers fill their columns with stories of crime, tragedy, and corruption in order to attract readers; this makes it seem that these are the only noteworthy things happening. Other papers, wishing to help their communities by keeping everyone happy, err on the other side and rarely print anything unpleasant.

The position of a particular news story on the page and the page on which it appears, the number of words used for it, whether or not it is illustrated, and the way in which it is headlined can slant news.

Remember our fictitious governor who was involved in a traffic accident? Let us assume that it was snowing, that he was driving down a hill where children were sliding on the sidewalk, and that his car went out of control, narrowly missed another one, and crashed into a tree. He was examined by a doctor but was found to be uninjured. Think of the different headlines that could be written for such a story: "Governor Escapes Death in Accident," "Governor to Face Court Charges in Accident," "Children Uninjured by Governor's Accident, Is Claim"—and so on.

News may be slanted by lack of time and manpower to pursue it thoroughly. A newspaper may get a tip that a Mr. Peter Smith has been victimized by the state highway department. A reporter is sent to investigate the incident.

He finds Mr. Smith, aged 79, living near a new highway but unable to have a driveway built between it and his house. He had previously lived at another location, but his land was confiscated by the highway department to make room for the new highway. Being too poor to hire a lawyer, he had taken the price offered for his land by the state. A neighbor had interceded with the state on his behalf and helped him buy back his original home, which had then been moved to its present spot. Once settled, he had planted a garden, bought a cow, built a henhouse, and *then* had found that the state would not allow him to build the necessary driveway. His only access to the outside world is a path a quarter of a mile long which leads to a secondary road. He cannot afford to turn this into a proper driveway because the only money he has is the amount the state paid him for his former property.

The reporter finds this a heart-rending story and returns to his office to write it. His editor looks it over carefully. It is interesting, the public should know about it if it is a typical incident, and it is true in the sense that it is reported exactly as Mr. Smith told it. If it turns out not to be the complete truth, the paper is not in danger of a libel suit, because the state cannot bring such a suit. (In our country, the government *is* the people, and we cannot sue ourselves. If a story accuses a specific government official of something that may harm his reputation, he can bring suit as an individual on the basis of personal injury.)

The editor suggests that the reporter telephone the proper state official and get the state's side of the story. The reporter makes the call and is connected with a man who has a desk full of important work and no inclination to talk. The official says he is sick and tired of hearing about Mr. Smith and of the way newspaper reporters distort facts. Here is another angle to the story. "State official angered by questions, has no sympathy for Mr. Smith, and accuses newspapers of distorting the truth." It becomes more colorful by the minute.

A good reporter does not stop there. He should insist on his right to know the facts and should explain that the story is going to be printed and he would like to make it as accurate as possible. (Most state officials and others in public life realize it is always better to talk to the press than to refuse to, no matter what they may happen to think of the individual reporter or newspaper concerned.)

A subsequent interview will present new facts. The state is involved in a large-scale operation of highway construction, and the property of Mr. Smith is one of many it has purchased. All such property has been evaluated by professional appraisers to determine its true value. Mr. Smith was informed, by letter, that he could buy back his original home at a modest price, as were all uprooted home owners. He was further advised, again by letter, that the property to which he had his house moved would not be allowed access to the new highway. Most new highways, such as this one, have limited side access in order to prevent dangerous cross traffic.

The state official might eventually become more friendly with the reporter and advise him that Mr. Smith is a well-known crank who has caused endless trouble. He may suggest that it would be wise to drop the whole story, since it is obviously not a case of right or wrong, but of a man who can get along with no one.

This changes the story entirely, and the reporter and the paper have now spent considerable time on it—time which would otherwise have gone to other stories. Is this the end?

Not yet. The reporter should check the official records and interview other state officials and those whose property has been purchased for the same highway. Out of all this time and effort may come a story that uncovers wrongdoing on the part of the state, or a story that is hardly worth writing and printing. Few newspapers have the facilities for following up every suggested story to this extent. *A story that is incomplete may be slanted because it omits some of the facts.*

Some stories may be both true and important, but misleading. Some years ago the late Senator Joseph McCarthy undertook a crusade to rid the government, schools, and churches of people whom he considered sympathetic to Communism. Speaking in the Senate (where his senatorial immunity made him safe from libel suits), he began to name people whom he said were Communists, Communist sympathizers, or "soft on Communism." Many of them were prominent people whose names were as newsworthy as the senator's.

It is news when any government official makes such statements. Many thoughtful editors did not believe the charges were true but they could not ignore their news value nor express their opinions in the news stories themselves. In order to handle the matter in what they considered the proper perspective, they printed their opinions on the editorial page, made a consistent effort to follow up on all of the accusations and give their readers the facts. Some published interviews with those accused giving their background and stature and with people who opposed Senator McCarthy's project.

To return to our original definition, news is an honest, unbiased, and complete account of events of interest or concern to the public. Professor George H. Morris of Florida Southern University, who was a newspaperman for many years before he became a teacher, characterizes news as "history in a hurry." He says "Read several papers, day after day, and eventually the truth will emerge."

No newspaper, because of the limitations of time and space, can print all of the facts that make the news in any one issue. No reader can understand what is happening by scanning any one issue of any one paper.

It is difficult for even the best newspapers to do a good job of gathering and writing the news. The good reader will evaluate it by reading carefully day after day and comparing the way identical stories are covered in papers with different viewpoints.

 POINTS TO CONSIDER

Duane Bradley: What Is News?

1. How can we define news? What are the commonest sources of news for a newspaper?

2. What are "man bites dog" and "meet the train" stories? What other kinds of newspaper stories are of value to the public?

3. What is meant by "slanted news"? What are some of the ways in which newspapers knowingly or unknowingly slant their news? Give some examples of how this may be done.

4. What are some of the qualities of a good newspaper reporter?

5. How can a newspaper story be both true and important and still be misleading?

6. How can the newspaper reader get the clearest and most objective view of the news?

What Is News?   **59**

How to Detect Propaganda

Clyde R. Miller
Language in Uniform, 1967

If American citizens are to have a clear understanding of present-day conditions and what to do about them, they must be able to recognize propaganda, to analyze it, and to appraise it.

But what is propaganda?

As generally understood, propaganda is expression of opinion or action by individuals or groups deliberately designed to influence opinions or actions of other individuals or groups with reference to predetermined ends. Thus propaganda differs from scientific analysis. The propagandist is trying to "put something across," good or bad, whereas the scientist is trying to discover truth and fact. Often the propagandist does not want careful scrutiny and criticism; he wants to bring about a specific action. Because the action may be socially beneficial or socially harmful to millions of people, it is necessary to focus upon the propagandist and his activities the searchlight of scientific scrutiny. Socially desirable propaganda will not suffer from such examination, but the opposite type will be detected and revealed for what it is.

We are fooled by propaganda chiefly because we don't recognize it when we see it. It may be fun to be fooled but, as the cigarette ads used to say, it is more fun to know. We can more easily recognize propaganda when we see it if we are familiar with the seven common propaganda devices. These are:

1. The Name Calling Device
2. The Glittering Generalities Device
3. The Transfer Device
4. The Testimonial Device
5. The Plain Folks Device
6. The Card Stacking Device
7. The Band Wagon Device

Why are we fooled by these devices? Because they appeal to our emotions rather than to our reason. They make us believe and do something we would not believe or do if we thought about it calmly, dispassionately. In examining these devices, note that they work most effectively at those times when we are too lazy to think for ourselves; also, they tie into emotions which sway us to be "for" or "against" nations, races, religions, ideals, economic and political policies and practices, and so on through automobiles, cigarettes, radios, toothpastes, presidents, and wars. With our emotions stirred, it may be fun to be fooled by these propaganda devices, but it is more fun and infinitely more to our own interests to know how they work.

Lincoln must have had in mind citizens who could balance their emotions with intelligence when he made his remark: ". . . but you can't fool all of the people all of the time."

Name Calling

"Name Calling" is a device to make us form a judgment without examining the evidence on which it should be based. Here the propagandist appeals to our hate and fear. He does this by giving "bad names" to those individuals, groups, nations, races, policies, practices, beliefs, and ideals which he would have us condemn and reject. For centuries the name "heretic" was bad. Thousands were oppressed, tortured, or put to death as heretics. Anybody who dissented from popular or group belief or practice was in danger of being called a heretic. In the light of today's knowledge, some heresies were bad and some were good. Many of the pioneers of modern science were called heretics; witness the cases of Copernicus, Galileo, Bruno. Today's bad names include: Fascist, demagogue, dictator, Red, financial oligarchy, Communist, muckraker, alien, outside agitator, economic royalist, Utopian, rabblerouser, troublemaker, Tory, Constitution wrecker.

"Al" Smith called Roosevelt a Communist by implication when he said in his Liberty League speech, "There can be only one capital, Washington or Moscow." When "Al" Smith was running for the presidency, many called him a tool of the Pope, saying in effect, "We must choose between Washington and Rome." That implied that Mr. Smith, if elected President, would take his orders from the Pope. Likewise Mr. Justice Hugo Black has been associated with a bad name, Ku Klux Klan. In these cases some propagandists have tried to make us form judgments without examining essential evidence and implications. "Al Smith is a Catholic. He must never be President." "Roosevelt is a Red. Defeat his program." "Hugo Black is or was a Klansman. Take him out of the Supreme Court."

Use of "bad names" without presentation of their essential meaning, without all their pertinent implications, comprises perhaps the most common of all propaganda devices. Those who want to maintain the status quo apply bad names to those who would change it. For example, the Hearst press applies bad names to Communists and Socialists. Those who want to change the status quo apply bad names to those who would maintain it. For example, the Daily Worker and the American Guardian apply bad names to conservative Republican and Democrats.

Glittering Generalities

"Glittering Generalities" is a device by which the propagandist identifies his program with virtue by use of "virtue words." Here he appeals to our emotions of love, generosity, and brotherhood. He uses words like truth, freedom, honor, liberty, social justice, public service, the right to work, loyalty, progress, democracy, the American way, Constitution defender. These words suggest shining ideals. All persons of good will believe in these ideals. Hence the propagandist, by identifying his individual group, nation, race, policy, practice, or belief with such ideals, seeks to win us to his cause. As Name Calling is a device to make us form a judgment to reject and condemn, without examining the evidence, Glittering Generalities is a device to make us accept and approve, without examining the evidence.

For example, use of the phrases, "the right to work" and "social justice," may be a device to make us accept programs for meeting the labor-capital problem which, if we examined them critically, we would not accept at all.

In the Name Calling and Glittering Generalities devices, words are used to stir up our emotions and to befog our thinking. In one device "bad words" are used to make us mad; in the other "good words" are used to make us glad.

The propagandist is most effective in use of these devices when his words make us create devils to fight or gods to adore. By his use of the "bad words," we personify as a "devil" some nation, race, group, individual, policy, practice, or ideal; we are made fighting mad to destroy it. By use of "good words," we personify as a godlike idol some nation, race, group, etc. Words which are "bad" to some are "good" to others, or may be made so. Thus, to some the New Deal is "a prophecy of social salvation" while to others it is "an omen of social disaster."

From consideration of names, "bad" and "good," we pass to institutions and symbols, also "bad" and "good." We see these in the next device.

Transfer

"Transfer" is a device by which the propagandist carries over the authority, sanction, and prestige of something we respect and revere to something he would have us accept. For example, most of us respect and revere our church and our nation. If the propagandist succeeds in getting church or nation to approve a campaign in behalf of some program, he thereby transfers its authority, sanction, and prestige to that program. Thus we may accept something which otherwise we might reject.

In the Transfer device, symbols are constantly used. The cross represents the Christian Church. The flag represents the nation. Cartoons like Uncle Sam represent a consensus of public opinion. Those symbols stir emotions. At their very sight, with the speed of light, is aroused the whole complex of feelings we have with respect to church or nation. A cartoonist by having Uncle Sam disapprove a budget for unemployment relief would have us feel that the whole United States disapproves relief costs. By drawing an Uncle Sam who approves the same budget, the cartoonist would have us feel that the American people approve it. Thus, the Transfer device is used both for and against causes and ideas.

Testimonial

The "Testimonial" is a device to make us accept anything from a patent medicine or a cigarette to a program of national policy. In this device the propagandist makes use of testimonials. "When I feel tired, I smoke a Camel and get the grandest lift." "We believe the John L. Lewis plan of labor organization is splendid; C.I.O. should be supported." This device works in reverse also; counter-testimonials may be employed. Seldom are these used against commercial products like patent medicines and cigarettes, but they are constantly employed in social, economic, and political issues. "We believe the John L. Lewis plan of labor organization is bad; C.I.O. should not be supported."

Plain Folks

"Plain Folks" is a device used by politicians, labor leaders, business men, and even by ministers and educators to win our confidence by appearing to be people like ourselves—"just plain folks among the neighbors." In election years especially do candidates show their devotion to little children and the common, homey things of life. They have front porch campaigns. For the newspaper men they raid the kitchen cupboard finding there some of the good wife's apple pie. They go to country picnics; they attend service at the old frame church; they pitch hay and go fishing; they show their belief in home and mother. In short, they would win our votes by showing that they're just as common as the rest of us—"just plain folks," and therefore, wise and good. Business men often are "plain folks" with the factory hands. Even distillers use the device. "It's our family's whiskey, neighbor; and neighbor, it's your price."

Card Stacking

"Card Stacking" is a device in which the propagandist employs all the arts of deception to win our support for himself, his group, nation, race, policy, practice, belief, or ideal. He stacks the cards against the truth. He uses under-emphasis and over-emphasis to dodge issues and evade facts. He resorts to lies, censorship, and distortion. He omits facts. He offers false testimony. He creates a smokescreen of clamor by raising a new issue when he wants an embarrassing matter forgotten. He draws a red herring across the trail to confuse and divert those in quest of facts he does not want revealed. He makes the unreal appear real and the real appear unreal. He lets half-truth masquerade as truth. By the Card Stacking device, a mediocre candidate, through the "build-up," is made to appear an intellectual titan; an ordinary prize fighter a probable world champion; a worthless patent medicine a beneficent cure. By means of this device propagandists would convince us that a ruthless war of agression is a crusade for righteousness. . . . Card Stacking employs sham, hypocrisy, effrontery.

The Band Wagon

The "Band Wagon" is a device to make us follow the crowd, to accept the propagandist's program en masse. Here his theme is: "Everybody's doing it." His techniques range from those of medicine show to dramatic spectacle. He hires a hall, fills a great stadium, marches a million men in parade. He employs symbols, colors, music, movement, all the dramatic arts. He appeals to the desire, common to most of us, to "follow the crowd." Because he wants us to "follow the crowd" in masses, he directs his appeal to groups held together by common ties of nationality, religion, race, environment, sex, vocation. Thus propagandists campaigning for or against a program will appeal to us as Catholics, Protestants, or Jews; as members of the Nordic race or as Negroes; as farmers or as school teachers; as housewives or as miners. All the artifices of flattery are used to harness the fears and hatreds, prejudices and biases, convictions and ideals common to the group; thus emotion is made to push and pull the group on to the Band Wagon. In newspaper articles and in the spoken word this device is also found. "Don't throw your vote away. Vote for our candidate. He's sure to win." Nearly everybody wins in every election—before the votes are in.

Propaganda And Emotion

Observe that in all these devices our emotion is the stuff with which propagandists work. Without it they are helpless; with it, harnessing it to their purposes, they can make us glow with pride or burn with hatred, they can make us zealots in behalf of the program they espouse. As we said at the beginning, propaganda as generally understood is expression of opinion or action by individuals or groups with reference to predetermined ends. Without the appeal to our emotion—to our fears and to our courage, to our selfishness and unselfishness, to our loves and to our hates—propagandists would influence few opinions and few actions.

To say this is not to condemn emotion, an essential part of life, or to assert that all predetermined ends of propagandists are "bad." What we mean is that the intelligent citizen does not want propagandists to utilize his emotions, even to the attainment of "good" ends, without knowing that is going on. He does not want to be "used" in the attainment of ends he may later consider "bad." He does not want to be gullible. He does not want to be fooled. He does not want to be duped, even in a "good" cause. He wants to know the facts and among these is included the fact of the utilization of his emotions.

Keeping in mind the seven common propaganda devices, turn to today's newspapers and almost immediately you can spot examples of them all. At election time or during any campaign, Plain Folks and Band Wagon are common. Card Stacking is hardest to detect, because it is adroitly executed or because we lack the information necessary to nail the lie. A little practice with the daily newspapers in detecting these propaganda devices soon enables us to detect them elsewhere—in radio, news-reel, books, magazines, and in expressions of labor unions, business groups, churches, schools, political parties.

 POINTS TO CONSIDER

Clyde R. Miller: How to Detect Propaganda

1. What is propaganda? What are its purposes? How does it differ from scientific analysis?

2. What are the seven common propaganda devices which Miller explains, and how do they work? Give examples from your own experience. Can you think of some other common propaganda methods? (See "The Ad and the Id," p. 5, and "Love According to Madison Avenue," p. 18.)

3. How can a novel, a movie, a TV show, or a song operate as a piece of propaganda using one or more of the common devices? Give some examples. (See the works listed under "Propaganda" and "Social Protest and Criticism" in the Thematic Table of Contents.)

4. What are some ways in which propaganda may be harmful in a free society? What are some ways in which it may be beneficial? Give some instances you know of.

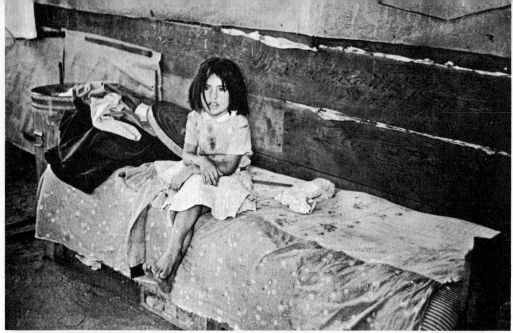

EVERY CALIFORNIA GRAPE YOU BUY HELPS KEEP THIS CHILD HUNGRY.

Under the leadership of Cesar Chavez, we have begun a farm workers' movement to free us from our lives of social and economic bondage. We ask only the same rights and benefits which the majority of American workers already enjoy. We believe that farm workers should be protected by the National Labor Relations Act. We demand that sanitary facilities be placed in the fields to protect both the farm workers and the consumer from disease. We ask for the right to live and work with dignity.

For three years thousands of us have been on strike against California grape growers. The growers have rejected all efforts to negotiate the dispute and have imported illegal labor to break the strike. The Government does nothing or little to stop it. For this reason, with the help of our friends across the nation, we have begun a boycott of ALL CALIFORNIA TABLE GRAPES in order to gain our rights.

We ask you to join us in our common cause. DON'T BUY CALIFORNIA GRAPES until the growers recognize Cesar Chavez and the United Farm Workers Organizing Committee. Together we will win the long and difficult struggle for human dignity and social justice.

DON'T BUY GRAPES

For more information, contact

UNITED FARM WORKERS ORGANIZING COMMITTEE, AFL-CIO

●Post Office Box 130, Delano, California 93215●
Telephone: (805) 725-1314
(From outside California, call the Boycott Department *collect*)

A Statement to the American Public

For two years you have been subjected to grossly misleading propaganda

You have been pressured by activists who would deny you the right to choose what you wish to buy or not buy

You have been harassed and intimidated by unruly pickets at grocery stores and supermarkets

You have a right to know:

THE POSITION OF CALIFORNIA TABLE GRAPE GROWERS

Regarding the Anti-Consumer Grape Boycott

The boycott of California table grapes was launched by Cesaz Chavez' United Farm Workers Organizing Committee, as a result of its near-total failure to organize farm workers in the California vineyards. Actively supported by Students for a Democratic Society, the Third World Liberation Front and other New Left groups, it seeks to inflict damage on *all* growers of a particular crop, including many hundreds of small farmers who employ no labor other than members of their own families.

The facts are:

- U.S. Department of Agriculture statistics show—and any impartial observer can verify—that wage rates for California farm workers are the highest in the continental United States.
- Vineyard workers receive even higher wages than the California average.
- Only a small percentage of vineyard workers are migrants.
- California farm workers are covered by more protective laws than farm workers in any other state.
- From the standpoint of increasing wages and improving working conditions, there is less justification for a boycott of California table grapes than for virtually any crop produced anywhere else in the United States.

The problem of farm labor disputes can only be solved by national legislation establishing ground rules for collective bargaining in agriculture. Thus, the controversy boils down to this:

What kind of legislation is fair to farm workers, farmers and consumers?

UFWOC demands legislation that would force workers to join a union—whether they wish to or not—without the benefit of a secret, impartially supervised election.

UFWOC demands legislation that places no restrictions on strikes and secondary boycotts.

These demands are unacceptable to California grape growers, and we believe to farmers of all crops everywhere in the country. We will not sell out the American consumer or our workers to Chavez' or anyone else's coercive tactics.

California grape growers support legislation that establishes fair collective bargaining in agriculture, including secret election procedures supervised by an Agricultural Labor Relations Board.

California grape growers support legislation that provides reasonable protection from disastrous crop losses due to strikes and boycotts.

Unlike manufactured goods, farm crops subjected to strikes cannot be placed back on a production line. In a matter of days, a farmer can lose his entire year's production and his farm as well.

From the standpoint of consumers, protection against interruptions in the free flow of the nation's food supply is even more important. People have to eat—every day of the year.

Concerned citizens interested in a peaceful settlement of farm labor disputes are urged to direct their energies toward enactment of fair Congressional legislation so that the question of farm worker representation can be settled in an orderly fashion, in all states, without coercion of workers, intimidation of grocery store owners and employees, and harassment of consumers.

We earnestly suggest to UFWOC and to responsible leaders within all of organized labor, that rather than resorting to false propaganda and violence, they join us with reason and logic in the peaceful resolution of equitable national farm-labor legislation.

CALIFORNIA GRAPE AND TREE FRUIT LEAGUE

E. Alan Mills, Executive Vice President • 717 Market Street, San Francisco, California 94103

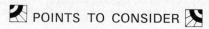

POINTS TO CONSIDER

Two statements on the California grape boycott

1. What propaganda devices can you find in these two statements on the California grape boycott?

2. Why does the United Farm Workers' statement show a picture of a child? Why doesn't the growers' statement include a similar appeal to emotion?

3. In both statements there are repeated references to people's rights. How are these used to arouse people's emotions? Can you find other similar attempts to arouse emotions?

4. What effect do the growers hope to gain by pointing out that SDS and other New Left groups support the boycott? Is this fact relevant to the issue?

5. How do the statements use statistics? Are the statistics and facts cited always relevant to the issue? Could the statistics have been rigged? How?

6. What questions would you put to each group in order to come to the clearest possible understanding of the true situation?

7. Which statement do you think is the most effective as propaganda? Why?

**Funny thing about advertising.
When it goes to work...so do the people.**

Why? Because advertising tells people about things they need and want. And the more they buy...the more must be produced. The result. More jobs.

That's why advertising is not an economic waste. That's why it pays to pay attention when well-meaning people start attacking advertising. They'll tell you advertising makes people want things they don't need. And they're right. Advertising builds dreams. But not idle ones. A new home, a new car, a trip. Maybe they're not lofty or awe-inspiring or earth-shaking. But they're one person's private dreams...and his alone. Put enough of them together and you'll know what made this country great.
Magazine Publishers Association.
An association of 365 leading U.S. magazines

Courtesy of the Magazine Publishers Association.

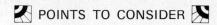 POINTS TO CONSIDER

Ad for Magazine Publishers Association

1. Is this statement advertising or propaganda? Why? What propaganda techniques can you find?

2. Why do you think the Magazine Publishers Association published this statement?

3. Do you believe, as the ad men seem to, that advertising is vital to our economy? Can you think of successful commercial enterprises that have never used advertising?

4. What is your opinion of the kind of dreams advertising builds ("a new home, a new car, a trip")? Do you feel that these are actually the sort of dreams that "made this country great"?

NEWS COVERAGE OF VIOLENCE IN CHICAGO AUGUST 28, 1968

The Village Voice, September 5, 1968

The Streets of Daleyland

by Jack Newfield

"At the southwest entrance to the Hilton, a skinny, long-haired kid of about seventeen skidded down on the sidewalk, and four overweight cops leaped on him, chopping strokes on his head. His hair flew from the force of the blows. A dozen small rivulets of blood began to cascade down the kid's temple and onto the sidewalk. He was not crying or screaming, but crawling in a stupor toward the gutter. When he saw a photographer take a picture, he made a V sign with his fingers.

"A doctor in a white uniform and Red Cross arm band began to run toward the kid, but two other cops caught him from behind and knocked him down. One of them jammed his knee into the doctor's throat and began clubbing his rib cage. The doctor squirmed away, but the cops followed him, swinging hard, sometimes missing.

"A few feet away a phalanx of police charged into a group of women, reporters, and young McCarthy activists standing idly against the window of the Hilton Hotel's Haymarket Inn. The terrified people began to go down under the unexpected police charge when the plate glass window shattered, and the people tumbled backward through the glass. The police then climbed through the broken window and began to beat people, some of whom had been drinking quietly in the hotel bar.

"At the side entrance of the Hilton Hotel four cops were chasing one frightened kid of about seventeen. Suddenly, Fred Dutton, a former aide to Robert Kennedy, moved out from under the marquee and interposed his body between the kid and the police.

"'He's my guest in this hotel,' Dutton told the cops.

"The police started to club the kid.

"Dutton screamed for the first cop's name and badge number. The cop grabbed Dutton and began to arrest him, until a Washington *Post* reporter identified Dutton as a former RFK aide.

"Demonstrators, reporters, McCarthy workers, doctors, all began to stagger into the Hilton lobby, blood streaming from face and head wounds. The lobby smelled from tear gas, and stink bombs dropped by the Yippies. A few people began to direct the wounded to a makeshift hospital on the fifteenth floor, the McCarthy staff headquarters.

"Fred Dutton was screaming at the police, and at the journalists to report all the 'sadism and brutality.' Richard Goodwin, the ashen nub of a cigar sticking out of his fatigued face, mumbled, 'This is just the beginning. There'll be four years of this.'

"The defiant kids began a slow, orderly retreat back up Michigan Avenue. They did not run. They did not panic. They did not fight back. As they fell back they helped pick up fallen comrades who were beaten or gassed. Suddenly, a plainclothesman dressed as a soldier moved out of the shadows and knocked one kid down with an overhand punch. The kid squatted on the pavement of Michigan Avenue, trying to cover his face, while the Chicago plainclothesman punched him with savage accuracy. Thud, thud, thud. Blotches of blood spread over the kid's face. Two photographers moved in. Several police formed a closed circle around the beating to prevent pictures. One of the policemen then squirted Chemical Mace at the photographers, who dispersed. The plainclothesman melted into the line of police."

The Battle of Chicago

Angry and defiant, the youths returned again the following night to Lincoln Park, and again were driven out—this time by stinging yellow clouds of tear gas from a specially equipped dump truck. Instead of dispersing, however, many of the youths moved downtown to Grant Park, in front of the Conrad Hilton. And it was there, soon after delegates had returned from the Amphitheatre, that National Guardsmen rumbled in and took up the police vigil against the youngsters. The spectacle of Army troops aligned against a college-age crowd, highlighted by the television lights and captured by television cameras set up in front of the Hilton, was a perceived reality that some observers could not bear. "You just had to do it, didn't you?" screamed an almost hysterical woman at a policeman. "You just had to do it." Then she broke down and cried. "My God," said another woman, "they're proving everything those kids have been saying."

The kids themselves relaxed, however, under assurances that the soldiers were not planning to drive them out of the park. Peter Yarrow and Mary Trask (two-thirds of the Peter, Paul and Mary folk trio) soothed the crowd by singing folk songs, and later the demonstration became an old-time revival meeting of sorts as individual demonstrators, joined for the first time by some delegates, stood on a makeshift podium and delivered testimonials of their faith in dissent over an electronic megaphone. One speaker urged observers in their hotel rooms across the street to "blink your lights if you're with us." At least fifteen lights in the Conrad Hilton flicked on and off. The kids cheered.

March: Eventually, most of the demonstrators drifted off, and by morning only 80 were left—along with 800 troops. But by midafternoon, the demonstrators' ranks in Grant Park had swelled again as the time approached for the moment of their avowed objective in Chicago—a march on the Amphitheatre at the time of the Presidential balloting.

The march never got started. Police and Guardsmen blocked all efforts to head south to the convention hall, but in their milling attempts to move on, the demonstrators had spilled out into the streets in front of the Hilton, only some 40 yards from the hotel's heavily guarded entranceway. Nervous police moved in several more platoons as the mass in front of the Hilton continued to grow, and then the cops began a slow sweep to clear Michigan Avenue. Spectators, television cameramen, everyone in the street and on the sidewalks was swept up until the crowd was backed up into a solid mass at the south end of the Hilton. "Pigs, pigs, pigs," the contemptuous youths began yelling. "Oink, oink, oink."

Then, without warning, 150 angry cops surged into the terrified crowd, and it didn't matter who was who. "We'll kill all you bastards," screamed a policeman as he kicked into the howling, terrified mob. He grabbed a youngster by his long brown hair, turned him around and jabbed a billy club into his groin. The youth, crying, fell to his knees, as another cop kicked him in the stomach. A plate-glass window in the hotel's drugstore gave way under the pressure of bodies. On the street, panicky youths trampled each other trying to get away. A jumble of bodies curled on the ground as police mercilessly pounded them to the pavement with their clubs. A young girl in a serape was sprawled on her back looking up at the onrushing police, begging them to stop hitting her. The police stepped on her stomach to get to the panicked crowds beyond her.

Finally, the police re-formed their lines, the scattered demonstrators regrouped and chanted, louder and louder, "Pigs, pigs, pigs." And for a while there was a standoff. But only for a while. The cops again charged into the crowd. "If they'd gotten beaten like this when they were kids," growled one policeman, "they wouldn't be out here starting riots."

The New York Times, August 29, 1968

Police Battle Demonstrators in Street: Hundreds Injured

by J. Anthony Lukas

Chicago, Thursday, Aug. 29   The police and National Guardsmen battled young protesters in downtown Chicago last night as the week-long demonstrations against the Democratic National Convention reached a violent and tumultuous climax.

About 100 persons, including 25 policemen, were injured and at least 178 were arrested as the security forces chased down the demonstrators. The protesting young people had broken out of Grant Park on the shore of Lake Michigan in an attempt to reach the International Amphitheatre where the Democrats were meeting, four miles away.

The police and Guardsmen used clubs, rifle butts, tear gas and Chemical Mace on virtually anything moving along Michigan Avenue and the narrow streets of the Loop area.

Uneasy Calm

Shortly after midnight, an uneasy calm ruled the city. However, 1,000 National Guardsmen were moved back in front of the Conrad Hilton Hotel to guard it against more than 5,000 demonstrators who had drifted back into Grant Park.

The crowd in front of the hotel was growing, booing vociferously every time new votes for Vice President Humphrey were broadcast from the convention hall.

The events in the streets stirred anger among some delegates at the convention. In a nominating speech Senator Abraham A. Ribicoff of Connecticut told the delegates that if Senator George S. McGovern were President, "we would not have these Gestapo tactics in the streets of Chicago."

When Mayor Richard J. Daley of Chicago and other Illinois delegates rose shouting angrily, Mr. Ribicoff said, "How hard it is to accept the truth."

Crushed Against Windows

Even elderly bystanders were caught in the police onslaught. At one point, the police turned on several dozen persons standing quietly behind police barriers in front of the Conrad Hilton Hotel watching the demonstrators across the street.

For no reason that could be immediately determined, the blue-helmeted policemen charged the barriers, crushing the spectators against the windows of the Haymarket Inn, a restaurant in the hotel. Finally the window gave way, sending screaming middle-aged women and children backward through the broken shards of glass.

The police then ran into the restaurant and beat some of the victims who had fallen through the windows and arrested them.

At the same time, other policemen outside on the broad, tree-lined avenue were clubbing the young demonstrators repeatedly under television lights and in full view of delegates' wives looking out the hotel's windows.

Afterward, newsmen saw 30 shoes, women's purses and torn pieces of clothing lying with shattered glass on the sidewalk and street outside the hotel and for two blocks in each direction.

It was difficult for newsmen to estimate how many demonstrators were in the streets of midtown Chicago last night. Although 10,000 to 15,000 young people gathered in Grant Park for a rally in the afternoon, some of them had apparently drifted home before the violence broke out in the evening.

Estimates of those involved in the action in the night ranged between 2,000 and 5,000.

Although some youths threw bottles, rocks, stones and even loaves of bread at the police, most of them simply marched and countermarched, trying to avoid the flying police squads.

Some of them carried flags—the black anarchist flag, the red flag, the Vietcong flag and the red and blue flags with a yellow peace symbol.

Stayed Defiant

Although clearly outnumbered and outclassed by the well armed security forces, the thousands of antiwar demonstrators, supporters of Senator Eugene J. McCarthy and Yippies maintained an air of defiance throughout the evening.

They shouted "The streets belong to the people," "This land is our land" and "Hell no, we won't go," as they skirmished along the avenue and among the side streets.

When arrested youths raised their hands in the V for victory sign that has become a symbol of the peace movement, other demonstrators shouted "Sieg heil" or "Pigs" at the policemen making the arrests.

Frank Sullivan, the Police Department's public information director, said the police had reacted only after "50 hard-core leaders" had staged a charge into a police line across Michigan Avenue.

Mr. Sullivan said that among those in the charge were Prof. Sidney Peck, cochairman of the Mobilization Committee to End the War in Vietnam, the group that is spearheading the demonstration. He said Professor Peck had struck James M. Rochford, Deputy Superintendent of Police, with his fist. Mr. Peck was arrested and charged with aggravated assault.

As the night wore on, the police dragnet spread from Michigan Avenue and the area around the Hilton throughout downtown Chicago.

On the corner of Monroe Street and Michigan Avenue, policemen chased demonstrators up the steps of the Chicago Art Institute, a neoclassical Greek temple, and arrested one of them.

As in previous nights of unrest here, newsmen found themselves special targets of the police action. At Michigan Avenue and Van Buren Street, a young photographer ran into the street, terrified, his hands clasped over his head and shrieking "Press, press."

As the police arrested him, he shouted, "What did I do? What did I do?"

The policeman said, "If you don't know you shouldn't be a photographer."

Barton Silverman, a photographer for the New York Times, was briefly arrested near the Hilton Hotel.

Bob Kieckhefer, a reporter for United Press International, was hit in the head by a policeman during the melee in front of the Hilton. He staggered into the UPI office on Michigan Avenue and was taken for treatment to Wesley Memorial Hospital.

Reporters Hampered

Reporters and photographers were repeatedly hampered by the police last night while trying to cover the violence. They were herded into small areas where they could not see the action. On Jackson Street, police forced a mobile television truck to turn off its lights.

Among those arrested was the Rev. John Boyles, Presbyterian chaplain at Yale and a McCarthy staff worker, who was charged with breach of the peace.

"It's an unfounded charge," Mr. Boyles said. "I was protesting the clubbing of a girl I knew from the McCarthy staff. They were beating her on her head with clubs and I yelled at them 'Don't hit a woman,' At that point I was slugged in the stomach and grabbed by a cop who arrested me."

Last night's violence broke out when hundreds of demonstrators tried to leave Grant Park after a rally and enter the Loop area.

At the Congress Street bridge leading from the park onto Michigan Avenue, National Guardsmen fired and sprayed tear gas at the demonstrators five or six times around 7 P.M. to hold them inside the park.

However, one group moved north inside the park and managed to find a way out over another bridge. There they met a contingent of the Poor People's Campaign march led by their symbol, three mule wagons.

Chase Youths

The march was headed south along Michigan Avenue and the police did not disrupt it, apparently because it had a permit. But they began chasing the youths along Michigan Avenue and into side streets.

The demonstrators were then joined by several thousand others who had originally set out from the park in a "non-violent" march to the amphitheatre led by David Dellinger, national chairman of the Mobilization Committee to End the War in Vietnam, and Allen Ginsberg, the poet.

The climactic day of protests began with a mass rally sponsored by the mobilization committee in the band shell in Grant Park.

The rally was intended both as a mass expression of anger at the proceedings across town in the convention and as a "staging ground" for the smaller, more militant march on the amphitheatre.

However, before the rally was an hour old, it, too, was interrupted by violence. Fighting broke out when three demonstrators started hauling down an American flag from a pole by the park's band shell where speakers were denouncing the Chicago authorities, the Johnson Administration and the war in Vietnam.

Four blue-helmeted policemen moved in to stop them and were met by a group of angry demonstrators who pushed them back against a cluster of trees by the side of the band shell. Then the demonstrators, shouting "Pig, pig," pelted the isolated group of 14 policemen with stones, bricks and sticks.

Grenade Hurled Back

Snapping their Plexiglass shields down over their faces, the police moved toward the crowd. One policeman threw or fired a tear-gas grenade into the throng. But a demonstrator picked up the smoking grenade and heaved it back among the police. The crowd cheered with surprise and delight.

But then, from the Inner Drive west of the park, a phalanx of policemen moved into the crowd, using their billy clubs as prods and then swinging them. The demonstrators, who replied with more stones and sticks were pushed back against rows of flaking green benches and trapped there.

Among those injured was Rennie Davis, one of the coordinators for the Mobilization Committee to End the War in Vietnam, which has been spearheading the demonstrations in Chicago.

As the police and demonstrators skirmished on the huge grassy field, mobilization committee leaders on the stage of the baby-blue band shell urged the crowd to sit down and remain calm.

The worst of the fighting was over in 10 minutes, but the two sides were still jostling each other all over the field when Mr. Ginsberg approached the microphone.

Speaking in a cracked and choking voice, Mr. Ginsberg said: "I lost my voice chanting in the park the last few nights. The best strategy for you in cases of hysteria, overexcitement or fear is still to chant 'Om' together. It helps to quell flutterings of butterflies in the belly. Join me now as I try to lead you."

So, as the policemen looked out in astonishment through their Plexiglass face shields, the huge throng chanted the Hindu "Om, om," sending deep mystic reverberations off the glass office towers along Michigan Avenue.

Following Mr. Ginsberg to the microphone was Jean Genet, the French author. His bald head glistening in the glare of television lights, Mr. Genet said through a translator:

"It took an awful lot of deaths in Hanoi for a happening such as is taking place here to occur."

Next on the platform was William Burroughs, author of "The Naked Lunch." A gray fedora on his head, Mr. Burroughs said in a dry, almost distant voice:

"I've just returned from London, England, where there is no effective resistance at all. It's really amazing to see people willing to do something about an unworkable system. It's not evil or immoral, just unworkable. And they're trying to make it work by force. But they can't do it."

Mailer Apologizes

Mr. Burroughs was followed by Norman Mailer, the author who is here to write an article on the convention. Mr. Mailer, who was arrested during the march on the Pentagon last October, apologized to the crowd for not marching in Chicago.

Thrusting his jaw into the microphone, he said: "I'm a little sick about all this and also a little mad, but I've got a deadline on a long piece and I'm not going to go out and march and get arrested. I just came here to salute all of you."

Then Dick Gregory, the comedian and Negro militant leader, took the platform. Dressed in a tan sport shirt and matching trousers with a khaki rain hat on his head, Mr. Gregory said: "You just have to look around you at all the police and soldiers to know you must be doing something right."

Many of the demonstrators in Grant Park had drifted down in small groups from Lincoln Park, where 300 policemen had moved in at 12:15 A.M. yesterday and laid down a barrage of tear gas to clear the area. About 2,000 young protesters had attempted to stay in the park despite an 11 P.M. curfew.

Time, September 6, 1968

Dementia in the Second City

The assault from the left was furious, fluky and bizarre. Yet the Chicago police department responded in a way that could only be characterized as sanctioned mayhem. With billy clubs, tear gas and Mace, the blue-shirted, blue-helmeted cops violated the civil rights of countless innocent citizens and contravened every accepted code of professional police discipline.

No one could accuse the Chicago cops of discrimination. They savagely attacked hippies, yippies, New Leftists, revolutionaries, dissident Democrats, newsmen, photographers, passers-by, clergymen and at least one cripple. Winston Churchill's journalist grandson got roughed up. *Playboy's* Hugh Hefner took a whack on the backside. The police even victimized a member of the British Parliament, Mrs. Anne Kerr, a vacationing Laborite who was Maced outside the Conrad Hilton and hustled off to the lockup.

Bloodletting.   Fortunately, there was no shooting. The demonstrators constantly taunted the police and in some cases deliberately disobeyed reasonable orders. Most of the provocations were verbal—screams of "Pig!" and fouler epithets. Many cops seemed unruffled by the insults. Policeman John Gruber joked: "We kind of like the word pig. Some of us answer our officers 'Oink, oink, sir,' just to show it doesn't bother us." The police reacted more angrily when the demonstrators sang *God Bless America* or recited "I pledge allegiance to the flag."

In some of the wilder fighting, the demonstrators hurled bricks, bottles and nail-studded golf balls at the police lines. During the first three days, the cops generally reacted only with tear gas and occasional beatings. But on Wednesday night, as the convention gathered to nominate Hubert Humphrey, the police had a cathartic bloodletting. Outraged when the protesters lowered a U.S. flag during a rally in Grant Park beside Lake Michigan, the cops hurled tear gas into the crowd.

The demonstrators, bent upon parading to the convention hall (Daley had refused a permit), regrouped in front of the Hilton, where they were surrounded by phalanxes of cops. Police warned the demonstrators to clear the streets, waited for five minutes for several busloads of reinforcements to arrive. And then the order was given.

Violent Orgy.   Chicago cops are built like beer trucks. They flailed blindly into the crowd of some 3,000, then ranged onto the sidewalks to attack onlookers. In a pincer movement, they trapped some 150 people against the wall of the hotel. A window of the Hilton's Haymarket lounge gave way, and about ten of the targets spilled into the lounge after the shards of glass. A squad of police pursued them inside and beat them. Two bunny-clad waitresses took one look and capsized in a dead faint. By now the breakdown of police discipline was complete. Bloodied men and women tried to make their way into the hotel lobby. Upstairs on the 15th floor, aides in the McCarthy headquarters set up a makeshift hospital.

The onslaught ended half an hour later, with about 200 arrested and hundreds injured. Elsewhere, the confrontation continued through the night. Then at 5 a.m. on Friday, with the convention ended, eleven policemen swarmed up to the McCarthy headquarters. They claimed that the volunteers had tossed smoked fish, ashtrays and beer cans at the helmeted cops below. With neither evidence nor search warrant, they clubbed McCarthy campaign workers. One cop actually broke his billy club on a volunteer's skull. Daley stood by his angry defense of his cops' conduct against the "terrorists," who, he snarled, "use the foulest of language that you wouldn't hear in a brothel house."

The demonstrators had chanted the night before: "The whole world is watching!" And it was. Newspapers and television commentators from Moscow to Tokyo reacted with revulsion to the orgy of violence in America's Second City. Thanks to Mayor Daley, not only Chicago but the rest of the U.S. as well was pictured as a police state. That impression may be unfair to a handsome and hospitable city, but it will linger long after Dick Daley's reign.

Law and Order, December 1968

The Strategy of Confrontation

The Hilton Encounter

. . . At 7:57 P.M., Dr. Abernathy and about 6 of his people came walking back toward the line. Just as Dr. Abernathy reached the line, several objects came flying out of the crowd, a roar went up and the chant "Let's go, Let's go" became a roar. The flags which were in the forefront of the crowd on the west half of Michigan surged forward and the violent disorder began.

The policemen at the surge point began to shove back and hit with their night sticks, missiles came flying out of the crowd and the rest of the police line charged into the crowd swinging their sticks. Many arrests were being made. Sidney Peck came up to Deputy Superintendent Rochford and assaulted him saying that "you are responsible for this" while pushing at him. An arrest was attempted by Sgt. Ray O'Malley but he was surrounded by demonstrators and beaten. The arrestees were struggling and screaming. One man was carried by four policemen and he grabbed one of the lead policemen by the ankle and all four of the police fell to the ground. The police got up and one of them kept hitting the man with his night stick. The policeman whose leg had been grabbed was yelling "The bast--d is biting me." It took two other policemen and an Assistant Corporation Counsel to disengage the policeman's leg from the mouth of the prisoner.

There was a great deal of violent action at this time. The arrestees were being literally thrown into the vans. One policeman carried a young teenager in his arms toward the rear and another escorted an elderly woman away from the mob. Missiles were coming from all over, from the north and from the east and south of the police line where the crowd in Grant Park was being held back by other police.

Simultaneously, the crowd next to the east wall of the Hilton on the sidewalk north of the entrance, began to surge to the south and to the east onto the sidewalk. The police were trying to hold them back at the south end and holding them in with the police lines on the east of the crowd. Some of the mob that had been around the loud speaker were pushing the crowd to the south. The police were pushing them north. Two windows were smashed in the east wall and about 6 of the crowd jumped in through the windows. Some police began swinging their night sticks. Some innocent bystanders may have been injured in this particular sweep.

The crowd was obviously stunned and began to move north on Michigan about 50 feet in front of the police line which was walking north toward them. On Michigan at the site of the initial clash, the street was littered with shoes, hats, rocks, Pepsi-Cola cans filled with sand, a black duffle bag filled with rocks and other debris. The time noted by both Deputy Rochford and Mr. Foran was 8:15 P.M.

National Review, September 24, 1968

If a Tree Falls and There Is No One to Hear, Is There a Sound?

The myth has jelled. In Chicago during the Democratic convention, defenseless kids (overexuberant in their idealism perhaps, but just kids) and concerned, ordinary citizens (just folks like you and me) were clubbed, manhandled and tossed into paddy wagons by those blue-helmeted beasts, the Chicago police. What for? Well, for gathering spontaneously, exercising their rights of free speech and assembly. Reporters and photographers were singled out for especially brutal treatment—an attack, clearly, on freedom of the press. Chicago stands shamed before America; America, before the world and, P.S., it's all the fault of that old fascist, Mayor Richard Daley.

There is nothing older than old news—but what about the news that never gets printed, or broadcast? *Is* it news? Is anyone interested in the question of just what it was that the police so "over-reacted" to? Probably not, but permit us a moment of iconoclasm.

1. The demonstrations in Chicago were not spontaneous, they were planned. Back in November 1967, Youth International Party (Yippie) leader Jerry Rubin invited readers of the *Village Voice* to the convention: "Bring pot, fake delegates' cards, smoke bombs, costumes, blood to throw. . . . Also football helmets." Early this year, the National Mobilization Committee to End the War in Vietnam (MOB) (headed by pacifist and self-proclaimed Communist David Dellinger) set up a "Chicago Project Committee." Rennie Davis was put in charge, with orders to "work closely" with Hayden and Rubin. On June 29, Hayden and Dellinger told a press conference that they were "planning tactics of prolonged direct action" (New Left language for anything that produces a confrontation with the System) for Chicago.

On August 9, Davis, Hayden and Yippie "organizer" Abbie Hoffman met to plan the demonstrations—MOB (the hardcore antiwar Left) and the Yippies (politically mobilized flower children) were operating jointly. Hoffman opened outdoor classes in snake-dancing, groin-kicking, cop-spraying and similar tactics. Students were reminded to try to be arrested in front of photographers. Three weeks before the convention, at a secret meeting presided over by Dellinger, a MOB official announced that press releases and statements for "victims of police brutality" had already been prepared.

2. Demonstrators were not denied their constitutional rights. MOB took the city to court, seeking parade and assembly permits—but with conditions that guaranteed, in advance, refusal. Davis sought permission for 200,000 people to march to the convention hall on nomination night, and for 150,000 to assemble at the Grant Park band shell—requests impossible to grant, given the need for security and traffic control. The actual number of Yippies, MOBbies and other protestors in Chicago during the week never amounted to more than 12,000— as Davis knew perfectly well; he wanted confrontations, not permits. MOB also insisted on being granted an assembly site "within eyeshot" of the International Amphitheatre—two sites, in fact, both on private property, whose owners chose not to make them available.

3. The Chicago police were very, very provoked. The psywar had been going on for weeks, in leaflets, underground papers and (whenever they would listen) the straight media: There would be violence, there would be 100,000, 200,000, 500,000 demonstrators, the Loop would be taken over, the Amphitheatre would be burned, and, over and over again, cops were pigs, fascists, beasts, brutes, doomed. During the week itself, in almost every confrontation with the demonstrators (and in all confrontations which erupted in violence), police were pelted with rocks, bottles, stones, bricks and golf balls with nails driven through them, and sprayed with caustic solutions, and always, howled at with the vilest insults imaginable: besides ordinary epithets, detailed references to their alleged sexual eccentricities, those of their wives, of their mothers.

Throughout the week, merchants in the Old Town area near Lincoln Park reported heavy purchases by Yippie types of oven spray (a caustic), hair spray (makes a dandy flame-thrower), flammables, blunt instruments, sharp instruments—a whole dimestore arsenal, and one that was used: The Department released a list of the 198 policemen who were injured in demonstrations, which includes such casualties as "Burns on face . . . sprayed in eyes by unknown chemical . . . human bite—elbow . . . hit in chest with brick . . . kicked in groin . . . abrasion to eye—unknown chemical . . . hit in groin and thigh with brick . . ." No Chicago policeman, by the way, fired a shot all week.

4. The news media distorted the hell out of all this. In their day-to-day coverage, national television and the wire services gave no hint of the provocations hurled at the Chicago police. Viewers saw only the nightsticks rising and falling; they never heard the unison chants of "Fuck the Cops" or saw the bags of human excrement thrown by the Yippies. And after the convention, when it was time to sum up, all the Respected Commentators could do was gangbang the cops. Perhaps because they were mad as hell—the police did, after all, club or otherwise injure 32 reporters and photographers, and hell hath no fury like a journalist when his comrades are kicked around. And still later, when Mayor Daley asked equal time to tell his and the police side of the story, the networks refused. Of course, it was all old news by then—and have you ever known a major news outlet to admit that it was ever wrong about anything?

The news media were awfully cozy with the demonstators, anyway. To get their stories, they went right in there among them—and a policeman handling a mob may not have the time to examine press credentials. Senator Gale McGee (D., Wyo.) reports that he saw a TV camera crew lead two hippie girls over to a line of National Guardsmen, then photograph the scene while the girls obligingly screamed "Don't beat me! Don't beat me!" And according to an undercover policeman, Rubin boasted that the networks advised him (via SDS headquarters) where their cameramen would be, so that he could plan his activities accordingly.

So. The police, some of them, did "over-react." A policeman is, after all, an average Joe with a wife, 2.54 kids and a mortgage; give Joe a nightstick and a badge and put him in front of a taunting, surging mob and you do not automatically get Sir Lancelot. Especially if he is badly under-trained in the handling of large crowds and super-especially if the crowds are out to get *him,* rather than some other target (a supermarket; a rock-n-roll idol) under his protection.

It may be, as Garry Wills suggests elsewhere in this issue, that the young demonstrators led their leaders more than the other way around—that is irrelevant; violence was planned, and sought, and occurred. It is certainly *not* true that the demonstrators were, as Senator Stephen M. Young (D., Ohio) claimed the other day, carefree youngsters "filled with enthusiasm for Senator Eugene McCarthy . . . singing, laughing, shouting and passing out McCarthy literature." (The nihilists were of course delighted to let befuddled McCarthyites into their ranks to be clubbed—they looked so respectable.) In "the kids'" view, a McCarthy nomination would have helped the System, and the System is what they are out to destroy. Our leaders, our courts, our news media and especially our police had best learn how to deal with that threat. Meanwhile, we should not say of the police (the British journalist Peregrine Worsthorne neatly put the words in our mouths), "This beast is dangerous—when attacked he defends himself."

The Washington Star, September 1, 1968

The Other Side of the Chicago Police Story

by Betty Beale

This columnist has just returned from Chicago—unbloodied, unpelted and even unbruised, thanks to the Chicago police.

It is time one member of the media gave the other side of the picture, because the public has the right to know.

Never has a law-enforcing group been more sorely tried. They received both bodily injury and unspeakably vile treatment from the hippies in Grant Park. Yet never at any time did I see policemen show more courtesy than the police of Chicago. Courtesy, of course, is only due people who show some courtesy themselves.

And, despite the difficult circumstances in which they had to maintain order, they managed to prevent fatal catastrophe.

We heard the word "overreacted" used a lot by commentators last week, and by busy politicians who were assuming that what they had been told was correct.

But if there was ever an overreaction to any fact of life during those seven days in Chicago, it was the overreaction of the media to any effort whatsoever to stop the hippies from the flagrant civil disorders and their disgusting disturbances of the peace.

Every time a newsman was hurt, the screams of protest went around the world, but how much was said about the newsmen who taunted the police or tried to get action for the TV cameras? A member of the Vice President's coterie heard two reporters having a great laugh in the coffee shop of the Conrad Hilton about how they agitated in Grant Park until the police started pushing them around.

Wyoming Senator and Mrs. Gale McGee and their two grown children walked over to the park to see for themselves what was going on, and they arrived when the changing of the National Guard troops was taking place.

Walking through a gang of hippies they saw two girls, one playing the flute. Then they saw a TV camera team lead the girls over to the exact place by the troops where they wanted them to stand. And when their camera started to roll, the girls cried, "Don't beat me! Don't beat me!" It takes no imagination to figure how this contrived scene would look on the screens in millions of American homes.

In the Convention hall, Mrs. McGee said a youth of about 15 sat in front of them and clapped hard at everything said that he liked and shouted four-letter words at everything he didn't like.

Instead of just grabbing him and removing him, as the police would have done in most civilized places, the police asked him first to stop it. But he paid no attention to them, so "they had to take him out," said Mrs. McGee. The cameras probably caught the big policemen bodily forcing the mere youth to leave, giving the television viewer the idea he had done nothing to provoke such reaction.

And what, by the way, has happened to the news media that provocation is left out of, or played down in, story after story?

Most announcements or headlines told what the police did to the hippies but left out or skimmed over what the hippies did to the public or police.

Senator Daniel Inouye, of Hawaii, World War hero and Democratic keynoter, said the hippies were throwing plastic bags of human excrement at the police and guards in Grant Park. They were also throwing rubber balls stuck with long nails aimed for the eyes. How would those commentators who thought the police "overreacted" have behaved if those things had happened to them?

For three straight minutes late Tuesday night, or rather early Wednesday morning, 3,000 hippies shouted in unison, directed by a leader, an obscene curse at the President of the United States. They were either cursing the police in the same way or calling them pigs. And I used to think that insulting an officer was against the law!

Why was an electronic amplifier allowed to remain in the park all day and night where obscenities were shouted until 4 a.m., I asked a police officer. There was a city ordinance against such use, he said, but if they arrested those using it they would only be fined and somebody might be killed in the process. If this wasn't underreacting, what is?

Mayor Daley was constantly referred to on the air in slurring accents as the boss of Chicago. He may be, and he is responsible, no doubt, for some bad as well as some good. But Chicago is only one city.

Two famous TV commentators were bossing the presentation of slanted news that affected the minds of millions of Americans in hundreds of cities. As Liz Carpenter [press secretary for Mrs. Johnson] said at the women's luncheon Thursday, in all the talk of brutality there had not been "one word about the TV network brutality—the commentator clubbing" of the mayor.

When the mayor fails to do what the majority of the people in Chicago want, they can at least vote him out. But no vote can stop the bossism of the airwaves where editorializing has been substituted again and again for straight reporting. One NBC commentator virtually campaigned for Teddy Kennedy throughout Tuesday evening.

In the past I have been proud to be a member of the Fourth Estate, but after this past week I feel a burning inward shame. In my mind, freedom of the press has always been necessary to liberty. The Bible states it most beautifully: "Ye shall know the truth, and the truth shall make you free."

But how much truth and how much biased opinion are the people, and especially the youth of America, getting?

The Other Side of the Chicago Police Story 87

A clean, well-combed, pretty young girl for Senator McCarthy was one of five of us who shared a taxi to O'Hare Airport Friday, and the conversation turned to what the hippies had done to convert the serious business of nominating a presidential candidate into a circus of vulgarity.

Unbelievably, she stood up for the right of the Grant Park crowd to curse the President in four-letter words. She had no respect for the highest office of our land.

When one of the men blamed Tom Hayden [cochairman of the National Mobilization Committee to End the War in Vietnam and a founder of the Students for a Democratic Society] for leading the youth to such actions, she said Tom was all right; he was a friend of hers.

I am not familiar with Hayden's record, but the fact that this young woman supported him and his undertaking indicated the truth had not reached her, as it is not reaching millions of young people.

Maybe the media had better ask itself why.

 POINTS TO CONSIDER

News Coverage of Violence in Chicago, August 28, 1968

1. All the news reports and articles from the seven popular magazines and newspapers cover the same events, but each gives a different picture of what occurred. What determines the picture which each publication chooses to paint of the event? Do you know some newspapers or magazines whose views of particular events you can guess even before you read them?

2. From reading the different accounts of the Chicago disorders presented by the seven publications, can you make any educated guesses about the views held by each of these publications on other social or political issues?

3. What are some of the ways that the news is slanted in each of these news reports or articles? (See Duane Bradley: "What Is News?" p. 55.) What kinds of progaganda devices or emotional appeals are employed in each of the news reports or articles? (See Clyde Miller: "How to Detect Propaganda," p. 62.) Which selections do you feel employ slanting, propaganda, and emotional appeals most skillfully? Which selections do you feel employ these techniques least skillfully? Why?

Pornography and Violence

Irving Younger

The Nation, August 14, 1967

Ian Brady and Myra Hindley were tried, convicted and sentenced last year in the Assize Court at Chester, England, for the murder of Edward Evans (17 years old) and Lesley Ann Downey (10 years old). Brady alone was convicted of murdering John Kilbride (12 years old). The killings were particularly atrocious. It appears that Brady and Hindley tortured and sexually abused the two children, as an extra fillip tape-recording the agonies of the girl. They buried the bodies on the moors outside Chester.

Of normal intelligence and without clinical symptoms of madness, the murderers were students of sado-masochism, sexual perversion and fascism, on which subjects they had accumulated a small library (e.g., *The Pleasures of the Torture Chamber, Sexual Anomalies and Perversions, Mein Kampf*). Their especial hero was the Marquis de Sade.[1]

Pamela Hansford Johnson has made rather a good thing out of these infamous murders. Assigned by the London *Sunday Telegraph* to cover the trial, she wrote it up for *Life,** and then published a book that, although silent on its genesis, is in fact an expansion of the *Life* article.**

Miss Hansford Johnson speculates whether society should not limit the freedom of the writer to write obscenity in order to lessen the risk that at other times and places other demons like Brady and Hindley may be driven by books to commit dreadful crimes. She gives no answers, resting on the hope that her book will set others thinking.

Let us try.

The issue is one of law, since the limitation of freedom is an end to which law is the means.

In Britain, by the Obscene Publications Act of 1959, a person may be imprisoned for publishing obscenity, which the act defines as any article whose effect is "such as to tend to deprave and corrupt persons" who are likely to be exposed to it.

In the United States, a federal statute makes it a felony to mail anything which is "obscene, lewd, lascivious, indecent, filthy or vile." Piling up words

* "Who's to Blame When a Murderer Strikes?" August 12, 1966.

** *On Iniquity,* Charles Scribner's Sons.

[1] Sado-masochism is the abnormal enjoyment of inflicting or suffering pain or abuse, often for sexual gratification. The term sadism—meaning the abnormal pleasure in causing pain—is derived from the name of the Marquis de Sade (1740–1814), a writer who studied and depicted this abnormality.

is no way to convey meaning. What exactly the American statute forbids is as difficult to say as what exactly the British statute forbids. So we pass directly to the initial query:

What are we talking about? The plain answer is that we are talking about pornography. The trouble with this plain answer is that it is impossible once and for all to define pornography. In a recent case, the Supreme Court announced that seven Justices have four different ideas of pornography. Justices Black and Douglas believe that government is utterly without power to suppress or control pornography, whatever it is. Justice Stewart would limit government's power to the suppression of "hard-core" pornography, which he cannot define. Chief Justice Warren, Justice Brennan and Justice Fortas think that obscenity is material that taken as a whole appeals to a prurient interest in sex, is patently offensive when measured by contemporary community standards, and is utterly without redeeming social value. Justice Harlan is of the opinion that redeeming social value has nothing to do with it.

If we do not concern ourselves unduly with the Supreme Court's verbalizations, we can read its many decisions on obscenity as follows: (1) there is something called pornography which, by the gambit of labeling it not-speech, the Court casts beyond the protection of the First Amendment to the Constitution; (2) because it is beyond the protection of the First Amendment, pornography may be forbidden, controlled or regulated; (3) it is bootless to try to define pornography in the abstract, for whatever the Court thinks *should* be forbidden, controlled or regulated *is* pornography; (4) the Court does not yet understand fully the considerations that determine whether material should be forbidden, controlled or regulated. Perhaps something of this was in Justice Stewart's mind when, in a case several years ago, he said that he couldn't define pornography, "but I know it when I see it."

In order to discourse rationally, we need to be somewhat less pithy than Justice Stewart, and so we shall posit a definition: pornography is material that deals with sexual life.

The considerations that determine whether pornography should be forbidden, regulated or controlled are not, after all, so very obscure. One way to illuminate them is to examine the value of pornography from the viewpoint of the pornographer, the pervert and the ordinary person.

An obvious value of pornography to the pornographer is its profitability. We can readily imagine a pornographer for whom pornography has no other value —the peddler of filthy post cards, of lubricious comic strips, of priapic motion pictures.[2] We can just as easily imagine a pornographer for whom pornography has some other value. Pornography may be the substance of comedy (*Gargantua and Pantagruel,* Book 2, chapters 21–22) or of tragedy (*Les Liaisons Dangereuses*). Pornography may supply the rhetoric to vivify an otherwise dull

[2] Lubricious means lewd; priapic means sexually stimulating.

text *(Ezekiel)*. Pornography may symbolize something not pornographic *(The Song of Songs)*.[3]

In short, pornography is important to art. None would object to curtailing the freedom of the pornographer whose sole motive is profit, if one could be sure that the artist's freedom to use pornography would not also be circumscribed. The problem seems to be that the law does not know how to tell the artist from the entrepreneur. The Supreme Court says that a redeeming social value is what divides art from commerce. How then [can it] tell whether a work has redeeming social value? Chief Justice Warren and Justices Brennan, Fortas and Stewart think *Fanny Hill* has it. Justices Clark, Harlan and White think not. When reasonable men cannot agree on the result, it may be that the formula is wrong.

To find out whether a certain pornographer is an artist, why not ask other artists? Their opinion will conclude the matter. Such a test would have two of the greatest virtues a law can have—simplicity and certainty. At a pornography trial, the defendant would call artists to the witness stand. If they testify that the defendant is an artist, the judge dismisses the case, for the artist should be exempt from punishment as a pornographer. If no artists believe that the defendant is one, the jury convicts him and the judge sentences him, for punishment should be the lot of the pecuniary pornographer.

What marriage manuals are to the innocent, pornography is to the pervert. Where else, if not in pornography, can he find out how to vent his passions. Not every deviate is as fecund of satisfactions as the copious de Sade.[4] Burning with a fire that he cannot name, let alone learn how to quench, his libido may boil over into brutish violence (one Jack the Ripper is enough), whereas, could he only read somewhere what men similarly situated have done in the past, he might well find some relatively harmless means of release.[5] Most of us have at one time or another asked, "What exactly is it that pederasts (for example), *do?*" The nascent pederast is no different.[6] What exactly is he to do? He finds the answer, as the rest of us have found it, in pornography.

The social utility of pornography to perverts has been insufficiently appreciated.

To ordinary persons, pornography is a pleasant diversion. It is absurd that the heavy weaponry of the law should be brought to bear on such a trifle. The

---

[3] *Gargantua and Pantagruel* is a novel (1535) by the French writer François Rabelais which points out faults in society by exaggerating them. *Les Liaisons Dangereuses* is a novel (1782) of sexual intrigue which reveals the decadence of mid-eighteenth-century Parisian high society. In the Biblical book of Ezekiel the prophet uses the images of harlotry to describe the sins of the people. *The Song of Songs* is a Biblical love poem in which young lovers describe the beauties of their loved ones. This poem is often interpreted as representing the spiritual love of God and man or of Christ and the church.

[4] Fecund means fruitful, prolific, or highly inventive.

[5] Libido is sexual desire.

[6] A pederast is a man who has a boy as a lover. Nascent means budding or developing.

lawyers themselves know that quixotry never justifies resort to the majesty of the law.[7] *De minimis non curat lex,* they say. The law does not concern itself with small things.

Ordinary persons do, however, concern themselves with their small children. If parents think it desirable, they may elect to supply their small children with pornography, but most, for self-evident reasons, will not. The latter object to the activities of any pornographer who caters to their children, for the very good reason that nobody relishes interference with his right to raise his children as he sees fit. So any law that forbids strangers to feed pornography to children will receive general approbation.

Ordinary persons believe that they can take pornography or leave it alone. Their picture of their sexual selves is one of sophisticated self-control. Accordingly, the pornographer who thrusts his merchandise on a disinterested or reluctant customer makes himself a stench in the nostrils of the community. Should the law interdict him, all would applaud.

This is not to say that pornography as an element of salesmanship must be forbidden. Without pornography, advertising would make dull reading indeed. The leer of the sensualist has long been recognized as a way to get people to buy. In *On Iniquity,* for example, Miss Hansford Johnson leers like a sensualist every 15 pages or so:

> There is not much doubt that the child was submitted to gross sexual indignities after the photographs were taken and, presumably, between the two periods when she seems to have been gagged. The transcript may be read in more than one way, but only one of them really makes some dreadful sense. . . .
> I wanted to attend the Moors Trial: also, I did not. The details of it had already sickened me. My imagination ran too freely. But there is no disguising the fact that a part of me was titillated. I wanted to know *all* the details, not solely because it was my job to do so, but because there was in them an element of repulsive stimulation.
> . . . It might have been better for me, an individual, if I had had nothing to do with this case at all. It has left a mark which I think will never quite be eradicated. People who talk about the trial, who have followed, even closely, the press reports, have small idea what it actually meant: what actually happened. What did happen to Lesley Ann Downey, as is generally agreed by those close to the case, I cannot put on paper.

Pornography is so deeply rooted in the tradition of literary salesmanship that it cannot be excised. Who would ever approve a law that might punish Pamela Hansford Johnson as a pornographer?

A failure to perceive the connection between advertising and pornography may explain the Supreme Court's decision in the Ralph Ginzburg case, surely one of the silliest opinions ever written. Recently the Court held publications such as *Lust Pool, Shame Agent* and *High Heels* to be not obscene. Yet Ginzburg was convicted (and sentenced to five years' imprisonment) for publishing *Eros,*

---

[7] Quixotry here means romantic fantasy.

a magazine devoted to charmingly romantic celebrations of sex, *The Housewife's Handbook on Selective Promiscuity,* a bland, clumsy and moralizing account of a lady's sexual experiences, and *Liaison,* a pamphlet containing articles on sex reprinted from professional journals. Recognizing that such material by its own tests is not obscene, the Supreme Court looked to Ginzburg's supposedly pornographic advertising to support the conviction. If it were not for Ginzburg's punishment, the opinion would be little more than cause for fun with the Court. Remembering his punishment, the angel of reason and justice must weep.

Granted! Miss Hansford Johnson might cry, but you have not faced up to the basic question, which is "whether, by making all books available to all men, we do not pay too high a price, if that price should be the death of one small child by torture."

When she suggests that literature drives men to torture and murder, Miss Hansford Johnson indulges in the pathetic fallacy of investing one's self and one's works with the power of miracles. Who has not walked in the street and seen a child suffering at nature's not always perfect hand—a little girl with palsy, perhaps, or a mongoloid boy?[8] Who has not then said to himself, "If I could buy normalcy for that child at the price of my sight (or my right arm, or both my legs, or my life), I would pay it." So with artists. How pleasurable to imagine that, if only they gave up their art, the children would be healed, would live.

Unfortunately for the poetry of things, there is no shred of evidence to think so. As Miss Hansford Johnson puts the question, it is too easy. Of course the death of one small child, by torture or otherwise, is too high a price to pay for "making all books available to all men." The problem, really, is whether, if we paid the price, one small child might live who otherwise would die. That answer nobody knows. Without proof, the sane legislator will not restrict the artist's freedom to create or the audience's freedom to consume.

Certain limitations on pornography, we see, would be wise and feasible. They can be expressed in a simple code. (1) "Pornography" means material that deals with sexual life. (2) It is forbidden to sell or give pornography to any person under the age of 18 who is not the child of the seller or giver. (3) It is forbidden to attempt to sell or give pornography to anyone who is unwilling to buy or receive it.

Here we have an answer to Miss Hansford Johnson's question. And once more Iago proves himself the most percipient of psychologists:[9] "If the balance of our lives had not one scale of reason to poise another of sensuality, the blood and baseness of our nature would conduct us to most preposterous conclusions."

---

[8] A mongoloid child has a birth defect which affects his appearance and often impairs his intelligence.

[9] Iago is the villain of Shakespeare's tragedy *Othello* who causes the downfall of the hero by cleverly playing upon his emotional weaknesses. Percipient means perceptive.

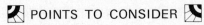

POINTS TO CONSIDER

Irving Younger: Pornography and Violence

1. What are some of the different definitions offered for "pornography" or "obscenity"? Why do you think it is so difficult for individuals and for social institutions to be more specific in their definitions or to be in closer agreement on their definitions?

2. What are some of the values to art found in pornography when defined in its broadest sense as "material that deals with sexual life"? How does the law attempt to differentiate between art that contains pornography and "hard core" pornography or "smut"? Why is this differentiation so difficult to make?

3. What does Younger consider to be the "sexual utility" of pornography to perverts and to ordinary persons?

4. How is pornography utilized as an element of advertising?

5. What relationships do some people make between pornography and criminal violence? To what extent do you feel that arguments stressing such relationships are valid? How does Younger react to these arguments?

6. What does Younger feel are the dangers of widespread censorship or legislation against pornography? Do you agree? What legal limitations does Younger believe would be useful to set on the sale of pornography? Do you agree?

TEEN SHOCKER I TURNED THE SCHOOL DANCE INTO A DRUG-FILLED SEX ORGY

Confession Secrets

MARCH
35c
MAC

wedding night bet—
"I'LL HAVE HER BEGGING FOR MORE!"
HE BRAGGED TO HIS FRIENDS

14-And My Stepfather Said,
"NOW YOU'RE RIPE FOR ME TO LOVE"

MY HUSBAND THINKS I'M
FRIGID,
BUT HIS BROTHER KNOWS I'M NOT!

VIRGIN NURSE
IN A SEX-CRAZED MADMAN'S WARD

Courtesy of Emtee Publications, Inc.

Psychiatrists Say Smut Won't "Motivate" You

Associated Press, August 24, 1969

Chicago (AP)—Most psychiatrists and psychologists who participated in a University of Chicago poll said they found no cases in which exposure to pornography caused antisocial sexual behavior.

Findings were based on questionnaires filled out by more than 3400 professionals in the mental health field.

The announcement said responses to questions show:

80% of the psychiatrists and psychologists said they had never encountered any cases in which pornography was a causal factor in antisocial sexual behavior.

7.4% did encounter cases in which they were somewhat convinced of a link between the two.

9.4% had cases in which they suspected, but were not convinced of, a link.

83.7% believed persons exposed to pornography are no more likely to engage in antisocial sexual acts than persons not exposed.

65.5% did not feel that eliminating censorship would reduce the desire for pornographic materials.

86.1% believed persons who vigorously try to suppress pornography are often motivated by unresolved sexual problems in their own characters.

64.9% believed censorship is socially harmful because it contributes to a climate of oppression and inhibition in which creative individuals can't express themselves adequately.

55.7% believed some form of censorship should be applied to pornography.

76.2% did not believe watching violence on TV or in movies tends to excite some persons or frequently leads to violent behavior.

Pornography was defined as photographs, drawings or printed material with no pretense of artistic value which depict sexual acts.

Pollyanna Digest

H. Marshall McLuhan
The Mechanical Bride, 1951

"Unpack your suitcase and live!" Between the covers of the *Reader's Digest* the sky is officially not cloudy all day. Here again we are home on the range and away from the cold-groin and blue-armpit world of the daytime serial. Here we meet not the gothic gargoyles of the lonely hearts, but the pep and bounce of the ozone plains where the deer and the antelope play. But just as these cheerful words are set in the song to a most mournful air, so the "keep smiling" creed of the *Digest* gets its meaning from the joyless intensity of commerce.

Since the merely practical man lives so much in a world of risk capital, liquidity preferences, and uncertain probabilities, he craves many kinds of reassurance and a spate of encouraging words. Poised on the bubble of business confidence, panic easily rises in his heart, even as he keeps the bubble floating along. Those prayerful imperatives which decorate the walls of the private chapels of commerce are easily understood in this context: THINK. SMILE.

The success story in a hundred guises is the formula of the *Digest*, as in such items on the present cover as:

Blind, He Teaches Those Who See.

Marriage Control: A New Answer To Divorce

Take a Cow to College And Make It Pay

Human Engineering at Boys' Ranch

In "Sunny—The Spirit of '76" there is a story about a little ranch girl:

> . . . The meanest old hammerheads under her tutelage became as cooing doves. All day long she worked with them and at night she sang about them. Sitting on the hearth, her blonde hair golden in the firelight, she'd cuddle the ranch guitar and croon heart-breakingly . . .
> "You ought to be on the radio," Noelke told her.

This is not just the *Digest* formula but will be found in most entertainment, business, and education. It can be stated very simply: Since there's a heap of goodness, beauty, and power in everybody and everything, let's extract it and then box it, bottle it, or can it, and hurry to market. The smart little pig went to market, the dumb little pig stayed home. But if some accident should keep the smart little pig at home, then bet your boots that little old home is going to bloom out into a $100,000 business, at least, and provide a lesson of comfort and solace to the entire community.

The endless use of the Barnum and Ripley technique of stressing the feasibility of the impossible as a challenge to curiosity and emulation results in the tediously terrific and the forcible feeble. If there is any harm done by the *Digest* or by any of the related entertainment industries, it is in supplanting better fare. It is the sheer presence of successful stupidity which commonly blocks and clutters the minds of those who might conceivably prefer something better. The *Digest* is also typical of all these agencies of mass diversion in eagerly creating an aura of intolerance around itself and its readers. Enfolded in its jovial, optimistic, and self-satisfied version of the higher things, the reader soon hardens into a man who "knows what he likes" and who resents anybody who pretends to like anything better. He has, unwittingly, been sold a strait jacket. And that is really as much as need be said about any of the effects of commercial formula writing, living, and entertainment. It destroys human autonomy, freezes perception, and sterilizes judgment.

The higher comedy is not to be found in the earnestness of *Digest* cheerfulness but in such displays as *The New Yorker* when attacking the *Digest.* In a book called *Little Wonder,* mainly reprinted from *The New Yorker,* the *Digest* was supposedly devastated. However, the author was much embarrassed at being unable to discover any sizable chinks in the moral armor of the *Digest* and its editors, and he was content to sneer at what was too evidently a lack of aesthetic dandyism in the earnest and convinced *Digest* makers. It was like a wrestling match between two men, each of whom was locked in a separate trunk. *The New Yorker* fan and the *Digest* addict are carried in different coaches through the same tunnel.

This fact is pointed out lest it be supposed that it has been argued here that there is value in merely attacking vulgarity and stupidity. Because today there is far too much of these commodities intermixed with valuable articles to make such a course desirable. What is needed is not attacks on obvious imbecility but a sharp eye for what supports and is now involved in it. It is from this habit of dissociation that the means of recreating shopworn values can come. As said earlier in "From Top to Toe," our situation is very like that of Poe's sailor in "The Maelstrom," and we are now obliged not to attack or avoid the *strom* but to study its operation as providing a means of release from it.

 POINTS TO CONSIDER

H. Marshall McLuhan: Pollyanna Digest

1. According to McLuhan, why does the *Reader's Digest* appeal so strongly to the "practical man"?

2. What is the formula which McLuhan says the *Digest* uses? Can you cite other uses of the same formula?

3. What does McLuhan mean by the "tediously terrific and the forcible feeble"? Can you think of examples of the same effect from other media?

4. How does the *Digest* create intolerance in its readers? Do other magazines do the same thing? How does this intolerance function as a mental "strait jacket"?

5. According to McLuhan, what harm does the *Digest* do? Do you agree?

6. Why does McLuhan feel there is no value in merely attacking "vulgarity and stupidity" in mass media and the popular arts? Do you agree? Explain.

7. McLuhan suggests that like Poe's sailor, we are trapped in a "maelstrom" of mass media and popular culture. Do you feel that movies, television, mass magazines, and other forms of popular culture are potentially dangerous to society? Explain. How can studying the operation of this maelstrom lead to a release from it?

The Playboy and Miss America

Harvey Cox
The Secular City, 1966

Let us look at the spurious sexual models conjured up for our anxious society by the sorcerers of the mass media and the advertising guild.[1] Like all pagan deities, these come in pairs—the god and his consort. For our purposes they are best symbolized by The Playboy and Miss America, the Adonis and Aphrodite of a leisure-consumer society which still seems unready to venture into full postreligious maturity and freedom. The Playboy and Miss America represent The Boy and The Girl. They incorporate a vision of life. They function as religious phenomena and should be exorcised and exposed.

Let us begin with Miss America. In the first century B.C., Lucretius wrote this description of the pageant of Cybele:[2]

> Adorned with emblem and crown . . . she is carried in awe-inspiring state. Tight-stretched tambourines and hollow cymbals thunder all round to the stroke of open hands, hollow pipes stir with Phrygian strain. . . . She rides in procession through

[1] Spurious means counterfeit or false.

[2] Cybele was an ancient Roman goddess of nature worshipped in elaborate festivals.

great cities and mutely enriches mortals with a blessing not expressed in words. They straw all her path with brass and silver, presenting her with bounteous alms, and scatter over her a snow-shower of roses.

Now compare this with the annual twentieth-century Miss America pageant in Atlantic City, New Jersey. Spotlights probe the dimness like votive tapers, banks of flowers exude their varied aromas, the orchestra blends feminine strings and regal trumpets. There is a hushed moment of tortured suspense, a drumroll, then the climax—a young woman with carefully prescribed anatomical proportions and exemplary "personality" parades serenely with scepter and crown to her throne. At TV sets across the nation throats tighten and eyes moisten. "There she goes, Miss America—" sings the crooner. "There she goes, your ideal." A new queen in America's emerging cult of The Girl has been crowned.

This young woman—though she is no doubt totally ignorant of the fact—symbolizes something beyond herself. She symbolizes The Girl, the primal image, the one behind the many. Just as the Virgin appears in many guises—as our Lady of Lourdes or of Fatima or of Guadalupe—but is always recognizably the Virgin, so with The Girl.

The Girl is also the omnipresent icon of consumer society.[3] Selling beer, she is folksy and jolly. Selling gems, she is chic and distant. But behind her various theophanies she remains recognizably The Girl.[4] In Miss America's glowingly healthy smile, her openly sexual but officially virginal figure, and in the name-brand gadgets around her, she personifies the stunted aspirations and ambivalent fears of her culture.[5] "There she goes, your ideal."

Miss America stands in a long line of queens going back to Isis, Ceres, and Aphrodite.[6] Everything from the elaborate sexual taboos surrounding her person to the symbolic gifts at her coronation hints at her ancient ancestry. But the real proof comes when we find that the function served by The Girl in our culture is just as much a "religious" one as that served by Cybele in hers. The functions are identical—to provide a secure personal "identity" for initiates and to sanctify a particular value structure.

Let us look first at the way in which The Girl confers a kind of identity on her initiates. Simone de Beauvoir says in *The Second Sex* that "no one is *born* a woman." One is merely born a female, and "*becomes* a woman" according to the models and meanings provided by the civilization. During the classical Christian centuries, it might be argued, the Virgin Mary served in part as this model. With

[3] An omnipresent icon is a portrait, usually of a religious figure, present everywhere at once.

[4] Theophanies are visible forms of a god.

[5] To be ambivalent is to have conflicting feelings toward a person or thing.

[6] Isis, Ceres, and Aphrodite are all ancient goddesses. Isis was the Egyptian goddess of motherhood and fertility, Ceres the Roman goddess of vegetation (especially grain), and Aphrodite the Greek goddess of love and beauty.

the Reformation and especially with the Puritans, the place of Mary within the symbol system of the Protestant countries was reduced or eliminated. There are those who claim that this excision constituted an excess of zeal that greatly impoverished Western culture, an impoverishment from which it has never recovered. Some would even claim that the alleged failure of American novelists to produce a single great heroine (we have no Phaedra, no Anna Karenina) stems from this self-imposed lack of a central feminine ideal.

Without entering into this fascinating discussion, we can certainly be sure that, even within modern American Roman Catholicism, the Virgin Mary provides an identity image for few American girls. Where then do they look for the "model" Simone de Beauvoir convincingly contends they need? For most, the prototype of femininity seen in their mothers, their friends, and in the multitudinous images to which they are exposed on the mass media is what we have called The Girl.

To describe the mechanics of this complex psychological process by which the fledgling American girl participates in the life of The Girl and thus attains a woman's identity would require a thorough description of American adolescence. There is little doubt, however, that such an analysis would reveal certain striking parallels to the "savage" practices by which initiates in the mystery cults shared in the magical life of their god.

For those inured to the process, the tortuous nightly fetish by which the young American female pulls her hair into tight bunches secured by metal clips may bear little resemblance to the incisions made on their arms by certain African tribesmen to make them resemble their totem, the tiger. But to an anthropologist comparing two ways of attempting to resemble the holy one, the only difference might appear to be that with the Africans the torture is over after initiation, while with the American it has to be repeated every night, a luxury only a culture with abundant leisure can afford.

In turning now to an examination of the second function of The Girl—supporting and portraying a value system—a comparison with the role of the Virgin in the twelfth and thirteenth centuries may be helpful. Just as the Virgin exhibited and sustained the ideals of the age that fashioned Chartres Cathedral, as Henry Adams saw, so The Girl symbolizes the values and aspirations of a consumer society. (She is crowned not in the political capital, remember, but in Atlantic City or Miami Beach, centers associated with leisure and consumption.) And she is not entirely incapable of exploitation. If men sometimes sought to buy with gold the Virgin's blessings on their questionable causes, so The Girl now dispenses her charismatic favor on watches, refrigerators, and razor blades— for a price.[7] Though The Girl has built no cathedrals, without her the colossal edifice of mass persuasion would crumble. Her sharply stylized face and figure

---

[7] Charismatic means having great spiritual power or charm for appealing to people and gaining their support.

beckon us from every magazine and TV channel, luring us toward the beatific vision of a consumer's paradise.[8]

Besides sanctifying a set of phony values, The Girl compounds her noxiousness by maiming her victims in a Procrustean bed of uniformity.[9] This is the empty "identity" she panders.[10] Take the Miss America pageant, for example. Are these virtually indistinguishable specimens of white, middle-class postadolescence really the best we can do? Do they not mirror the ethos of a mass-production society, in which genuine individualism somehow mars the clean, precision-tooled effect?[11] Like their sisters, the finely calibrated Rockettes, these meticulously measured and pretested "beauties" lined up on the boardwalk bear an ominous similarity to the faceless retinues of goose-steppers and the interchangeable mass exercisers of explicitly totalitarian societies.[12] In short, *who* says this is beauty?

The caricature becomes complete in the Miss Universe contest, when Miss Rhodesia is a blonde, Miss South Africa is white, and Oriental girls with a totally different tradition of feminine beauty are forced to display their thighs and appear in spike heels and Catalina swim suits. Miss Universe is as universal as an American adman's stereotype of what beauty should be.

The truth is that The Girl can*not* bestow the identity she promises. She forces her initiates to torture themselves with starvation diets and beauty-parlor ordeals, but still cannot deliver the satisfactions she holds out. She is young, but what happens when her followers, despite added hours in the boudoir, can no longer appear young? She is happy and smiling and loved. What happens when, despite all the potions and incantations, her disciples still feel the human pangs of rejection and loneliness? Or what about all the girls whose statistics, or "personality" (or color) do not match the authoritative "ideal"?

The Playboy, illustrated by the monthly magazine of that name, does for the boys what Miss America does for the girls. Despite accusations to the contrary, the immense popularity of this magazine is not solely attributable to pinup girls. For sheer nudity its pictorial art cannot compete with such would-be competitors as *Dude* and *Escapade. Playboy* appeals to a highly mobile, increasingly affluent group of young readers, mostly between eighteen and thirty, who want

---

[8] Beatific means bringing bliss or joy.

[9] Noxiousness is harmfulness or injuriousness. A Procrustean bed is a rigid standard which everyone is supposed to fit (from the Greek legend of a highwayman who bound his victims to an iron bed and stretched them or lopped off part of their legs to make them fit it exactly).

[10] To pander is to act as an agent for something illicit or disreputable.

[11] An ethos is a set of values.

[12] The Rockettes are a chorus line of dancers who are featured in the elaborate musical shows at Radio City Music Hall in New York. They and the Miss America candidates are compared to well-trained rows of soldiers parading for a dictator or to the anonymous mass of workers in a state with rigid government controls.

much more from their drugstore reading than bosoms and thighs. They need a total image of what it means to be a man. And Mr. Hefner's *Playboy* has no hesitation in telling them.

Why should such a need arise? David Riesman has argued that the responsibility for character formation in our society has shifted from the family to the peer group and to the mass-media peer-group surrogates.[13] Things are changing so rapidly that one who is equipped by his family with inflexible, highly internalized values becomes unable to deal with the accelerated pace of change and with the varying contexts in which he is called upon to function. This is especially true in the area of consumer values toward which the "other-directed person" is increasingly oriented.

Within the confusing plethora[14] of mass media signals and peer-group values, *Playboy* fills a special need. For the insecure young man with newly acquired free time and money who still feels uncertain about his consumer skills, *Playboy* supplies a comprehensive and authoritative guidebook to this forbidding new world to which he now has access. It tells him not only who to be; it tells him *how* to be, and even provides consolation outlets for those who secretly feel that they have not quite made it.

In supplying for the other-directed consumer of leisure both the normative identity image and the means of achieving it, *Playboy* relies on a careful integration of copy and advertising material. The comic book that appeals to a younger generation with an analogous problem skillfully intersperses illustrations of incredibly muscled men and excessively mammalian women with advertisements for body-building gimmicks and foam-rubber brassière supplements. Thus the thin-chested comic-book readers of both sexes are thoughtfully supplied with both the ends and the means for attaining a spurious brand of maturity. *Playboy* merely continues the comic-book tactic for the next age group. Since within every identity crisis, whether in teens or twenties, there is usually a sexual identity problem, *Playboy* speaks to those who desperately want to know what it means to be a man, and more specifically a *male,* in today's world.

Both the image of man and the means for its attainment exhibit a remarkable consistency in *Playboy.* The skilled consumer is cool and unruffled. He savors sports cars, liquor, high fidelity, and book-club selections with a casual, unhurried aplomb.[15] Though he must certainly *have* and *use* the latest consumption item, he must not permit himself to get too attached to it. The style will change and he must always be ready to adjust. His persistent anxiety that he may mix a drink incorrectly, enjoy a jazz group that is passé, or wear last year's necktie

---

[13] Mr. Riesman says that a young person's character is formed less by his family than by friends his own age and by the mass media which sometimes take the place of human friends.

[14] A plethora is an overabundance, an excess.

[15] Aplomb is assurance or poise.

style is comforted by an authoritative tone in *Playboy* beside which papal encyclicals sound irresolute.[16]

"Don't hesitate," he is told, "this assertive, self-assured weskit is what every man of taste wants for the fall season." Lingering doubts about his masculinity are extirpated[17] by the firm assurance that "real men demand this ruggedly masculine smoke" (cigar ad). Though "the ladies will swoon for you, no matter what they promise, don't give them a puff. This cigar is for men only." A fur-lined canvas field jacket is described as "the most masculine thing since the cave man." What to be and how to be it are both made unambiguously clear.

Since being male necessitates some kind of relationship to females, *Playboy* fearlessly confronts this problem too, and solves it by the consistent application of the same formula. Sex becomes one of the items of leisure activity that the knowledgeable consumer of leisure handles with his characteristic skill and detachment. The girl becomes a desirable—indeed an indispensable—"Playboy accessory."

In a question-answer column entitled "The Playboy Adviser," queries about smoking equipment (how to break in a meerschaum pipe), cocktail preparation (how to mix a Yellow Fever), and whether or not to wear suspenders with a vest alternate with questions about what to do with girls who complicate the cardinal principle of casualness either by suggesting marriage or by some other impulsive gesture toward a permanent relationship. The infallible answer from the oracle never varies: sex must be contained, at all costs, within the entertainment-recreation area. Don't let her get "serious."

After all, the most famous feature of the magazine is its monthly foldout photo of a *play*mate. She is the symbol par excellence of recreational sex. When playtime is over, the playmate's function ceases, so she must be made to understand the rules of the game. As the crew-cut young man in a *Playboy* cartoon says to the rumpled and disarrayed girl he is passionately embracing, "Why speak of love at a time like this?"

The magazine's fiction purveys the same kind of severely departmentalized sex. Although the editors have recently improved the *Playboy* contents with contributions by Hemingway, Bemelmans, and even a Chekhov translation, many of the stories still rely on a repetitious and predictable formula. A successful young man, either single or somewhat less than ideally married—a figure with whom readers have no difficulty identifying—encounters a gorgeous and seductive woman who makes no demands on him except sex. She is the prose duplication of the cool-eyed but hot-blooded playmate of the foldout.

Drawing heavily on the fantasy life of all young Americans, the writers utilize

[16] Papal encyclicals are letters of religious directive from the Pope to the bishops of the world.

[17] Extirpated means destroyed completely.

for their stereotyped heroines the hero's schoolteacher, his secretary, an old girl friend, or the girl who brings her car into the garage where he works. The happy issue is always a casual but satisfying sexual experience with no entangling alliances whatever. Unlike the women he knows in real life, the *Playboy* reader's fictional girl friends know their place and ask for nothing more. They present no danger of permanent involvement. Like any good accessory, they are detachable and disposable.

Many of the advertisements reinforce the sex-accessory identification in another way—by attributing female characteristics to the items they sell. Thus a full-page ad for the MG assures us that this car is not only "the smoothest pleasure machine" on the road and that having one is a "love affair," but most important, "you drive it—it doesn't drive you." The ad ends with the equivocal question "Is it a date?"

Playboy insists that its message is one of liberation. Its gospel frees us from captivity to the puritanical "hatpin brigade." It solemnly crusades for "frankness" and publishes scores of letters congratulating it for its unblushing "candor." Yet the whole phenomenon of which *Playboy* is only a part vividly illustrates the awful fact of a new kind of tyranny.

Those liberated by technology and increased prosperity to new worlds of leisure now become the anxious slaves of dictatorial taste makers. Obsequiously[18] waiting for the latest signal on what is cool and what is awkward, they are paralyzed by the fear that they may hear pronounced on them that dread sentence occasionally intoned by "The Playboy Adviser": "You goofed!" Leisure is thus swallowed up in apprehensive competitiveness, its liberating potential transformed into a self-destructive compulsion to consume only what is *à la mode. Playboy* mediates the Word of the most high into one section of the consumer world, but it is a word of bondage, not of freedom.

Nor will *Playboy's* synthetic doctrine of man stand the test of scrutiny. Psychoanalysts constantly remind us how deep-seated sexuality is in the human being. But if they didn't remind us, we would soon discover it ourselves anyway. Much as the human male might like to terminate his relationship with a woman as he would snap off the stereo, or store her for special purposes like a camel's-hair jacket, it really can't be done. And anyone with a modicum of experience with women knows it can't be done. Perhaps this is the reason *Playboy's* readership drops off so sharply after the age of thirty.

Playboy really feeds on the existence of a repressed fear of involvement with women, which for various reasons is still present in many otherwise adult Americans. So *Playboy's* version of sexuality grows increasingly irrelevant as authentic sexual maturity is achieved.

Thus any theological critique of *Playboy* that focuses on its "lewdness" will

[18] Obsequiously means obediently or submissively.

misfire completely. *Playboy* and its less successful imitators are not "sex magazines" at all. They are basically antisexual. They dilute and dissipate authentic sexuality by reducing it to an accessory, by keeping it at a safe distance.

Freedom for mature sexuality comes to man only when he is freed from the despotic powers[19] which crowd and cower him into fixed patterns of behavior. Both Miss America and The Playboy illustrate such powers. When they determine man's sexual life, they hold him in captivity. They prevent him from achieving maturity.

POINTS TO CONSIDER

Harvey Cox: The Playboy and Miss America

1. Why did the writer use such uncommon words as "theophanies," "surrogates," and "encyclicals"? What does this reveal about the audience for whom he is writing?

2. In what sense does Miss America resemble a religious figure in American culture?

3. What value system in our culture does Miss America represent? What is the danger of identifying too closely with this system?

4. Why do you think there have been no Negro Miss Americas?

5. How is the value system represented by *Playboy* like the value system represented by Miss America?

6. What "needs" does *Playboy* fulfill for its readers? What is the *Playboy* image? How realistic is it?

7. In what sense is *Playboy* magazine, despite its photos of attractive girls, basically an antisexual magazine?

8. In what way can *Playboy's* "playmate of the month" be compared to the products which Morton Hunt discusses in "Love According to Madison Avenue"? (p. 18).

[19] Despotic powers are tyrannical powers.

Ideas for Investigation, Discussion, and Writing

Journalism

1. Using the appropriate journalistic approach, write an article of about three hundred words reporting some news event. The report should be as complete as possible including, if at all feasible, statements from the principal persons involved. Necessary background material should also be supplied as well as any other facts and details needed to give as complete and accurate an account of the event as possible. Supply the item with a headline and a subhead. Also indicate in what sort of newspaper this article would be likely to appear as well as where it would be likely to appear in the newspaper.

2. Write two news articles dealing with some controversial, contemporary event or issue. Slant the first article sharply toward one point of view, and slant the second article just as sharply toward the opposite point of view. Since slanting, to be effective, must not be obvious, it is advisable to confine yourself to the facts of the matter—or as will more likely be the case, some of the facts—as reported by newspapers and other media.

3. Cover a major news event such as a speech or demonstration which you are certain will be reported in the local newspaper or newspapers. Write an essay in which you compare your own recollections and impressions of the event with the version of the event presented by the newspaper. Using this comparison, come to some conclusion about the newspaper story. What aspects of the event were most emphasized. Why? What, if any, was the overall bias of the article? What "angle" did the article seem to be playing up? Was the article slanted? Did it make use of propaganda devices?

4. Write a letter of about three hundred words to the editor of your local paper concerning some controversial problem or issue. In this letter use at least five of the seven propaganda devices discussed in the essay "How to Detect Propaganda" (p. 65).

5. Write an essay analyzing and discussing as propaganda a portion of a political address. (You can find the texts of speeches in newspapers and in *Vital Speeches of the Day* in your library.) What propaganda devices can you find? What specific purpose is each device intended to serve? How effectively does it actually fulfill its purpose? Keeping in mind that the basic goal of propaganda is to focus attention on the emotions of an issue and not on the facts, evaluate the passage as a whole and give reasons for your conclusions.

6. Describe in an essay the editorial profile of a particular newspaper. How might you characterize the general editorial tendencies of the paper over the past ten years? What editorials or editorial campaigns can you cite as examples of this tendency? Are there exceptions or special cases? How are these explained? What are some of the paper's more specific editorial likes and dislikes? Can you cite examples of these particular idiosyncrasies? Do you feel that the editorial policy of the paper reflects, on the whole, the honest and consistent opinion of the editors and publisher, or can you see other pressures or interests at work?

7. Using evidence from the ads, covers, articles, fiction, cartoons, photographs, and other features of a particular mass magazine, analyze and discuss the magazine's image. As he reads the magazine, what sort of person is the reader supposed to feel he becomes? What identity does the magazine give to those who are willing to suspend consciousness of their own identity while reading the magazine? How do the various features of the magazine help the reader slip into this temporary role? How does this image, e.g., the *Playboy* male or the *Cosmopolitan* female, compare with the sort of people who actually read the magazines? Is the disparity greater for some magazines than others? Is the disparity a source of potential harm? How?

8. Four of the articles in the section on popular music first appeared in well-known magazines. "The Music of Protest" appeared in *Saturday Review*, "Soul Is Selling" appeared in *Esquire*, "Fancy Rock" appeared in *The New Republic*, and "Rock for Sale" appeared in *Ramparts*. How much can you tell from each of the articles about the attitudes and style of the magazine in which it appeared? Compare and contrast the attitudes and styles of the four articles.

PART THREE

CARTOONS

The main purpose of the cartoon is to entertain, and these drawings entertain millions daily in comic books, magazine cartoons, newspaper comic strips, and editorial cartoons. But while they entertain, cartoons also reflect our feelings about the ideal or the heroic qualities in human nature (consider "Prince Valiant," "Superman," "Steve Canyon," or even "Mary Worth"), or they reflect our sense of the weakness and absurdity of individual behavior and the workings of our society (consider "Blondie," "B.C.," and "Grin and Bear It"). Many newspaper comic strips whose main purpose is to entertain often contain large admixtures of political and social satire. Such popular strips as "Dick Tracy," "Little Orphan Annie," "Li'l Abner," and "Pogo" offer very evident social satire, while other widely read strips such as "Peanuts," "Miss Peach," and "The Wizard of Id" present social satire in a subtler form.

When, in the second half of the nineteenth century, Thomas Nast made the political cartoon popular in the United States, (Nast created the Republican elephant and the Democratic donkey), a corrupt politician known as "Boss" Tweed said of the cartoons which were destroying him: "I don't care a straw for your newspaper articles, my constituents don't know how to read; but they can't help seeing them damned pictures." Political cartoons now appear in almost every newspaper and news magazine where they augment the editorials and influence the opinions of the people who read the articles as well as of those who do not.

**"Now, Where Was I? Oh, Yes — Why Don't All
The Poor People Get Out And Work!"**

Copyright 1969 by Herblock in The Washington Post.

"We'll Get Anybody That Could Try To Get Us
—— If We Don't Get Ourselves First"

Copyright 1969 by Herblock in The Washington Post.

RUNAWAY

THE TREE OF KNOWLEDGE

BOOKMARKS

Herblock and Bill Mauldin: Editorial Cartoons

1. What issue of national political or cultural importance is being commented upon in each of the cartoons?

2. What parallel or symbolic situations or emblems have the cartoonists created to express the important issues?

3. In what sense is every editorial cartoon really an "argument by analogy"?

4. Although these cartoons all comment on serious issues, they are funny. Why?

5. Why are almost all editorial cartoons critical rather than complimentary?

Quo Peanuts?

Martin Jezer
The Funnies: An American Idiom, 1963

A noted psychiatrist arrived at his office one morning to find a newspaper clipping tacked to his office door. The clipping was that morning's *Peanuts,* and scrawled across it was a message from a patient which read: "Dear Dr.——, I have discovered what is wrong with me, and there is no need for me to continue treatment."

Among its other nosegays,[1] the comic strip *Peanuts* probably holds the distinction of being clipped out of more newspapers and posted on more bulletin boards, lockers, and walls than any other of its newsprint relatives on the comic page. Perhaps it has not outstripped (no pun intended) the "pin-up girl" in sheer numbers of walls decorated, but it is now as common to see a group of men (and the distaff side as well) ogling a *Peanuts* pin-up as it is to witness a similar celebration of pulchritude on paper.[2] *Peanuts* elicits chuckles and the "pin-up

[1] A nosegay is a small bouquet—in this sense, an appealing or noticeably good quality.

[2] The distaff side is the feminine side; pulchritude is feminine beauty.

gal" a deep breath or two—or perhaps a healthy sigh—yet the two are similar in that they appeal to the psychological needs of their audience of onlookers.

Interestingly enough, the popularity of *Peanuts* in the crowded comics field is due not to the inherent humor of the strip, but to the manner in which it is interpreted by its readers. Charles M. Schulz, the man behind the *Peanuts* drawing board, has created a strip which appears to deal—at its simplest level—with a group of ingenious cherubim who say and do things in an innocent, yet adult, way. Each individual strip has its gag or its entertaining punch line, but the psychological overtones of the strip strike a responsive chord only when the characters are taken as a Gestalt and perceived in reference to contemporary American life.[3]

If it were not for a peculiar characteristic of its doting audience, *Peanuts* would exist solely on the first, obvious level of meaning. But it is precisely *because* a substantial sector of the *Peanuts* patronage is composed of a better-educated class of people—people who are preoccupied with layman's psychology —that the strip can be viewed as a psychological reflection of contemporary life. Certainly the plethora[4] of articles in the popular magazines that deal with psychology attest to the extreme interest in that subject. Schulz, of course, is not unaware of this: in a *Newsweek* interview published in March, 1961, he ventured an opinion as to why the strip is so popular. "Well, it deals in intelligent things— things that people have been afraid of," he declared. "Charlie Brown represents the insecurity in all of us, and our desire to be liked." Schulz declined to psychoanalyze Snoopy, but he did define Lucy as "the dominant one in every family, the little girl who has no doubts about who is going to run the show." Surely there are several—who knows how many?—thousand *Peanuts* fans who would be delighted to put Snoopy on the couch, and possibly as many interpretations of his behavior. And, all shaggy dog dogmas aside, it is important that people hunt for and find psychological gems in *Peanuts.* What is even more important— many of these armchair analysts strike truth in their probes beneath the surface of a lowly comic strip.

The humor in *Peanuts,* then, has a dimension apart from the obvious gag level. This is because the characters in *Peanuts* are reflections of ourselves, and we are funnier than any make-believe character could possibly be. By laughing at *Peanuts,* we recognize our silly selves. We are, in a sense, part of the strip.

This type of subjective humor is very popular today, and not merely in the comic strip. The comedian of an earlier day expected the audience to do nothing more than *react* to whatever he said or did. Today, however, we are not only the audience but also the "straightmen." Mort Sahl, Lenny Bruce, and Shelley Berman expect—in fact, *count* on—the shock of recognition. Their stock in trade is the human race, its foibles and follies, and their success requires our acknowl-

---

[3] A Gestalt is a pattern of behavior.

[4] A plethora is an overabundance, an excess.

edgement that it is indeed *us* they are using as the butt for levity. In this manner, a community of interest—albeit self-interest—is established.

This mutual identification is further advanced by an *additional* role the audience plays in the creation of the modern comedian's material. The so-called "hip" comedian can exist only because the audience is also "hip" and in-the-know. Credit the mass media for this: the audience knows what is in the news and behind the news and they therefore know what is funny about the news. Thus when Mort Sahl mentioned "Ike," he had only to add the word, "golf," to pull laughter from an audience that was predisposed, or in a psychological state of "set," to laugh at such a reference. One has only to visit a cabaret where Sahl or one of his brethren is playing to realize that there is a conspiracy between performer and audience: he wants them to laugh and they are already aware of what to laugh at. Otherwise they wouldn't be there.

This type of in-group or "hip" humor plays its part in *Peanuts* as well. An audience already concerned with psychology is only too ready to apply it to any situation in which the *Peanuts* peewees find themselves. Just as Mort Sahl supplied the situation, so does Charles Schulz. In each case, it is the audience which supplies the frame of reference that makes the situation humorous.

Since the beginning of the comic strip medium, there have been many entries based on the antics of children. *Peanuts* is unique in that it utilizes an adult frame of reference—in a strip where there are *no* adults—for its true appreciation. The children in *Peanuts* are not mischief makers, as the comic strip children of yore. They are not even engaged in a war against the adult world, as happens in such a comparatively recent strip as *Dennis the Menace*. Like the earlier comedians, Dennis is funny for what he does, not why he does it. The humor in *Dennis* is explicit, and needs not even the tinge of psychology for its success. (Not that it isn't possible to read into the li'l monster's motives, just as we wonder —and shudder—at the happy violence of our own children.) Dennis is an extroverted child in a not-*as*-extroverted world, and the difference between the two is good fun for the reader. Because he works at it—that is, at being a child— Dennis records a high degree of laughs for his efforts.

Now take Charlie Brown. The last thing he would do is work for laughs. He has too much trouble co-existing in a world which, for all ostensible purposes, is composed of kids. Just once he wants to be a *winner,* but—as the Fates (and Schulz) would have it—he's a born loser. Accordingly we don't laugh at *what* Charlie does, but at *why* he does what he does (or more often, doesn't do). Charlie would be a pathetic figure if we didn't recognize the tinge of Everyman in him. What's more, he is a great guy for sacrificing himself on a cross of human vanity: seeing Charlie take the third strike for the umpteenth time reminds us that we are *not* alone in our failures and, what is more, that the embarrassing situations we were ashamed of are, in truth, extremely funny.

Although Charlie Brown is representative of a long tradition of bumbling funnymen, he is portrayed in a new light. Two classic losers were the Charlie

Chaplin character and Stan Laurel of Laurel and Hardy. Like Charlie Brown, they were incapable of accomplishing anything but failure, but when we laughed at either Chaplin or Laurel, it was because they gave us security: no matter how badly off we were, here were two characters who made winners out of us, if only by contrast. With Charlie Brown, the humor is far more subjective; we laugh not because we are better off than Mr. Schulz's Mr. Brown, but because we *are* that Mr. Brown. Good grief! We have finally found someone who is every bit the bumbling fumbler we might once have been!

An obvious compatriot of Charlie Brown is Jules Feiffer's Bernard. He, too, is a natural loser. He, too, is incapable of coping with the enemy—which in this case, is called Society. The analogy is further strengthened by the fact that Feiffer has used a number of the same situations to depict Bernard's penchant for failure as has Schulz in depicting Charlie Brown's.

One example finds Bernard calling his answering service and telling the operator that he is Nelson Rockefeller . . . and he wishes to speak to Bernard. The operator, who has been overwrought because no one ever calls Bernard, bursts into tears. As Schulz draws it, Charlie Brown, feeling lonely as usual, calls the operator and asks her to tell him a story. Both Bernard and Charlie, by their actions, communicate the great fear of being alone that characterizes our outer-directed society. Bernard is ashamed, because he knows that being alone is somehow *wrong*. Charlie, not old enough to read Riesman's *Lonely Crowd,* doesn't know yet that being alone is almost tantamount to being guilty of a moral wrong.[5] But he feels guilty anyway, because his friends constantly remind him of his plight. That, in Charlie Brown's world, is what friends are for.

If Charlie Brown's problem is that he is an inner-directed person in an outer-directed society, his failure in life is simply his inability to adjust to that society. Unable to perceive his own predicament (so often the human condition), he constantly recasts himself in one of life's little dramas where the ending is foretold; no matter how hard he tries or how high his hopes, poor Charlie is going to fall on his face.

Schulz's visual characterization of Charlie Brown indicates Charlie's personalty. His entire physical appearance can only be described as "bland." His round, humpty-dumpty face is bland, his clothes are bland, and the few facial expressions he essays are bland. By his very blandness, he is a graphic portrayal of the ciphers who inhabit the world of Whyte's *Organization Man,* and who have adopted blandness as a positive image.

Yet of all the characters in *Peanuts,* Charlie Brown is the only one to face life

---

[5] David Riesman's *The Lonely Crowd* is a book which observes that many Americans are unhappy because they base their lives on conforming to the standards of other people (other-directed or outer-directed) rather than shaping their own ideals (self-directed or inner-directed), preferring the approval of society to self-satisfaction. (See "The Playboy and Miss America," note 13, p. 101.)

without the benefit of a false crutch of security. Linus has his blanket, Schroeder has his toy piano, and the three girls have Charlie Brown. Though Charlie is often tempted to adopt the identities of his peers for security, he quickly gives it up and goes back to his own reliable role as St. George looking for the dragon.

Once Charlie went out and bought himself a blanket of outer-flannel, hopeful that it might give him the same security it does Linus. But what was likely for Linus proved illogical for a loser like Charlie Brown. Similarly, a number of times he has tried to emulate Schroeder by taking up music but, as that eminent pianist explained to him, Beethoven never wrote anything for piano and cigar-box banjo.

Charlie's friends, an outer-directed crew, are all capable of pragmatically adjusting to their ever changing society. Charlie, who answers only to his own muse, continues to act according to his own inner logic (which at least is admirable for its consistency), regardless of what the consequences might be. The outcome: defeat, but not capitulation. Though innumerable fences are marked with the accountings of Lucy's victories over Charlie in checkers, he continues to play checkers with Lucy—and he continues to lose. We know, Lucy knows, and Charlie Brown knows that he will lose, yet he keeps playing. Charlie has no more chance of winning at checkers than he does of flying his kite, but he refuses to concede that the impossible won't someday happen—that he *will* best Lucy over the checkers board and that he *will* manage to get the kite in the sky, where it belongs, and not in a tree, where neither he nor the kite belongs. Somehow, in the past, the tree has always come between him and the sky, but a Charlie Brown can outlast any tree.

Here we can readily identify with Charlie Brown, because we have all been in situations where repeated failure has made success unlikely. Yet we persist, and we endure, just as Charlie Brown does. Only by such persistence can we someday succeed, and if Charlie puts his kite away in the garage, neither he nor the kite will *ever* make it. So Charlie keeps flying his old kite, and someday he may just clear that tree . . . and the next day he will beat Lucy at checkers, Patty at marbles, and have Violet tell him that she loves him. Maybe that's the day when all men will love each other, and Charlie will belong to that larger community of man, not just to the kids in the neighborhood. Charlie wants that, surely, and so do we all. His persistence in the face of failure mirrors our own hope that man will someday sail his kite in the clearest of skies.

Meanwhile Charlie must play the stoic. So what if the others talk about him behind his back, plan parties so as *not* to invite him, and snub him at every opportunity? This is the way it has *always* been. It's only when they point out to him that they do not like him that Charlie, reared on Dr. Spock, recognizes how psychologically necessary it is for him to be loved and accepted by his friends. And he *has* to worry because, according to the experts' criteria, he is an unhappy child. Perhaps he doesn't feel like an unhappy child, but *that* must be due to a shortcoming in his psychological adjustment. Similarly, the Charlie

Browns of our adult world too often fret and pout and become neurotic contemplating the neuroses they should have. In both cases, a little knowledge causes a lot of anxiety.

Charlie also has the burden of living in the age of the decline of the American male. In addition to being dominated by females, the American male is constantly being reduced in stature by contrast with the males of other countries who repeatedly surpass him in manliness, gentleness, charm, *savoir-faire,* and whatnot-else. Charlie Brown has to put up with such odious comparisons, but he persists in asserting his masculinity. Once, when Patty and Violet informed him that they could no longer play with him because he was a "roughneck," he could hardly contain his triumph. A manly grin was evidence that, on occasion, the worm does turn.

Of course the other girls are small fry, figuratively speaking, when stacked up against Lucy. She is not only the world's greatest fuss-budget, she is—if I may be so presumptuous—a perfect representation of the modern American female. Worse yet, she has had a touch of education (play school, nursery school, and picnic school), and this acquired superiority predisposes her to the cynicism *sui generis*[6] to the sophisticate. After reading in a book: "The boy sees a slide. . . . The boy wants to go down the slide. . . . The boy is afraid to go down the slide," Lucy tosses aside the book and declares with great nonchalance: "The boy is a hopeless case." After all, Lucy knows her psychology. When Patty tells her to stop crying, Lucy yowls: "Waddya mean don't cry?!! . . . Why should I deprive myself of an emotional outlet?"

Lucy has all the weapons of womanhood. When she can't have her way, Lucy doesn't hesitate to throw a temper tantrum. Another ploy is the slow sulk, and the Ultimate Weapon is an *extremely* loud voice that causes all the other characters, victims of an irrepressible force, to perform reverse somersaults whenever Lucy unleashes her vocal chords. If guile and sophistication won't work, Lucy reasons, it doesn't hurt to have the lungs of a top sergeant.

Lucy has but one weakness—her infatuation for Schroeder. And of course Schroeder is infatuated with Beethoven and will have no truck with less intellectual pursuits. "Sigh," Lucy moans as Schroeder rejects her, "I'll probably never get married. . . ."

Schroeder, then, is the answer to an otherwise female-dominated society. Included in the cast of leading ladies, in addition to Lucy, are Patty, Frieda, and Violet. Violet is the cutest and most feminine, so naturally Charlie Brown develops a crush on her. Alas, poor Charlie Brown—he cannot even compete with Snoopy the dog, upon whom Violet showers all her affection. But Charlie doesn't demur on a crush that easily. In one particularly touching scene, he prepares to present a Valentine to his Violet. After rehearsing what he is going to say to her, Charlie finally musters the courage to make the actual presentation.

[6] *Sui generis* means in a class by itself.

Handing the Valentine to Violet, he says: "This is for you, Violet . . . Merry Christmas."

This delightful, yet poignant, episode illustrates the essential difference between the humor of *Peanuts* and the humor of Charlie Chaplin. As Al Capp noted in his fine essay on Chaplin some years ago, the hobo always fails to win the girl because he is nothing more than a hobo, and therefore not good enough for her. We are also better than a hobo, and we might very well have succeeded in winning the pretty girl. Secure that we are better off than Chaplin's hobo, we are able to laugh at him. In contrast, we laugh at Charlie Brown's failure to win the pretty girl because we can remember a time when, like Charlie, we became flustered in the presence of a girl we liked and did something embarrassing. We laugh at Charlie because he reminds us that we are not alone.

Though each has his weaknesses, Linus and Schroeder are greater successes in the game of life than Charlie is. Linus has his security fetish all right, but he occasionally proves himself by tossing the ball into the basket (after Charlie, of course, has missed), and by building a house of playing cards (after Charlie has created chaos from the same cards). Linus also puts his blanket to some practical use. Killing a fly with the flick of his blanket, he pronounces himself "the fastest blanket in the West." But don't expect Linus to let go of that blanket, for he is aware that children need security for their psychological well-being, and Linus wants to keep security well in hand.

Ironically enough, Schroeder was introduced to the toy piano by Charlie Brown, who explained that although it is a difficult instrument it *is* possible to play songs on it. Schroeder then proceeded to sit down and play Beethoven despite the fact that, as Charlie pointed out, "the black keys are painted on." Schroeder panics, however, when confronted with a real piano—the number of keys at his disposal proves too much for him. And don't think that *this* doesn't provide grist for the gristmill of psychiatry the country over.

Whatever his failings at the keyboard, Schroeder is the pride of all the music lovers who read *Peanuts.* An important annual event in the strip is the celebration of Beethoven's birthday, and the custom has spread to more than a few college campuses. Taken symbolically, Schroeder is the representation of the modern creative artist, and his problems are the problems of the creative artist in a mass society. When Lucy asks him to play *Three Blind Mice* for her brother, Schroeder's retort is: "Only three years old and already I'm forced to go commercial." Wise young Schroeder knows his Philistines.

The humor in the microcosmic world of *Peanuts* is the humor of the human race. Because it is far easier to laugh at comic strip characters than at ourselves, we esteem Charlie Brown—in his case, all the world loves a loser. In an earlier day, when we could escape to a wide open frontier of opportunism, a figure like Horatio Alger was symbolic of the times.[7] Today, when there is no place to run

[7] Horatio Alger was the author of a series of novels in which a young man by dedication, persistence, and hard work became a success in the eyes of society.

to, and we must adjust inward rather than escape outward, our ideal symbol is Charlie Brown.

So people from all walks of life tack *Peanuts* to the walls of their offices and classrooms. And together with their co-workers and schoolmates, they share a sense of security: they are not alone in the world. Scientists, professional people, and creative talents can find something even more personal in the image of Charlie Brown. It is not unlikely that, in following their own paths to success in their chosen fields, they were often unable to adjust to the society of their childhood companions. While others played, they studied, and like Charlie they were outcasts. Since they eventually proved their worth to society, so might Charlie Brown. In one particularly engaging sequence, Schulz has Charlie build a snowman quite unlike any other snowman built by children. It is Charlie Brown's own abstract expressionistic version of a snowman. It is unique. Underneath Charlie's bland exterior some talent may exist. At least there is hope. . . .

POINTS TO CONSIDER

Martin Jezer: Quo Peanuts?

1. Why is "Peanuts," a comic strip about children, more popular with adults than with children?

2. What are some of the sources of humor in "Peanuts"? How does this comic strip allow us to laugh at ourselves?

3. What adult personality types are represented by Charlie Brown, Lucy, Schroeder, and Linus? If the children act like adults, who in the strip acts like a child? In what ways?

4. What is Charlie Brown's main weakness? What is his main virtue? Why do we enjoy laughing at him? What is the difference in why we laugh at Charlie Brown and why we laugh at Snoopy?

PEANUTS

PSYCHIATRIC HELP 5¢

THE DOCTOR IS [IN]

I HAD TO GO TO THE SCHOOL NURSE YESTERDAY BECAUSE MY STOMACH HURT...

YOU WORRY TOO MUCH, CHARLIE BROWN... NO WONDER YOUR STOMACH HURTS...YOU'VE GOT TO STOP ALL THIS SILLY WORRYING!

HOW DO I STOP?

THE DOCTOR IS [IN]

THAT'S *YOUR* WORRY! FIVE CENTS, PLEASE!!

THE DOCTOR IS [IN]

© 1968 by United Feature Syndicate, Inc.

PEANUTS

IN KITE-FLYING, THE RATIO OF WEIGHT TO SAIL-AREA IS VERY IMPORTANT

THIS RATIO IS KNOWN AS "SAIL LOADING" AND IT IS MEASURED IN OUNCES PER SQUARE FOOT...FOR EXAMPLE, A THREE-FOOT FLAT KITE WITH A SAIL AREA OF FOUR AND ONE-HALF SQUARE FEET SHOULD WEIGH ABOUT TWO OR THREE OUNCES...

YOU KNOW A LOT ABOUT KITES, DON'T YOU, CHARLIE BROWN?

YES I THINK I CAN SAY THAT I DO...

THEN WHY IS YOUR KITE DOWN THE SEWER?

© 1967 by United Feature Syndicate, Inc.

PEANUTS

STRIKE THREE!

"HEY, KID, WHO TOLD YOU YOU WERE A BALL PLAYER? BOO!! BOO!!"

"GET OFF THE FIELD, KID!"

"WE CAN DO WITHOUT YOUR KIND, KID!"

"WHERE'D YOU LEARN TO PLAY BALL, KID, IN KINDERGARTEN?!!!" HA! HA! HA! HA! HA! HA! HA! HA! HA! HA!

SPRING LAKE summer camp FUN! RECREATION! COMPANIONSHIP!

SIGH

© 1967 by United Feature Syndicate, Inc.

⬛ POINTS TO CONSIDER ⬛

Charles Schulz: Peanuts Cartoons

1. To what extent do these cartoons illustrate the points which Martin Jezer makes in his article, "Quo Peanuts"?

2. What similar problem does Charlie Brown have in each comic strip? How do Lucy's and Linus's personalities compare or contrast with Charlie Brown's?

3. How do the problems and personalities of Charlie Brown and his friends relate to the problems and personalities of adults?

4. What seems to be the source of humor in these strips? Is it the very same in all of them, or is there any difference?

5. How does the drawing style contribute to the meaning and humor of "Peanuts"?

Who Reads the Funnies—and Why?

Edward J. Robinson and David Manning White

The Funnies: An American Idiom, 1963

The comic strip pages are probably the most misunderstood parts of an American newspaper. Misunderstood by whom? Obviously not by the readers of the funnies in newspapers, who number from eighty to one hundred million every day, but by the managing editors of the nation's press, who are aware that comic strips attract a lion's share of their readers but give short shrift to the composition of this highly read section of the paper. These same editors are aware that about twice as many readers faithfully follow their favorite comics as read an editorial. However, this is not to say that comic strips are as "important" as editorials. But it is disconcerting to an editor's equanimity when the editorial page, which is put together with great thought and planning can't "pull" the readership that the taken-for-granted collection of daily or Sunday comic strips invariably attracts.

Some years ago, Dr. Charles Swanson analyzed approximately forty thousand news-editorial-feature items that had appeared in 130 American newspapers over the period from 1939 to 1950. Fifty thousand adult readers over a period of twelve years were interviewed regarding what they read in their respective newspapers. The category that ranked highest was "the comics," with an average male readership of 58.3 per cent and an average female readership of 56.6 per cent. The next highest category was "war" (World War II did, of course, occur during the period of these surveys) with an average readership of 34.6 per cent, about half that of "comics." Are we to deduce that the funnies are more important to the average newspaper reader than news about the greatest war in history? The answer, naturally, is no. But by the same token these figures do suggest that the comic strips, for whatever reasons, have a very strong appeal to what is known as the "mass audience." Although the Continuing Study of Newspaper Reading surveys, summarized by Dr. Swanson, verified that the comic strip was by far the most widely read section of the newspaper, they did not give any answers as to why this was so.

Our study of the young readers of comic strips revealed, not surprisingly, that comics reading remains an extremely popular activity (with 99 per cent of the boys and 97 per cent of the girls indicating regular reading of one or more strips daily and Sunday). We found that the strips chosen by our sample, both as most frequently read, and as favorites, were consistently the humorous, non-narrative type of strip. These data refute the theory posited by various critics of the medium that children seek violence and sensationalism from the comic strips.

We learned that the main reason children like comics and continue to read them was the positive pleasure obtained, e.g., "comics are fun," "relaxing," "make me feel good," etc. Our previous study of highly-educated adults revealed precisely the same reason.

How does a youngster picture the adult reader of comics? Our survey indicated children generally imagine that such adults are of higher education and social status. But when we asked adults what kind of person reads comic strips, they predominantly visualized the comic strip reader as someone of less education and generally of lower social-economic status. In short, to the kids there is no social stigma attached to reading comic strips, but to adults there seems to be considerable ambivalence about comics reading.

This adult conflict is further reflected in the children's belief that many grownups read comic strips but pretend not to do so. The main reason for this pretense, children think, is the feeling of embarrassment or shame felt by the adult reader. Significantly, the feeling of guilt connected with comic strip reading on the part of adults was perceived by children in the earliest grades and remained constant throughout, including the ninth graders.

Children use comics quite extensively as a form of socializing with their schoolmates. Seventy-five per cent of the children in our sample discussed comic strips (situations, content, characters) with their friends at school.

On the basis of these pilot studies of adult readers and children, we embarked on a full-scale national survey of who reads comics, and why. During January, 1962, interviewers of the Opinion Research Corporation surveyed 1,360 adults randomly chosen by means of a probability sample of the nation. Our survey questionnaire consisted mainly of twelve sentence-completion items, designed to elicit a spectrum of the reader's attitudes toward comic strips, as well as a few additional open-ended questions. This was essentially the same measurement device (with some refinements) that had proved effective in our two pilot studies.

Our questionnaire was designed both to probe the reader's attitudes toward comics reading in general and to probe his attitudes toward comics in particular. Questions from both categories were randomly distributed throughout the questionnaire.

Below we summarize our findings in terms of answers to a series of basic questions, the sum total of which spells out who reads comics, and why.

How many people in the United States read the funnies? Our survey distinguished between those who read Sunday comics regularly (i.e., each Sunday), less frequently (two or three times a month), infrequently, or not at all. Assuming our data are representative, more than 100 million Americans, from the very young to the very old, read one or more comic strips in their Sunday newspapers, and, of these, about 90 million are regular readers. Previous studies have shown that Sunday readers of comics are also those who read the strips daily, and it would be reasonable to suppose that the number of daily readers is only slightly smaller than the Sunday audience. A popular strip which runs in the largest circulation Sunday newspapers may easily be read by 30 to 40 million readers every Sunday. In terms of reader exposure to such popular strips as Blondie, Dick Tracy, or Li'l Abner, to cite just three which are always very high in polls, one must multiply 40 million by 52 separate weeks, thereby obtaining a yearly reader exposure index of more than two billion. It is fairly obvious that no other single mass medium offering, whether a hit movie or even the most successful television program, begins to attract so enormous a mass audience.

How does this readership break down as to age, education, occupation, and sex differences? For regular Sunday comic readers, the peak reading years are between thirty and thirty-nine, followed by a slow decline thereafter, with the lowest readership in the "over seventy" category. All previous surveys have shown that fewer older people tend to read comics; one is tempted to speculate that this merely reflects the declining activity in old age of all forms of reading and/or participating in entertainment.

Regarding education: as the survey progresses from grade school students through to those attending college, the percentage of regular readers increases by a factor of almost two. Even those who have completed college and have had some graduate study read more comics than those with eighth-grade educations or less.

With respect to occupations and regular comics reading, it should therefore not surprise us that professional, technical, managerial, and, to a somewhat lesser extent, craft and clerical workers have the highest proportion of readers. These occupational categories generally require individuals with higher education.

What do Americans think about this leisure activity called comic strip reading? More than 50 per cent of them regard comic strip reading in positive pleasure terms, e.g., "enjoyable," "fun," "relaxing," and "entertaining." Only one in six respondents viewed comics in negative terms, with such epithets as "foolish," "silly," "dull," and "poor reading."

In a related question, we asked our respondents to free-associate to the sentence, "When I think about reading the comics, I am reminded of . . ." The dominant responses were in terms of being reminded of one's own childhood and youth, in naming a specific strip, and in being reminded of pleasure, humor, or happy times. Only one out of twenty respondents voiced any negative association.

Another facet of the public's attitudes toward comic strip reading was derived by asking the interviewees what they felt all comics readers had in common. Twenty-five per cent said that comics readers have positive personality characteristics, e.g., are "intelligent," "human," "imaginative," and "optimistic." Only five per cent responded in derogatory terms, such as "stupid," "of low mentality," or ones who "lack interest in good books."

To find out how the individual perceived his own reading of comic strips, we first asked the interviewees to indicate why they personally read comic strips. Sixty-three per cent replied in terms of the above-mentioned positive pleasure responses. From these and previously mentioned responses, we conclude that comics reading is primarily a pleasure-seeking activity, rather than a negative escapism, as some have suggested.

As we are so often told by psychoanalysts, pleasurable activities are frequently accompanied by guilt feelings. We asked ourselves, to what extent does this hold true for comics reading? To find the answer to this question we had to turn the respondent's attention away from himself (since obviously we couldn't ask him if he felt guilty about comics reading). We asked him to complete the following sentence: "The main reason some people do not let on to others that they read the comics is . . ." Seventy-five per cent of the responses were variations of guilt, shame, or fear that their intellectual and/or social status would be lowered. Only 3 per cent of the respondents questioned the implications of the query itself. This finding agrees completely with data we gathered in our first study, where the sample emphasis was on the college-educated individual. Because we wanted to find out at what age this ambivalence toward comics reading could be perceived, we asked the identical sentence-completion in our study of the eleven hundred children (third through ninth grades). We learned that the third-grader perceived this adult ambivalence as clearly as the ninth-grader. The idea that adults like to read the funnies but are ashamed to admit it is in evidence extremely early.

Why do adults feel this way? Although we do not have the full answer to this question, some insight was provided by still another sentence-completion which read as follows: "Of all the occupational groups in our country, I would say that the one that reads comics the most is . . ." Fifty-four per cent of the conventional occupational categories cited were from the lowest end of the occupational continuum, including laborers, unskilled workers, etc. Is it any wonder, when the respondent thinks that the average reader of comics is of low status and education, that he would be reluctant to see himself a member of this readership group? Rather, we suspect that he fancies himself as the exception and thereby neatly rationalizes his pleasure-seeking comics reading.

In our children's readership study, just the opposite was true. The children perceived the truth: the more highly-educated occupational elite are among the most avid readers of comics. Contrary to the general adult population's idea of who reads comics, the higher status group readers are the rule rather than the exception.

What do adult Americans think about people who do not read the funnies? The second largest response category must be regarded as a neutral assessment, with about 26 per cent of the nonreaders thus described. By "neutral," we mean describing a person by his occupation and/or personality in such a way that a value judgment could not be made. One might expect a neutral response from adults, as contrasted with our children's study, in which non-comic strip readers were definitely seen as an "out" group. In spite of this adult tendency toward greater permissiveness, the category (27 per cent), or nearly one in four of the respondents, described the nonreader in negative personality terms, e.g., a "stuffy person," a "sour puss" with a "pessimistic outlook on life." Finally, 18 per cent visualized such nonreaders as too busy or too wrapped up in their work to read comics.

Some critics of the funnies stridently claim that comics reading is bad for children. What does the general public think? We approached this question through two related sentence-completions.

One was: "People who claim that reading comic strips is bad for children are . . ." This evoked the following associations: Fifty-seven per cent said that such claimants are foolish, ignorant, silly, or at the very least, wrong. Only 12 per cent agreed with the premise of the sentence completion itself (very likely these 12 per cent were part of the same "hard core" of respondents who answered each sentence in a manner negative to comics). Consistent with their answer, 77 per cent of the respondents said they felt that the appeal of comics to kids lies in the pleasure and humor that the comics provide.

POINTS TO CONSIDER

Edward J. Robinson and David Manning White: Who Reads the Funnies —and Why?

1.   About how many people read a popular Sunday newspaper comic strip during a year? How does this audience compare in size with that of other popular art forms, such as that of a popular song, a weekly television show, a popular movie, etc? Compare some figures.

2.   Why are newspaper comic strips so very popular? Are there any differences in the reasons why children read comic strips and why adults read comic strips?

3.   Why do you think that better-educated people read comic strips more frequently or more regularly than people with less education?

4.   Why do some adults feel guilty about reading comic strips? Is this same feeling of guilt present in adults' enjoyment of any other popular art forms?

5.   Which kinds of comic strips tend to be the most popular? Why? Which comic strips are your favorites? Why?

6.   Why do some people feel that comic strips and comic books are harmful to children? Do you think they may be harmful? Why or why not?

Text in cartoon panels:

I WAS A LONER AS A CHILD.

DISTRUSTFUL OF STRANGERS. KEPT TO MYSELF. DIDN'T GET INVOLVED.

GREW UP STRONG. HONEST. NICE TO EVERYONE. NEVER LOST A FIGHT.

GOT TO BE AFFLUENT. FORCED INTO OBLIGATIONS. EVERYONE MADE DEMANDS. NOBODY GRATEFUL.

MADE ENEMIES. GOT INTO MORE FIGHTS. HARDER TO WIN THAN IN THE OLD DAYS.

ENEMIES SURROUNDED ME. ATTACKED FROM WITHOUT. CONSPIRED FROM WITHIN.

ID GO MAD IF I DIDN'T FIND A WAY TO GET MY MIND OFF MY TROUBLES.

I KILL.

©1967 Jules Feiffer 9-8

Dist. Publishers-Hall Syndicate

POINTS TO CONSIDER

Jules Feiffer: "Uncle Sam" cartoon

1. In what ways is this cartoon similar to traditional political cartoons such as those of Herblock and Bill Mauldin? What perspectives does it add to the traditional approach? What propaganda techniques does Feiffer use to persuade us of his point of view?

2. How does the cartoon use drawing and satirical techniques similar to those used in *Peanuts?*

3. What specific historical facts is Feiffer commenting on? Why doesn't he have Uncle Sam mention things like the world wars, student protests, Vietnam? Do you think this vagueness makes the cartoon sequence more or less effective? Explain.

4. What personality traits does Feiffer give to Uncle Sam? How do these personality traits become comments on U.S. government policy?

Ideas for Investigation, Discussion, and Writing

Cartoons

1. What does the drawing style contribute to the effect of a cartoon? Compare the drawing styles of several humorous cartoons—such as "Peanuts," "Beetle Bailey," "L'il Abner," and "The Wizard of Id"—with the drawing styles of several adventure or romance cartoons—such as "Juliet Jones," "Steve Canyon," "Dr. Kildare," and "Batman." How are the styles appropriate to the subjects?

2. Using some or all the published collections of "Peanuts" cartoons, write an essay discussing the changes in the comic strip over the years. How has the drawing style changed? How have the characters' personalities changed? How have their relationships to each other changed? Assuming that these changes were at least to some degree a popular demand, what conclusions can you make about what Americans find amusing? Do you find that these changes reflect changes in our whole society? How?

3. Compare similar comic strips from different countries. (For example, "Dagwood" versus "Andy Capp.") What differences are there in characters and their relationships to each other? To what extent do these differences reflect differences in the social attitudes and values of the two countries?

4. List and discuss the various character sterotypes used in cartoons. Psychiatrists, for instance, are usually pictured as middle-aged men with dark goatees and dark horn-rimmed glasses. Include examples from magazines and other sources. Do you think these conventions are really necessary? Why? Is there a way in which they could be considered harmful?

5. Write an essay comparing cartoons found in magazines such as *Playboy, Esquire,* or *True* with cartoons found in *Ladies Home Journal,* or *Redbook,* or *Look.* What differences are there? How do these differences reflect the appeals and attitudes of the respective magazines in which the cartoons appeared?

6. Using a number of sample cartoons, discuss the use of political cartoons as propaganda. What advantages does the cartoon offer the propagandist? In what ways is the cartoon less effective as a propaganda medium than the printed word, television, or radio?

7. Draw several propaganda cartoons dealing with unusual topics or topics concerning your school. Write an explanation of the propaganda devices you use in the various cartoons and the stylistic conventions you employ.

8. Draw several humorous cartoons. For each cartoon write a discussion which includes an explanation of any stylistic conventions used, an indication of what magazines the cartoon would be likely to appear in, and for what audiences the cartoon is intended.

9. Write an essay discussing the animated cartoon as an artistic medium. What peculiar advantages does the medium offer? Can you cite examples of cartoons which utilize these aspects of the medium? Why do you think most animated cartoon features are humorous in nature? What are some of the drawbacks to the animated cartoon as an artistic medium?

10. What supernatural features have we come to associate with still and animated cartoons—such as miraculous recoveries by characters that are beat up, blown up, shot up, or otherwise assaulted? What is the significance of these conventions? How can they be compared to dream images, or how can they be considered "poetic license"? How would you attempt to explain these conventions to someone who has never seen them?

PART FOUR

RADIO AND TELEVISION

We sometimes find it difficult to think about our radios and television sets as mass media—mere pieces of machinery. Yet they greet us with news and music in the morning, keep us company as we drive to or from school or work, baby sit for our children and provide a large part of their education, entertain us in the evening, and soothe us to sleep at night.

Many social scientists believe that television has had more influence than any other mass communications medium in affecting the political and social philosophy of contemporary Americans—especially among the young people who grew up with it. Television has affected our feelings about politics by inviting us into the conventions and bringing us face to face with the candidates; it has affected our feelings about violence in our cities and on our campuses by giving us closeup views of the disorder; and it has affected our feelings about war by bringing the ugliness and the pain of the battlefields into our living rooms.

Television has upgraded our general level of education with news coverage, special reports, and talk shows, as well as with the programs and series specifically labeled "educational." And schools are discovering, to their embarrassment, that students learn more about certain important subjects from watching their television sets than from sitting in classrooms. It is not surprising, therefore, that television, both public broadcasting and closed circuit, has moved into many classrooms.

Radio and television both have greatly affected the popular arts. Radio has been particularly influential in broadening people's tastes in music as well as for producing a quick turn-over in popular songs. Television, despite some of its poor drama, has encouraged some good playwrights and produced some good plays. By offering inexpensive entertainment which competes with movie theatres and by showing movies, television has stimulated the movie industry to produce for showing in theatres films which cannot be shown advantageously or appropriately on TV—more technical, more spectacular, more sophisticated, or more daring films. Television has also affected the book publishing industry. By raising the general level of public knowledge, TV encourages people to buy books. On the other hand, it lures some people away from books by providing a competitive source of entertainment and escape.

Unfortunately, the inferiority of so much television programming stems from the economic forces that control so much of the industry. Most broadcasting in this country is commercial—that is, paid for by advertisers—and programs are selected and retained, not for their quality so much as for the number of viewers they can reach and convert into customers. This practice of broadcasting to consumers rather than to people and of programming more for immediate financial advantage than for the public welfare alienates many viewers and has, thus far, prevented television from realizing its full educational and cultural potential.

No Exit

Robert Lewis Shayon

Life with the mass media in the privacy of home, where you can make choices, is difficult enough: the true test of character comes when one is confronted by the media in public. I flunked the test in recent weeks, in a plane over the Pacific, a restaurant in Philadelphia, a home in Boston, a taxi in New York, and a motel near the Canadian border. The last stop taught me a lesson and I pass it on to all fellow-sufferers in this sermon for a hot summer afternoon. Flying to Honolulu, there was a mix-up in my ticketing and I couldn't get dinner aboard the plane. I offered to pay the stewardess, but she said she couldn't sell me dinner, and I ruefully watched her throw the food away—but I got a free movie in color. I didn't want the movie: I wanted to do some work; but the lady in back of me cheerfully inquired if I would lower the back of my chair so she could see Frank Sinatra. The sound track was blissfully secreted in the plug-in earphones; but there loomed Sinatra on the rectangular screen ahead; and fuming, I finally quit and suffered the mob their taste. Back on the mainland a few weeks later, I dined at a small, pleasant restaurant in Philadelphia, enveloped by the *high-volume* signal of a local radio station. I knew it would be fruitless (and bad form) to ask the manager to switch off; but I couldn't resist asking him why he kept the station on.

The other diners would immediately complain, he said, if he tuned out. "People need it," he shrugged. "They really don't listen, but it makes a noise in the background and it permits them to talk. If there was silence, there wouldn't be any conversation. It would be dead in here."

The Boston experience came shortly after. I visited a home in the suburbs, where a woman was alone. She sat in a large room: the TV was on (it was early afternoon); but she was intent on a cross-word puzzle. Two rooms away, the radio was turned on, playing to nobody. In New York, another day, I got into a taxi at Penn Station. It was the evening rush hour; the hot city's garment center was clashing and raucous with west-side traffic: the cabbie had his dashboard radio belting above the din. I moaned inwardly but hid my frustration with another taxicab survey. "Do you have that radio on all the time?" I asked in a friendly fashion. "All the time. Never without it a minute," the driver answered.

"What do you usually listen to?" "Nothing," said the driver. "I don't hear a thing. No program. No commercial. I just have it on." "But why?" He turned the knob and shut off the radio. "See for yourself," he said. "I'd miss it. It's monotonous without it, driving all day." He turned the radio on again. "People get in the cab and start telling me their troubles. Like the guy who said he loved his wife but was going out with another dame. What should he do? he asks me. What do I care what he does? But I can't tell him that, so I turn up the radio real loud . . . like this . . . and they keep on jabbering away . . . and once in a while I throw them a yeah . . . yeah . . . yeah . . . but I don't hear a thing . . . not them . . . not the radio . . . nothing."

A few weeks after that, I was in Potsdam, New York, on a lecture engagement. I had breakfast at a motel's restaurant. The cheery waitress had her transistor radio atop the refrigerator the other side of the counter—and with my orange juice I had some bright and early upbeat country music. The local newspaper couldn't assuage my resentment. "Is there no surcease anywhere from this ubiquitous, tribal, electronic collectivism?" I grumbled to my All-Bran.

Suddenly I stopped in the middle of a grumble. The announcer had spoken a familiar name—mine. Along with other items of local news, he was mentioning the talk I was scheduled to give at a nearby college that morning. The music came on again; I went back to the newspaper; but I had been hit—dead on target. All that horrible noise which other people listened to—had instantaneously been transformed into something clear and significant when the right index clue had come up—my own specific involvement. I recalled the taxi-driver who had said: "The only time I listen is when they come on with traffic-bulletins. Then I tune in—with my mind." At all other times the medium of radio was without message: its sound, to him, was shelter from the job's monotony, escape from the unwanted signals of his passengers. To the lady in the Boston home, the unattended TV and radio sets were barriers against loneliness: to the diners in the Philadelphia restaurant the radio's chatter and music were curtains for privacy. The transistor atop the refrigerator in the Potsdam motel met some felt need of the waitress, probably without verbal content. The excommunication of boredom—or fear: this was the meaning of the color movie aboard the plane bound for Hawaii. There is no escape: the public media have interlocked us all. The only response is to learn tolerance—each to his own involvement.

POINTS TO CONSIDER

Robert Lewis Shayon: No Exit

1. What services, other than providing news and entertainment, do radio and TV provide for the public? Give some examples from your own experience.

2. Why do restaurants, stores and shopping centers, doctors' and dentists' offices so often provide continuous background music? (See Vance Packard's "The Ad and the Id," p. 9.)

3. What is the significance of Shayon's title? Do you ever feel that media over which you have no control—such as background music or someone else's radio or TV—is a nuisance? When? Can anything be done about it?

Growing Influence Of Black Radio

Robert E. Dallos
The New York Times, November 11, 1968

"Say it loud, baby. I'm black and sure enough proud of it."

Speaking into the microphone, paraphrasing the title of a James Brown hit, is Chris Turner, a Memphis [Tennessee] disk jockey.

He sits in a small cluttered studio of radio station WDIA (Theme: "More Soul Power per Hour."), whose programing is aimed at the black community. He wears a Dashiki (an African style shirt) and when he's not playing records on Memphis's most popular radio station, he devotes most of his spare time to a militant group ("we don't do any burning up or anything like that") called the Black Knights.

The twenty-two-year-old disk jockey and his colleagues around the country work for a rapidly rising number of lucrative, mostly white-owned "soul stations" beamed at the black community. The audience is estimated at 25 million, of which about 5 per cent is white.

Approximately $35 million worth of advertising is placed with these stations annually. In 1960 the figure was $10 million.

Today [1968] there are 528 stations programming anywhere from an hour to the entire broadcasting day for blacks, an increase from 508 last year and 414 in 1964.

Of these, 108 stations aim all of their programing at Negroes, compared with 50 eight years ago and only one in 1947, according to Howard Bernard Company, a New York company that sells advertising for thirty-five black-oriented stations. All but eight of the black stations are owned by white interests.

The soul stations play mostly rhythm and blues music—a few play only gospel music—and the disk jockeys are almost exclusively Negro. Musical performers, both live and on record, are also generally black and most of the commercials are made by blacks in a familiar idiom.

Jive Talk Disparaged

Coca-Cola, for example, makes a number of rhythm-and-blues commercials for black radio using recording stars, including Aretha Franklin, Joe Tex and Ray Charles. Kent Cigarettes uses the black Chicago disk jockey Ed Cook (Nassau Daddy) to narrate some of its commercials and rhythm-and-blues groups to provide the music, and Lou Rawls does the commercial for Cold Power detergent.

"Our men have to speak well," says Zenas Sears, the bearded, white vice president of WAOK, one of Atlanta's three black stations. "It's been clean up the language or get off the air in this city. No more *y'all* or other jive talk. Racial pride is a very important part of the business."

Soul stations are also devoting an increasing number of hours to discussions of topics of special interest to blacks. The programs enable community leaders —both black and white—to talk to the stations' large audiences and they allow frustrated blacks to call in and "sound off."

In New York, WWRL, for example, broadcasts a weekly ninety-minute talk show entitled "Tell It Like It Is," during which listeners may call to take part in discussions on such topics as "Welfare in New York City," "The Negro and the Draft," and "The Ghetto School Crisis."

Another WWRL program focuses on Negroes who have successful careers. It is titled "Spotlight on Your Future" and sponsored by Lever Brothers Corporation. It is designed to "show youngsters in disadvantaged areas what they can achieve with proper education and training."

New York's other black station, WLIB, won a Peabody Award, one of broadcasting's highest honors, for its "Hot Line" program.

Soul stations have also been performing other important community functions. These vary from city to city and depend on local needs.

KXLW in St. Louis, for example, gives thirteen weeks of spot announcements to Negroes starting businesses and WCHB in Detroit helped find food, clothing and shelter for victims of the 1967 summer riot.

But there are critics who say that the efforts of many white-owned Negro stations take the forms of "safe" public service. For example, one critic who asked not to be identified, said the stations run campaigns urging black children to stay in school, but they would do little to lead and organize movements to correct the underlying conditions that cause the youngsters to fall behind and quit.

Helping to "Cool It"

After the assassination of the Rev. Dr. Martin Luther King, Jr., . . . [in April 1968], most black radio stations dropped all their advertising and played only religious music and reports concerning the murder. They were cited by officials in many areas of the country for having helped to avoid local disorder. . . .

Station KGFJ in Los Angeles was praised in a city council resolution for having been "instrumental in keeping racial trouble from developing" and maintaining "a helpful, informative approach to assist in easing tensions when any trouble did have an opportunity to blossom."

But it is the music, news and chatter of the black stations that have proved extremely popular and caused audiences to increase rapidly.

Washington has a 63 per cent black population, and most of its members are regular listeners of station WOL. In addition, WOL also has a fairly large white audience, mostly teen-agers. As a result the station has maintained its number one position in the twenty-three-station area for the last two years.

The same is true in other cities. In Memphis, WDIA has been the top rated station of twelve for years as is WVON in Chicago.

The spending power of the nation's 22 million Negroes is currently running at $35 billion annually, according to the Department of Commerce. By 1970 the figure is expected to reach $45 billion.

And major companies are now recognizing this. There are almost two dozen concerns, according to the Howard Bernard Company, who spend $100,000 a year advertising on Negro radio. These include General Foods, Colgate-Palmolive, Humble Oil, General Motors and R. J. Reynolds.

The Sonderling Broadcasting Corporation, which owns four black stations, recently raised its advertising rates from $10 to $52 a minute in Washington (WOL), from $20 to $36 in Memphis (WDIA) and from $18 to $60 in New York City (WWRL).

"Over-all Negro radio is a cheap buy," says William Lilios, the Howard Bernard Company's director of research. "In cities like New York, Chicago and Washington general market stations with comparable-sized audiences charge two to three times as much."

The revenues of Atlanta's WAOK will near $600,000 this year, according to Mr. Sears, compared with $450,000 in 1966. Sonderling's Oakland, California, station, KDIA, was grossing $165,000 a year when the company acquired it in 1959. Currently it is grossing between $600,000 and $700,000.

But while many advertisers are flocking to black radio, some local advertisers —notably restaurants, banks, clothing and department stores—are boycotting black radio for fear of attracting too many Negroes and consequently losing their white customers.

One of Atlanta's five largest banks has refused to advertise on WAOK, according to Mr. Sears. He declined to identify it for publication. "They just don't want the Negro business," he said. "They tell us: 'A few we don't mind. But we don't want too many.'" He adds that some clothing stores still boycott the station and a large car dealer canceled an advertising campaign recently because too many Negroes turned up at its show rooms.

But a spokesman for the bank in Atlanta about which Mr. Sears complained, said that his institution had advertised on black radio when a specific appeal was being made to the Negro community.

> The inherent problem [he said] and we hope it will be solved soon, is that the average income level of the Negro is still too low. There are certain things blacks are not in a position to buy. They don't have checking accounts, they don't have that much money.

WDIA's manager, Bert Ferguson, who founded his station twenty years ago and stayed on after selling out to Sonderling, says his ad salesmen are often told "we're glad to have those [blacks] who come into the store. But we don't want to make a specific appeal. It would have a bad effect on the market we're used to."

Robert Elliot, director of radio for Atlanta-based Rollins, Inc., which operates four black stations, says two or three businesses in Norfolk, Virginia, still refuse to advertise on its station, WRAP. But he notes that a bank—he declined to identify—that had always refused, signed on last month for the first time because "it realized the significance of the black business."

> There's been a gradual loosening of restrictions by local advertisers [Mr. Ferguson said]. The reason: The civil rights movement and the plain and simple fact that the Negro has more money to spend.

Public Service Function

Perhaps one of the most important functions of black stations is the public service they render. This was recognized by Nicholas Johnson, a member of the Federal Communications Commission, who recently told a convention of black disk jockeys that it is not enough to play soul music.

> Soul radio is big business [he said]. It is also big responsibility. Many institutions have tried to reach the destitute and alienated millions who seek a richer future in the hearts of our cities. The schools have tried. The Office of Economic Opportunity has tried. Newspapers have tried. . . . Only one institution has consistently succeeded. This is Negro-oriented radio.

Memphis station WDIA, founded in 1947 as the first radio station to devote itself exclusively to blacks, has long broadcast along personal lines.

For example, the following public-service announcements were made recently on the station's "Night Hawk" show.

> A billfold was lost at the bus station, 1324 Kennedy, contained money and papers. Call 9461708.

> A small brown German shepherd dog strayed from home. Dog answers to the name of Poochie. Mrs. Edna Grayson of 1451 Parkway South is offering a $10 reward for Poochie.

WDIA's Bert Ferguson says that

> this might all sound silly to whites. But whites have their daily newspapers and whites have more money. To a Negro the loss of a $3 umbrella is a major loss. We will run anything that has to do with the Negro community in Memphis.

Other black stations perform similar public service work.

One important way that many blacks are aided by the stations they listen to is in finding jobs.

Radio station KATZ in St. Louis broadcasts local job opportunities five times a day. and WVOL in Nashville, which has been broadcasting job openings for some years, is currently campaigning to get what it terms "upgraded job offers for Negroes." In Augusta, Georgia, WAUG broadcasts job offers directly from the state employment office.

News and editorials concerning items of interest to the black community are also carried by most soul stations, WAOK, for example, carried taped interviews with Julian Bond, the Georgia legislator, from the Democratic National Convention, and with other black delegates.

Some stations, though, are wary about putting news items on the air when they concern racial disturbances.

> Our news is screened [says Robert Meeker, the white president of KCOH in Houston] so that when an individual with treasonous motives says "go out in the street and kill and burn," we do not report this.

WERD in Atlanta bans all news of racial unrest while such incidents are in progress.

> The news policy of this station [said Bert Weiland, the white vice president and general manager] is not to report violence of any kind while it is going on. I strongly feel that TV and radio contribute to the incitement of riot. I do not consider this censorship.

But WERD believes it is serving the public interest with another type of broadcasting. Six times a week it produces two-minute vignettes about the contributions of blacks to American history under the title of "Our Noble Heritage." These are made available to black stations in other parts of the country.

◪ POINTS TO CONSIDER ◪

Robert E. Dallos: Growing Influence of Black Radio

1. What kinds of programs are being broadcast on black radio stations? What kinds of services do these stations provide to black communities? What kinds of services do they provide to white communities as well?

2. In what sense is "soul radio" big business?

3. What social trends are reflected in the large increase in black radio stations over the past eight to ten years?

4. In what sense is "racial pride a very important part of the business"? Why is jive talk disparaged on Atlanta's black radio stations? How do you think the idea of what constitutes racial pride for Negroes may differ between blacks and whites?

5. What mass media and popular art forms other than radio and music have shown a noticeable increase in black participation or in the reflection of black culture in the past five to ten years? Why?

The Impact of TV on American Politics

Emmet John Hughes

The New York Times, November 11, 1968

Has the power of television—now dramatized by the device of debate—really revolutionized the democratic process? Is the change more apparent than real? For better or for worse?

So stunning are the factors of size of audience and speed of communication on the grand scale that the very rhythm of political life does seem revolutionized. And a case can be at least plausibly argued that American political history has been decisively affected, these last eight years, by this revolution in technique.

Three witnesses—three of America's political giants—can be summoned to lend evidence to that case.

Richard M. Nixon in 1952 dramatically appeared on national television to explain to all the homes of America how he had financed his home, his career, his whole life—in a performance that made Checkers the nation's most famous dog since F. D. R.'s Fala. Hours, even minutes before that telecast, Mr. Nixon stood an excellent chance of making history as the first candidate on a national ticket ever to be stricken from the lists in mid-campaign as an insufferable embarrassment to his own party.

So nearly definite was this stern verdict of the party leaders that it is not enough to note that television remarkably served the man: it saved him. No other kind of apologia—nothing but television, with impact both massive and instantaneous could have spared Mr. Nixon swift retirement to the little town of Whittier, California, whose residents thronged the streets, just a few weeks ago, to hail the 1960 Presidential nominee.[1]

Dwight D. Eisenhower in 1956 spent an agonizing late spring in slow recovery from major surgery, following his earlier heart attack. His decision to run for re-election trembled in doubt for weeks; even the thought of it would have made

[1] The success of Richard Nixon's 1968 campaign for the Presidency can be attributed largely to his skillful use of television. Nixon's TV campaign is well documented in Joe McGinniss's best-selling book *The Selling of the President, 1968* (New York, Trident Press, 1969).

a weaker man tremble. But it is hardly conceivable that even he would have elected to wage a national campaign were it not for the fabulous facilities of television to ease and simplify the ordeal.

John F. Kennedy in 1960 found his spring offensive for the Democratic nomination fatefully committed to the primary battle for West Virginia. His most ominous problem was the state's massive and pervasive hostility to a Catholic candidate. Only the most full and personal kind of campaign—directly reaching and affecting tens of thousands—could counter popular passions so diffuse, so widespread. And only television made such an effort conceivable.

Three different men, in three different years: for all of them, the road to this political moment took its crucial turning around the same extraordinary fact.

Towering personalities and dramatic incidents aside, the impact of television on American political life can be reckoned in a number of other ways. These are ways less crisply clear, yet perhaps more seriously historic and lasting.

First, TV makes political life itself more fluid and more volatile. Men can surge or stumble with astonishing speed—either triumphing over obscurity or tripping over a hasty or graceless public word or gesture. And issues can become as mercurial as individuals: A single performance before a sufficiently massive audience can virtually end an issue or precipitate one.

In the golden days of radio, the nightmare of performers in the studio was the mumbling of some indiscretion or vulgarity a moment before the microphone was dead. Now the politician almost lives before a live "mike" and camera. His world is tapped.

Second, TV forces much of the backstage machinery of political life to endure the same exposure. Conventions tend to become not national caucuses of politicians, but public spectacles, designed less for deliberation (or dealing) among the participants than the delight (or entertainment) of an audience. It is at least debatable whether this makes the event itself more sober or merely more contrived.

It is equally debatable whether the effect upon the audience is one of visual education, in a serious sense, or one of visual enjoyment just a notch or two above the level of the peepshow. What is not in doubt is the fact that the people *see* more.

Third, TV dramatically tends to nationalize political life. The citizen who can watch and hear Presidential candidates from his easy chair feels understandably less excitement than his father at the prospect of a "live" appearance in the local auditorium of a Congressman or even a Senator. Local political clubs—as centers of political life—tend to suffer and sag in appeal.

The firing of local partisan zeal, then, requires ever more prestigious names —as close to the top of the ticket as one dare demand. Ultimately, this could dictate, of course, greater dependence of all local tickets upon the national ticket.

Fourth, TV can strikingly shift political advantage toward those officeholders with easiest access to a national medium; these are national officeholders. It seems hardly an accident that 1960 has been notable for the fact that three of the four candidates on the national tickets come from the U.S. Senate—traditionally inferior to state governorships as sources of national candidates—while the fourth candidate, Henry Cabot Lodge, has enjoyed unique exposure on national television.

In the future of television, it would seem doubtful if the most distinguished governor, whatever his record or his personality, could come close to national candidacy without finding a way, first, to establish his identity as nationally as Washington leaders.

Fifth, accenting the person and the personal, TV both imposes new demands and offers new opportunity to the individual politician. This transcends the level of a Kennedy's concern with his hair or a Nixon's anxiety about his eyebrows (both appropriately adjusted for the current campaign). In the meeting—or the muffing—of issues, it puts new and heavy stress on the man himself.

Thus, for example, one astute political commentator, watching last spring's West Virginia primary, anticipated Senator Kennedy's massive victory on the basis of one response, discovered universally among all citizens queried a fortnight before election. This was the simple fact that all who had seen the Senator on television had reacted favorably, even if grudgingly. Enough television, then, logically would prevail. It did. But it underscored the fact that there could have been no effective substitute for this entirely personal attack on the political problem.

Sixth, TV obviously quickens the tendency of big politics to resemble big business. The cost of campaigning, of course, soars: the relatively easy political struggle of 1956 cost the G.O.P. some 2 million dollars for television and radio. The eager novice, in this televised political life, can afford to start unknown—but not unfinanced.

POINTS TO CONSIDER

Emmet John Hughes: The Impact of TV on American Politics

1. What examples does Hughes give of the instances in which TV influenced national politics? What more current and even more dramatic instances can you cite?

2. What are the six important influences which Hughes lists of TV upon American politics? Can you think of some examples to illustrate these influences? To what degree do you feel that each is a good or a bad in-influence? See Vance Packard, "The Ad and the Id" (p. 9).

3. What propaganda devices are commonly employed in TV political campaigning? See Clyde Miller's "How to Detect Propaganda," (p. 64). What instances can you recall in which a candidate's own campaign propaganda backfired and worked against him?

A Riot on TV

John Gregory Dunne
The New Republic, September 11, 1965

No one wants to impugn the courage, ingenuity, and virtuosity of the broadcast journalists in Watts. But the very nature of television, with its pressing need to fill the gaping maw of dead air, mitigates against reasoned analysis of a running civil disturbance.[1] Consciously or not, electronic journalism is essentially show business, and show business demands a gimmick. With its insatiable appetite for live drama, television turned the riots into some kind of Roman spectacle, with the police playing the lions, the Negroes the Christians. The angle, in this case, was that the Christians were winning.

Not only did television exacerbate[2] an already inflammatory situation, but also, by turning the riots into a Happening, may even have helped prolong them. One channel went so far as to score its riot footage with movie "chase" music. The situation was made to order for the late-night call-in shows, which cater to what one critic calls "a twilight world of the lonely, the subliterate, the culturally deprived." The riots gave these disembodied voices in the night a chance to vent their private furies against "these people," a euphemism for "Negroes" on station after station. "What do these people want. . . . Why don't they get jobs like decent people. . . . These people remind me of animals." . . .

No rumor, however unsubstantiated, went unreported. Hovering over the riot scene in a helicopter, a reporter for KTLA suddenly announced, "There's a report that one or two policemen are surrounded, so we're going up that way for a look." The report was unfounded, but by the time that was established, there were other unconfirmed stories on the air. The Shrine Auditorium was on fire, the Minute Men were invading Watts, a contingent of Hell's Angels was even now careening down the Harbor Freeway toward the riot area; all were false alarms. Even when there was nothing new to report, the pitch was maintained—looting at Vermont and 83rd, a shooting at Central and 39th, a car gunned down running a roadblock at Broadway and 47th—until quite isolated events blurred into holocaust and a riot became a massacre.

In fact broadcast coverage of the riots only deepened my own conviction that a thousand words are worth one picture. The most disturbing effect of televised news coverage is that, like LSD, it tends to create a heightened and often spurious reality of its own. No newspaper, no magazine has television's

---

[1] A gaping maw is an empty gullet or stomach; to mitigate here means to moderate or to lessen the opportunity.

[2] To exacerbate is to aggravate or to make more intense.

awesome ability to maintain the momentum of an event. Watts is a vast sprawling ghetto, fifty miles square. Normally the dweller in such a peculiarly horizontal slum, in such an immense area, would hear of an incident with the police only the next day, if at all, when he read it in the newspaper. With 24-hour on-the-spot news coverage, however, reality for the viewer in the eye of the storm became not the quiet outside his own bungalow, but the place, often miles away, where the action was.

And the screen affected as well the viewer who was not in the storm at all, the man who could sit in his family room 30 miles away and watch a continuous and indiscriminate feast of violence, death, and destruction. Since only high points are reported, an incident soon becomes a skirmish, a skirmish a full-scale war. Moreover, a microphone tends to create news, often where there is none. . . .

By virtue of the microphone in his hand, an electronic journalist is automatically a participant in any story he covers, particularly in one as volatile and fluctuating as a riot. There is no rewrite man to temper his immediate emotions, no time to reflect before a typewriter upon what he has seen. He is forced to shoot from the lip, as are those he interviews. When a microphone is thrust before an official's face, there is nothing off the record, no chance for a later strategic retreat. He is frozen in the position of defending himself at all costs, giving blanket absolution to his adherents, accepting no blame at all.

Because it is so dependent upon action, television runs the risk of being manipulated far more than the other news media. Who can blame a picket for alerting the networks before going out on the line? . . .

POINTS TO CONSIDER

John Gregory Dunne: A Riot on TV

1. How does the fact that commercial television is primarily an entertainment medium affect the way in which a news event is covered on TV?

2. What are some of the ways in which television can "slant" the news? See Duane Bradley's article, "What is News?" (p. 53) and compare news slanting on TV with news slanting in newspapers. Which ways of slanting news do the media have in common? Does TV have any ways of slanting news that newspapers do not?

3. How does TV news coverage differ in approach from newspaper news coverage? What are the particular advantages and disadvantages of each in terms of what they can convey and of how they can affect society?

No Let-up Noted in TV Violence

United Press International, July 7, 1969

St. Louis Post-Dispatch

Philadelphia, (UPI): A task force analyzing television for the national commission for the causes and preventions of violence has concluded television portrays "a largely violent America . . . with a mostly violent past and a totally violent future."

Investigators from the Annenberg School of Communications at the University of Pennsylvania examined televised plays, cartoons and films during the first week of October, 1967 and again in October 1968.

Their results showed no decrease in violence.

In both years violence prevailed in eight out of 10 prime time or Saturday shows. Half of all the leading characters in the plays committed violence, one in 10 turned killer, and one in 20 was killed.

"The casualty count of injured and dead was at least 790 for the two weeks . . . one in every 10 acts of violence resulted in a fatality," the report stated.

Investigators found half of all the killers reached a happy ending because "good guys" inflicted as much violence as "bad guys."

The study concluded that CBS featured the least violence; ABC was "the most violent in many respects," NBC "declined slightly in some respects."

"AND NOW FOR THOSE OF YOU WHO LIKE VIOLENCE, HERE IS THE WORLD NEWS ROUNDUP."

Is There Really Any Violence on TV?

Rick DuBrow
St. Louis Post-Dispatch, May 14, 1969

Is there really too much violent entertainment on television?

Or is it just possible that the basic problem is that there isn't enough real violence shown at all in the weekly melodramas?

What I mean is this:

When somebody is shot or stabbed or otherwise done in on a television show, it is usually such a neat and clean job of killing that the viewer feels little or no pain at seeing a death.

How can there be horror when the process of killing and dying is not merely repetitive—but virtually palatable in the terms of real ugliness?

I think perhaps the numerous deaths on television have been no more responsible for killing feeling in viewers than the more pertinent fact that the slayings have not been particularly unpleasant.

And I'm not so sure television's current "anti-violence" trend of cutting away from actual killings at the crucial moment is a good idea.

My own feeling is that if you really want to generate a fear, a hatred and a horror of death on television—that is, take a positive instead of negative approach—then killing should be shown as it genuinely is.

And I think there would be such a feeling of revulsion by the public that its requests for less violence would be steeped in much more real feeling—so much, in fact, that viewers would understand the correlation between the genuine deaths in the Vietnam news and the phony ones in melodramas.

For example, what if a fellow on "Gunsmoke"—instead of merely getting shot in the arm or leg—was plugged in the groin? You don't see that sort of thing happen very often on television.

What if somebody on "The High Chaparral"—instead of getting a scalp wound or dying neatly—were shot right square in the eye, for all viewers to see?

What if a villain or a good guy in "Hawaii Five-O" had half his head blown off, in full view, before a nation of watchers settling down to watch some nice clean killing?

What if a woman in a melodrama was shot to pieces? What if someone's mouth or ears were ripped off by a knife or gun wound?

You say it's too horrible. You cringe and say that's not the sort of stuff one should see on television. A network executive would say it would be tasteless.

I disagree. What is horrible and what is tasteless is to see antiseptic death, the way it hardly ever really happens. That is dishonest. That is immoral. That is the worst possible kind of lie. It glamorizes killing. It glamorizes the so-called romance of dying in a melodrama.

The truth could set a lot of people in television free.

◤ POINTS TO CONSIDER ◥

Rick DuBrow: Is There Really Any Violence on TV?

1. How does the usual depiction of violence on TV and in movies differ from the violence in real life? (Compare DuBrow's comments with William Saroyan's in "Love, Death, Sacrifice, and So Forth," p. 195.)

2. How does DuBrow feel that depictions of violence on TV can be lessened? What do you think of his method?

3. What does DuBrow suggest is the danger of depicting "antiseptic" violence routinely on TV? Do you agree that the routine depiction of violence, of any kind, on TV is undesirable? Why or why not?

4. Does DuBrow's theory help to explain why many people who do not seem to mind the routine violence of TV drama protest the broadcasting of real war and of disorders in our cities and on our college campuses?

Smith and the Telly

Alan Sillitoe
The Loneliness of the Long Distance Runner, 1959

Night after night we sat in front of the telly with a ham sandwich in one hand, a bar of chocolate in the other, and a bottle of lemonade between our boots, while mam was with some fancy-man upstairs on the new bed she'd ordered, and I'd never known a family as happy as ours was in that couple of months when we'd got all the money we needed. And when the dough ran out I didn't think about anything much, but just roamed the streets—looking for another job, I told mam—hoping I suppose to get my hands on another five hundred nicker so's the nice life we'd got used to could go on and on for ever.[1] Because it's surprising how quick you can get used to a different life. To begin with, the adverts on the telly had shown us how much more there was in the world to buy than we'd ever dreamed of when we'd looked into shop windows but hadn't seen all there was to see because we didn't have the money to buy it with anyway. And the telly made all these things seem twenty times better than we'd ever thought they were. Even adverts at the cinema were cool and tame, because now we were seeing them in private at home. We used to cock our noses up at things in shops that didn't move, but suddenly we saw their real value because they jumped and glittered around the screen and had some pasty-faced tart going head over heels to get her nail-polished grabbers on to them or her lipstick lips over them, not the crumby adverts you saw on posters or in newspapers as dead as doornails; these were flickering around loose, half-open packets and tins, making you think that all you had to do was finish opening them before they were yours, like seeing an unlocked safe through a shop window with the man gone away for a cup of tea without thinking to guard his lolly.[2] The films they showed were good as well, in that way, because we couldn't get our eyes unglued from the cops chasing the robbers who had satchel-bags crammed with cash and looked like getting away to spend it—until the last moment. I always hoped they would end up free to blow the lot, and could never stop wanting to put my hand out, smash into the screen (it only looked a bit of rag-screen like at the pictures) and get the copper in a half-nelson so's he'd stop following the bloke with the money-bags. Even when he'd knocked off a couple of bank clerks I hoped he wouldn't get nabbed. In fact then I wished more than ever he wouldn't because it meant the

[1] Five hundred nicker is five hundred pounds (worth about $1200), the amount Smith's mother received in insurance and compensation when her husband died and which accounted for the family's sudden wealth.

[2] His lolly is his loot, his treasure.

hot-chair if he did, and I wouldn't wish that on anybody no matter what they'd done, because I'd read in a book where the hot-chair won't a quick death at all, but that you just sat there scorching to death until you were dead. And it was when these cops were chasing the crooks that we played some good tricks with the telly, because when one of them opened his big gob to spout about getting their man I'd turn the sound down and see his mouth move like a goldfish or mackerel or a minnow mimicking what they were supposed to be acting—it was so funny the whole family nearly went into fits on the brand-new carpet that hadn't yet found its way to the bedroom. It was the best of all though when we did it to some Tory[3] telling us about how good his government was going to be if we kept on voting for them—their slack chops rolling, opening and bumbling, hands lifting to twitch moustaches and touching their buttonholes to make sure the flower hadn't wilted, so that you could see they didn't mean a word they said, especially with not a murmur coming out because we'd cut off the sound. When the governor of the Borstal[4] first talked to me I was reminded of those times so much that I nearly killed myself trying not to laugh. Yes, we played so many good stunts on the box of tricks that mam used to call us the Telly Boys, we got so clever at it.

POINTS TO CONSIDER

Alan Sillitoe: Smith and the Telly

1. How can you tell that Smith lives in England? Do the English TV programs and commercials sound much like their American counterparts?

2. Why are TV ads often much more influential than ads in other media, such as movies, billboards, magazines, and newspapers?

3. What is the relationship between Smith's reaction to TV advertising and his reaction to "cops and robbers" films and to political speeches on TV?

4. What influences does TV advertising seem to have on Smith's philosophy of life? Do you think that Smith is at all typical of TV watchers or that he is an unusual case? (Compare this selection with the Hollywood premiere excerpt from Nathanael West's *The Day of the Locust,* p. 199.)

---

[3] A Tory is a member or supporter of England's Conservative political party.

[4] The governor of the Borstal was the director of the reformatory where Smith was sent for stealing some money.

Ratings and Mass Values

Harry J. Skornia
Television and Society, 1965

Probably no single factor is more responsible for the principal practices of commercial United States broadcasting than the use made of ratings. Ratings determine, in large part, what programs will be retained and which will be dropped. It will be noted that the programs offered in the first place, however, are determined by the broadcaster.

Ratings and the use made of them have been repeatedly condemned—and not only by the usual critics of television. LeRoy Collins, former president of the National Association of Broadcasters, has called them "a maze of statistics built from scanty facts" and has noted that investigations into how they operate "call into question the truth of any rating delivered today." David Sarnoff has said that the rating services do not mean what they say and do not say what they mean. Robert Hurleigh, president of the Mutual Broadcasting System, has called ratings based on 0.0003 per cent of the population meaningless. They have been criticized as "much ado about (practically) nothing," in view of the millions of dollars and the showy electronic computers used to extrapolate[1] microbe-sized figures based on inadequate evidence into "public opinion." Probably never have so many people and dollars been engaged to prove so much from so little.

Ratings are based on the premise that stations should broadcast What the Public Wants. This premise should be examined.

Journalists a few years ago were criticized for providing too little news about nuclear fallout. Editors explained that before press coverage of this problem could be increased, the public must demand it. The chicken-and-egg relationship in such a statement is obvious. From what, if not from news, is the public to know that such information is available? Or how is the public to know that fallout is or was reaching dangerous levels, and therefore should be considered news? The market for news items, like that for products, can be either created or not created.

Years ago speakers, artists, and writers had things to say; the media available —print, podium, and radio—dictated only its form. The commodity viewpoint reverses this. Now the communicator asks: What do you want said? The dangers of carrying the What-the-Public-Wants practice to an extreme are obvious. Only in so commercially controlled an environment as broadcasting is such a perversion of the very definition of news imaginable. Do you go to a lecture to hear what a man wants to say about a subject? Or do you go to have him tell you what

[1] To extrapolate is to project an estimate based upon a limited amount of information.

you want to hear? Does an atomic scientist change his subject from fission to his latest trip through the Alps because it would be more entertaining and he has excellent slides available?

But this is only a small part of the problem. The slogan "Give the public what it wants" implies, first, that the public knows what it wants; second, it implies that the public is an *it* instead of a *they;* third, it implies that there is a clear and accurate way for wants to be transmitted to the decision makers.

The Canadian scholar Alan Thomas has analyzed the roles people play in relation to television as Audience, Market, and Public. As Audience, people are a series of unconnected homes or individuals. Because they are so unconnected and isolated from each other, they cannot set standards, as Frank Stanton and others say they do. The Audience exists only from moment to moment. The Audience's vote is expressed by ratings. And ratings count sets rather than people or likes and dislikes in general.

As Market, the people become buying units, economic rather than human entities. Market success is measured by sales and profits; i.e., dollars. Market, too, is temporary. It is created by advertising.

As Public, people exist in their capacity as citizens. People who may vote *for* a program as audience, through ratings, may also vote as Public (citizens) *against* the program if they find the sponsor dishonest. As a part of the Public, a man may even support stricter government regulation to correct indecencies, dishonesty, rigging, deceit, excessive violence, or any objectionable content in the very programs he voted *for* as audience, and may even have voted for as market, by buying the product. The role of Public makes the citizen ask himself what is the *responsible* thing to do, rather than merely what he likes or wants. This role is the only continuing and rational one of the three.

Only in the role of Public do the people operate as a nation. Only in this role have they an objective and accurate mechanism for voting. That is the ballot box. The Public has voted for the creation of regulatory agencies by voting for congressmen who wrote legislation to create them. As Audience or Market, people may want lewd programs, or dope; as Public, or citizens, however, they will ask for limitations on both. . . .

The Public regulates. The Audience watches programs and laughs at regulation violations. And the Market buys. Only in their role as the Public do the people recognize their duties and needs as well as their wants in the perspective which democracy requires. To quote ratings is not to quote the Public; it is only to quote Audience—to quote appetite instead of hunger, want instead of need, irresponsibility instead of responsibility, short-term instead of long-term, irrationality instead of rationality. Yet Audience is the constituency which the broadcast industry so often quotes (by ratings) in support of its programming. . . .

It is natural for broadcast leaders to rely on ratings, since they conceive of television as a mass medium. Yet what is a mass? And can television viewers be considered a mass? Television viewers, as we have seen, behave at different times in different roles. At one moment they are a part of one group; the next moment they are part of another of the several minorities. But no one of these units is stable from moment to moment. Nor is any one a majority except, possibly, fleetingly. That is why the term *mass,* which implies such stability, does not describe a dynamic and open society.

The job of such a democratic society is the formation of individuals. Totalitarianism, under whatever name it may operate, reduces man to a unit or a cog. Whether he be thus dehumanized for political, economic, racial, religious, or broadcasting reasons is of less significance than that he *is* dehumanized, less than free and less than fulfilled.

Management of television and radio in the United States decided to apply mass-production techniques to broadcasting, not because they were inevitable or better but because they were more profitable. As the reasons are examined for considering television and radio as mass rather than minority or pluralistic media, it appears that they are mass media principally because they were *made into* mass media by their uses and their users. United States broadcasting aims at the largest possible audience available at any given time. Yet one of the dangers of thinking of the media in terms of the mass is that as the size of a group grows, so does the number of compromises which need to be made to avoid talking over the heads of lowbrow members or antagonizing certain minority members.

In a mass-dominated society individual features become blurred. We see only faceless crowds. The symbol of the society becomes the blank look, the look of people whose irrational appetites are manipulated by an elite who control mass media. Nothing could be more of a contradiction or parody of true democracy than this mass or "cultural" democracy.

While Frank Stanton and his compatriots have said for the United States commercial system that a mass medium must concern itself with the common denominator of mass interest, the BBC's first director general, Lord Reith, has never considered television and radio to be mass media.[2] He sees not a mass but a series of different publics, each of which must be treated with respect; not as targets for advertisers, but as human beings capable of cultural and intellectual *growth.*

Robert Sarnoff[3] has said that television is "the broadest of mass media." Yet in education, which has always avoided mass tactics by making age, grade-level, subject-matter, and other non-mass divisions, television has been marvelously successful. Doctors learning from specialized television uses how to save patients' lives by new surgical and radiation techniques illustrate non-mass uses. Talk-back and question techniques by radio, providing instantaneous feedback,

[2] Frank Stanton is the president of CBS. The BBC is the British Broadcasting Corporation, England's government-operated television network.

[3] Robert Sarnoff is the president of NBC.

daily illustrate non-mass techniques in the use of radio and television. Radio stations KPFA in Berkeley and WFMT in Chicago, "class" stations with small but loyal audiences composed largely of culturally oriented individuals and community leaders, illustrate non-mass uses. All serve their areas. All reach large groups, but preserve them integrally as desirable and separate minorities. All are in a fair way to disproving the mass concept of Frank Stanton, who claims that every mass medium must "cater to the middle" or cease to exist.

Mass culture is fabricated by technicians and profit-seeking administrators who find that the mass status of the people requires less trouble and less imagination, and yields higher return on investment. The analogy to industrial production is obvious: The bigger the volume and the fewer the styles or models, the bigger the profits. . . .

Philosophers and historians have warned of the dangers to be faced unless the American can shake himself loose from the hypnotic influence of totalitarian mass behavior and psychology. The American seems to be becoming more unable to demonstrate the individuality which democracy requires. Continuing hypnotism, emulsification, and homogenization of men by the media is the opposite of what our nation needs. . . .

However painful to present broadcast leadership, and even if it reduces profits, the dehumanization of democratic man by television and radio must be halted if democracy is to survive. At least two steps are needed if the present dangerous mass concept dominating the use of television and radio is to be stopped. The first is to introduce into the one-way system we now have the much more rapid feedback that leaders in a democracy require. This involves recognition of the fact that television and radio are first of all instruments of democracy rather than of commerce. The leaders of the broadcast system also require more dependable feedback than ratings provide. Channels must be found through which the members of the public can express themselves to leaders of all kinds. This will mean setting aside air time for serious, unrigged discussions. It will require the introduction of the kind of *talkback* that has been developed by education. The use of telephone lines has been described whereby listeners and viewers may participate while educational television programs are on the air. By the reservation of a few frequencies for the viewer and for feedback, the great dialogue which democracy requires is still possible. Old ballot approaches devised two hundred years ago are too slow today. Electronic guidance in the form of reaction to dialogue, and the feeding in of ideas on an instantaneous basis from the people to government, are now possible. If commercial media do not provide this service, government itself must have its own broadcast and feedback system to make it possible. It is electronically feasible now to have instantaneous feedback from every television viewer in the United States. A few rating services already are using, or misusing, such devices. Broadcasters can know instead of guessing about qualitative reactions of viewers. Many practices which are denounced today as economically unfeasible can become realities tomorrow—but only if the present monopoly is broken and the present mass concept of the media abandoned.

Second, programming for the cultural subgroups of the nation must replace mass-audience programming. This is not to say that fewer people should be served. It is to say only that fewer people will be served at a time. Selective viewing and selective programming must be promoted. Instead of reaching a majority by homogenizing most programs, a majority would be accumulated by adding together the many individual minorities who want something more specific than the present fare.

It is ridiculous to believe that television and radio are not innately as capable of non-mass uses as the book, the magazine, or the film. The principal obstacle to such development is the mass-media concept now prevalent.

Ratings *could* be useful. But they are now being used to defeat rather than to serve the public interest. Good editors have reported that when readership surveys have revealed low interest in foreign news, they have used these surveys as guides for *improving* or *increasing* their foreign news, not for replacing it with comics. Ratings should challenge rather than defeat.

The people of the United States need to be lifted to the level of today's problems. The media, more than the schools or any other institutions, can do this. So far, the problems have been lowered or watered down. We have heard that education, culture, or many other things cannot be forced down people's throats. Yet soap operas have been. And so have westerns, quizzes, wrestling, game shows, thirty-year-old movies, and professional sports.

Judge Learned Hand challenged the allegation that the people have consented to what exists. They have not. They are only too unorganized, too inert, or too uninformed to do anything about it. The only true rating of what the people want must take into account what they would choose if it were offered, if they clearly saw its importance, and if they were left alone and allowed to act rationally.

Lord Reith of the BBC gave his view of the responsibility of leadership as early as 1924. He said: "As we conceive it, our responsibility is to carry into the greatest possible numbers of homes everything that is best in every department of human knowledge, endeavour, and achievement, and to avoid the things which are, or may be, hurtful. It is occasionally indicated to us that we are apparently setting out to give the public what we think they need—and not what they want, but few know what they want, and very few what they need. There is often no difference. . . . In any case it is better to over-estimate the mentality of the public than to under-estimate it."

POINTS TO CONSIDER

Harry J. Skornia: Ratings and Mass Values

1. What are television ratings? Who conducts the ratings, and how are they determined? How representative are they?

2. What is wrong with the premise, on which ratings are based, that television should broadcast "what the public wants"?

3. What are the distinctions between the viewers of television as audience, as market, and as public? How does the determining of TV programming primarily by ratings ignore these distinctions?

4. What are the dangers to a democratic society of applying mass-production techniques to broadcasting? Compare what Skornia says about "mass-dominated society" with what Erich Fromm says about "personality packages" (p. 5).

5. What are some of the educational "non-mass" uses of television?

6. What two steps does Skornia suggest for halting the "present dangerous mass concept dominating the use of television and radio"? What do you think of his suggestions?

7. Why do you think that TV ratings have affected television differently when comparing them with the ways that readership surveys have affected magazines or newspapers? How could TV ratings be used to improve television?

"How long must I endure this insult
to my intelligence?"

Drawing by Handelsman; © 1969. The New Yorker Magazine, Inc.

Ideas for Investigation, Discussion, and Writing

Radio and Television

1. Interview a number of people of different ages and interests to discover if they listen to the radio, how much they listen, and what they like to hear. What groups listen to radio the most? What groups listen the least? What varied services does the radio perform for its different kinds of listeners?

2. Speak with some station managers and disc jockeys of local radio stations to learn how they arrange their programs, select their music, and schedule their advertising. What people or groups of people are the most influential in determining kinds and scheduling of programs, music, and advertising?

3. What functions can radio perform better than other mass media? How well do you feel it performs these functions? How could it improve its performance of these functions? What additional functions, if any, do you think it could or should perform?

4. What are some of the different services which TV provides its various viewers? Ask some people of different ages and interests for their opinions. To what extent do these services overlap those offered by other mass media? Which services does TV seem to be able to perform especially well?

5. Compare the kinds of weekday daytime TV shows, the kinds of weekend daytime TV shows, and the kinds of evening TV shows to determine the audiences of each. How do the products or services advertised at these times and the styles of the commercials appeal to the audiences for which they are intended?

6. What effect has television had upon the education and upon the social activities of our society? How do you evaluate these effects?

7. In what ways does television news reporting differ from news reporting by other mass media? What advantages and limitations does TV news reporting have? How do you think it could be improved?

8. What are some of the different ways in which TV broadcasting can be financed? What are advantages and disadvantages of each? What services are currently offered by subscription television stations in this country?

9. What qualities account for the sustained popularity of some TV drama series and situation comedy series shows of the past and present, such as "I Love Lucy," "Leave It to Beaver," "Beverly Hillbillies," "Perry Mason," "Gunsmoke," and "Bonanza"? Why are some of these shows just as popular in other countries as they are in the United States?

PART FIVE

PHOTOGRAPHY AND
MOTION PICTURES

Photography and motion pictures share the properties of both media and popular arts. As media, they bring to the mass audience visual reproductions of people, places, and events which otherwise only the privileged few could see. They also enable us to record these images for future reference. Specialized processes, such as microphotography and slow motion or time-lapse motion pictures, allow us to see things we could not see without their aid, increasing our interest in the world beyond our immediate environment while augmenting our knowledge of it. At the same time, photography and motion pictures have colored and intensified our feelings about the subjects they record. A commonplace scene or person may appear glamorous or ugly in a photograph; a commonplace event may seem important when recorded on film. The very experience of seeing an event glowing from a screen adds to its fascination and often heightens its reality.

As popular arts, photography and motion pictures both reflect and influence our society. Photojournalism has aroused public pride as well as public concern about the state of society and world events and has hastened many social reforms. Commercial photography is big business: modern advertising and packaging could not exist without it. Fine art photography has affected the nature of other more traditional visual art forms, such as painting, and has modified our ideas about what is and what is not art.

Motion pictures have largely replaced theatre as the popular dramatic art form. In content, popular motion pictures mirror the issues of society, while in style—both dramatic and technical—they mirror its emotional state. Current film acting style tends toward low-key realism, but camera and editing techniques—and special techniques such as animation—are complex and imaginative. Like popular fiction, journalism, and television—and sometimes in connection with these other media and art forms—movies tend to create their own heros and ideals and to make "improvements" upon reality which, at times, are more convincing than reality itself. Certainly the image which many foreigners have of Americans as corpulent cutthroats in Cadillacs was established largely by our widely exported Hollywood films. Today, American motion pictures exert a double influence both at home and abroad: They appear not only on the movie screens of thousands of theaters, they appear on the television screen in millions of homes.

Basic Visual Elements of the Photograph and the Motion Picture

Fredric Rissover

Still Photography

Some people who admire drawing and painting used to argue that photography really is not an art form because it is not personal and creative—it simply reproduces its subject objectively. But few people hold this opinion any more. One reason may be that museums of fine art, like New York's Museum of Modern Art, have been displaying outstanding photographs in their galleries. Another reason may be that with the tremendous use of photography in journalism and advertising, the general quality level has risen as increasingly talented artists have come to work in the medium. As more good photography is produced and reproduced in great quantity, people who are exposed to it grow to admire and appreciate it. A third reason is that movies—photographs in motion—have called the attention of the public to the artistry of good photography.

All good photography demands that the photographer have a "good eye"; that is, he must be able to recognize the raw material which will provide good subjects for his photographs. An appealing photo often has an unusual or expressive or revealing subject. It may capture interesting forms or details. It may depict contrast or conflict in design or in action and emotion. Frequently, the photograph which attracts us most and lingers longest in our memories is one which presents vividly a specific subject or situation but which also suggests that the specific subject may be representative of the universal.

But spotting an appealing subject is just the beginning. When the photographer has found his subject, he must decide how to treat it. Like any other artist, he has a variety of ways that he can interpret his subject. The good photographer, consciously and instinctively, combines the elements of his art to achieve the effects he desires.

Perhaps the most immediately apparent element of the photographer's art is "framing": isolating a subject from its surroundings. In no other art form is the element of isolation so obvious and striking as it is in photography—in both still photos and movies. A commonplace and not particularly interesting object or detail is often called to our attention and becomes fascinating simply because the observant photographer has put a frame around it and isolated it for us on a piece of paper or a movie screen.

The element of framing in photography calls our attention to the composition of details, just as it does in painting. We notice the distribution of shapes and sizes, of textures, of lights and darks; and we notice the interplay of horizontal, vertical, diagonal, and curving lines. The element of framing also makes us

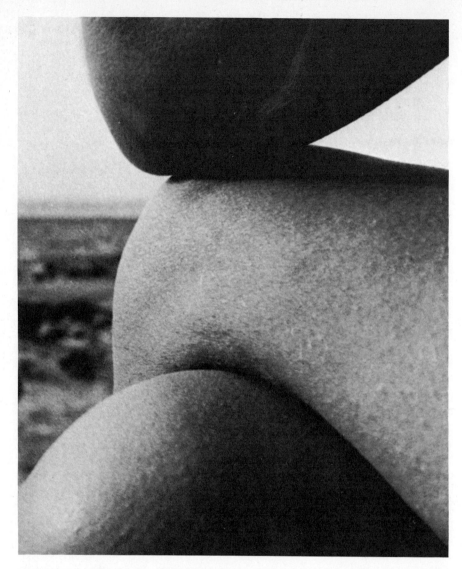

Photograph by Bill Brandt. Rapho Guillumette.

aware of the ways in which similar or different objects exist near to or together with each other. This side-by-side relationship between the details within the frame is called "juxtaposition in space."

A good example of how photography can call our attention to the commonplace is seen in the picture just above. The subject is simply an elbow and two knees, but the special view of them which the photographer gives us trans-

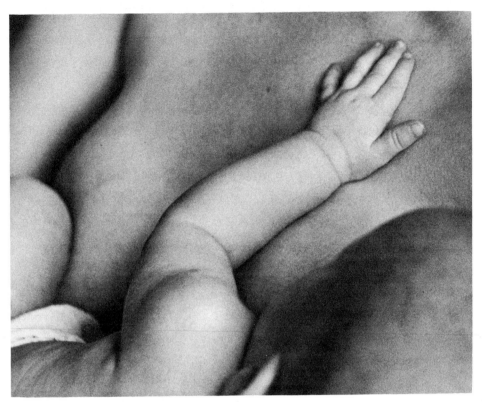

Photograph by Wayne Miller. © Magnum Photos.

forms them into something new. The tight framing which detaches them from the rest of the body turns them into abstract shapes resembling a piece of modern sculpture. The lighting which provides striking highlights and shadows and which brings out a grainy quality in the skin suggests the solidity and roughness of carved stone.

Another example of effective framing can be seen in the photo above. In this picture of a mother nursing her baby, we see only the mother's bosom, the head of the baby, and the arm of the baby clinging to the mother. This limitation of subject forces us to concentrate on the idea of the mother's gift and the child's dependency rather than on the mother-and-child relationship in general. It also seems to blend the parts of both bodies into one harmonious pattern, as if to suggest that the mother and her child are, at this time, like a single being. Interesting juxtaposition in space is illustrated by the photo on page 170 in which a young boy on his way to school contrasts dramatically with the setting in which he walks—a bombed-out section of a city.

Closely related to the element of framing as an important component of the

Photograph by Otto Hagel. © *Otto Hagel.*

photographer's art is the element of "scale," or "relative size." The photographer can depict the relative importance of his details by comparing them to each other in size. Or he can greatly exaggerate or diminish the size of his subject or details to express his feelings about them.

In the photo of the young pianist on page 171, the hands appear huge to suggest both the forcefulness of his playing and the importance of his hands and his music to his life. The two photos of mothers and their children, on pages 172 and 173, offer an interesting comparative study in relative size. In the picture to the left, the tall mother towers protectively over her two small children. The difference in size here is captured by the photographer but not created by him. In the picture to the right, however, the photographer places the little girl and the baby in the foreground and the mother behind them, making the mother look smaller by comparison and perhaps suggesting the all-absorbing importance of the two children to their mother who looks lovingly at them.

A third element of the photographer's art which greatly influences the effect of his picture is the "visual angle." Interesting visual angle is an important way

Photograph by Henry Crossman, ASMP.

Basic Visual Elements of the Photograph and the Motion Picture   171

Photograph by Consuelo Kanaga.

Photography and Motion Pictures

of creating the illusion of depth. It also provides a way to present the subject in an unusual or provocative manner. Further, it can affect our interpretation of the subject just as the element of relative size can. A low shooting angle in which we look up at the subject tends to make the subject look larger and more impressive; a high shooting angle in which we look down at the subject tends to make the subject look smaller and weaker.

Notice how in the photo of the man in the swamp, on page 174, the downward visual angle, combined with the relatively small size of the man and the framing of branches and leaves, makes the man appear to be a part of his surroundings and greatly influenced by them. By contrast, in the photo of the young man on page 175, the upward visual angle and the contrast of the bold face and fist

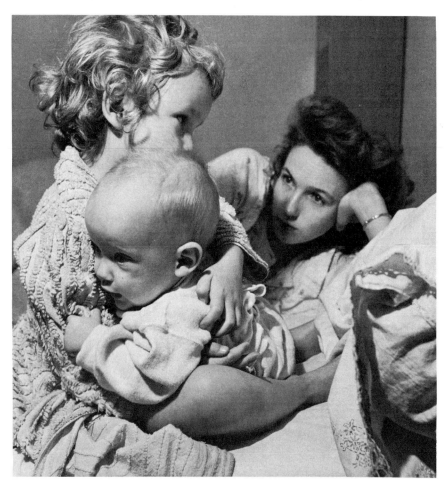

Photograph by Wayne Miller. © Magnum Photos.

Basic Visual Elements of the Photograph and the Motion Picture　　173

against the plain background emphasize the forcefulness of the man and his attempt to stand out from or even dominate his surroundings.

Along with framing, relative size, and visual angle, there are several special optical effects which the photographer may employ. One of these is the regulation of the amount and quality of light in his pictures. With good use of light and dark obtained through natural or artificial lighting, filters, and various exposure times, the photographer can call attention to significant details and wash other details in obscuring glare or shadow. He can bring out textures and

Photograph by Ted Polumbaum. Life *Magazine, © Time Inc.*

Photography and Motion Pictures

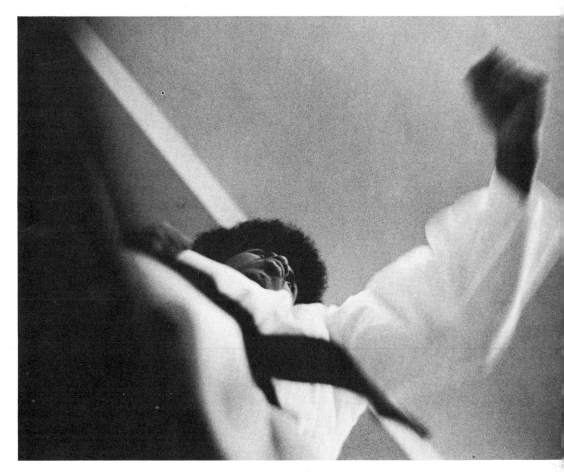

Photograph by Howard Sochurek.

heighten or lessen the solidness, opaqueness, or sharpness of his details, thereby affecting the mood of the picture.

The photo of the sculptor at work on a portrait bust, on page 176, uses light
and shadow effectively to contrast the softness of the curtains with the solidity
of the sculpture and to create a similarity between the appearance of the artist
and of his creation which suggests the close relationship of the two. The picture
of a flock of sheep standing near the entrance of a cave, on page 177, combines
effective framing with effective use of light. The framing creates the illusion that
the sheep are emerging from the cave in a spiral pattern like the unwinding of the
mainspring of a watch. If the picture had not been so closely framed, the illusion
would have been lost as we saw the groups of sheep and individual sheep
wandering in all directions farther from the cave. The lighting is bright enough
to bring out the whiteness of the sheep, but not so intense as to wash out the

textures of the sheep's wool and of the rocky hillside. The white sheep stand out just enough from the white and grey rock to appear different from it, but they blend in closely enough to suggest their harmony with it—their close relationship to their natural environment. The black shadows in the cave, around the legs of the sheep, and above and below the sheep contrast with the whiteness of the sheep, reinforce the spiral pattern of the sheep and the hillside, and provide a kind of natural frame within the picture.

By use of "sharp" or "soft focus" or by use of the two in contrast, the photographer affects the mood of his picture. Most pictures have sharp focus in which all the details are as clear as their size and the amount of light permit. But sometimes the photographer uses soft focus; that is, he chooses to blur the outlines and details of his picture to suggest an unreal, ideal, or dreamlike quality. Sometimes he uses both sharp and soft focus in the same picture to accentuate the illusion of depth or to contrast solid reality with the dreamlike.

In the portrait of the young man on page 175, a blurring of the arm and fist records his defiant gesture. In the picture of the little girl on her father's shoulders, page 178, the blurring of the background focuses our attention on the main figures, while the soft focus in the foreground helps to impart a mood of dreamlike idealism to the happy moment.

Photograph by George Krause.

Courtesy of AT&T.

"Multiple images" and "time exposures" form another group of optical effects which the photographer may use to advantage. Multiple images can depict imaginative or distracted states of mind by superimposing representations of mental images upon the images of solid reality, as in pictures illustrating visions or ghosts. The picture on page 179 was made by combining parts of several different negatives to create a multiple print with the vivid but unreal quality of a dream. Multiple and time exposures often translate time into space by blurring images to suggest motion or speed or by capturing in one picture a series of actions or a continuous action performed over a period of time. The photo on page 180 of a lady doing a physical fitness exercise employs multiple exposure in order to record in one image the separate movements she performs over a brief period of time. Thus, it translates her graceful motion into an attractive still pattern.

A fourth optical device which the photographer may use to create expressive pictures is "deliberate distortion," which may be achieved with lenses, prisms, mirrors, or filters when the picture is taken or by some chemical or mechanical

Photograph by Jerry Uelsmann.

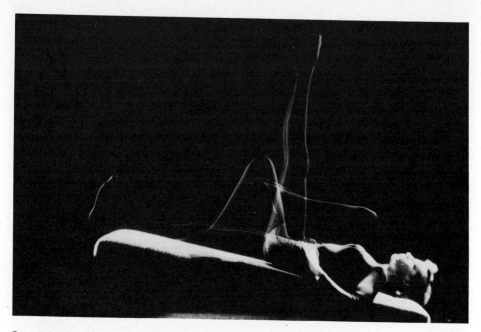

means in the developing process. Distortion may suggest unreality or unusual mental states such as those created by mind-expanding drugs, it may create the macabre or the grotesque, or it may call our attention to the forms and patterns of common things by presenting them in an unusual way. Although deliberate distortion is not unusual in still photographs, it probably appears more frequently in movies.

Motion Pictures

Movies make use of all the elements of the art of still photography. The movie-maker is concerned with framing and juxtaposition in space, scale or relative size, visual angles, and special optical effects, such as amount and quality of light, sharp and soft focus, multiple and time exposure, and deliberate distortion.

Framing in motion pictures, as in still pictures, focuses the attention of the viewer on a limited subject and points up relationships between details. Sometimes in movies framing is used especially to prevent the viewer from seeing some details or some of the action. This may be done to build suspense, to prevent the viewer's seeing something particularly painful or ugly, or to force the viewer to imagine details for himself. Sometimes this can be used as a comic device if the viewer is led to imagine something one way and then is shown something quite different.

A special kind of framing which changes the normal dimensions of the screen picture is known as "masking." In masking, part of the picture is blocked out to make it appear tall and narrow, especially wide, or even circular. This is used to reinforce particular details such as knights in combat on a tall castle tower, a covered wagon caravan crossing a broad prairie, or an approaching pirate ship seen through a spyglass.

Relative size functions in movies as it does in still photos to suggest relative strength or importance; however, in movies the relative sizes change quickly with movement of subject or camera. The overall scale of the picture depends upon the distance of the camera from the subject and upon the lens used. The extents of view and the scales of size range from the long shot, which depicts a very restricted view on a large scale—a view of a distant-city skyline with buildings the size of sugar cubes—to detailed views of an eye or a trigger finger filling the whole screen. Special effects often are created with models or miniatures representing full-sized objects, such as ships in sea battle or towns attacked by monsters, or with images of people or objects of one size superimposed upon images of people or objects of another size to depict ghosts, midgets, or giants.

Visual angle is important in movies because it is so expressive and because it can change so rapidly to create a number of cumulatively effective impressions. Action viewed from a great height often suggests detachment while action viewed from below suggests victimization. Unusual camera angles can suggest odd or distressing circumstances or troubled states of mind. As with framing, visual angles can be employed to limit what the viewer can see or to create deliberate ambiguity. Often in movies the camera will adopt the point of view of a character for some part of the action.

The special optical effects used in still photography—controlling amounts and quality of light, sharp and soft focus, multiple and time exposures, and deliberate distortion—appear commonly in movies. In many cases, their use in movies is more complex and expressive than it is in still photos because the added elements of time and motion permit more variations and combinations.

In addition to the artistic elements shared with still photography, motion pictures make use of a number of other expressive visual elements related to movement within individual shots and to movement between and among shots. A movie "shot" is the action recorded on film during a single running of the camera—the action recorded between "roll 'em!" and "cut!" Shots range from a few seconds to a few minutes. Theoretically, a whole feature-length film could be made in one shot, but (except for a few experimental oddities) this is never done because to do so would rob the film of one of its most expressive techniques.

Movement within individual shots involves three basic components—movement of the subject, movement of the camera, and regulation of time. Movements of the subject can be horizontal, vertical, or diagonal, in or out, or some combination of these. In general, horizontal movement is less strong than vertical movement, and neither is as exciting as diagonal movement. Movement in toward the camera is usually more forceful and often suggests that action is about to occur, whereas movement away from the camera is less forceful and often suggests a suspension of action. Movement in more than one direction, of course, tends to be more exciting than movement in a single direction, just as fast movement is more exciting than slow movement. All these generalizations, however, are open to exceptions.

Movements of the camera generally have the same emotional effects as movements of the subject. Horizontal motion is calmer, vertical action is stronger, and diagonal motion is more exciting, relatively speaking. Motion toward a subject is usually stronger than motion away from a subject. Movement in which the camera swings or pivots horizontally, vertically, or diagonally, is commonly known as "panning," while movement in which the camera focuses toward or away from the subject is called "zooming in" or "zooming out." Usually, the faster the panning and zooming are done, the more exciting they tend to be. Movement of the whole camera which concentrates upon and follows a particular subject, such as a moving car, is generally called "tracking."

Control of motion and time within individual movie shots helps to determine the dramatic effects of a film. If the film is shot at slower-than-normal speed and projected at normal speed, the motion will be faster than usual. Fast motion is used occasionally in comedies to exaggerate the awkwardness of some action or the hectic nature of a slapstick chase scene. If the film is shot at faster-than-normal speed and projected at normal speed, the motion will be slower than usual. Slow motion is sometimes used to give film action the quality of a dream or a memory. Often it is used to slow down the action of a natural process (like bird flight) or of a sports event (like a pole vault or a football play) to reveal all the details of motion.

In general, the moviemaker regulates time for dramatic effect in the same way a playwright does. If details are important, they may be dwelt upon, whereas, if details are not important, they may be passed over quickly. This means that unimportant action lasting, say, an hour in reality may be represented on film in thirty seconds, while important action lasting five minutes in reality may take half an hour to present in all its dramatic significance on film. Very rarely does time in a film approximate time in reality.

In using the element of time for emphasis, however, the film maker has an advantage over the playwright. The film maker is not as restricted as the playwright to single physical points of view. He can employ, in addition to action within single shots, movement between and among shots. If for example, he wants to show a bit of action from a number of different angles or distances, he can splice together a number of different shots. Splicing together shots can move action instantly from one setting to another and suggest changes in time or circumstance. Movement from shot to shot can compress time if the movement is quick or involves many omissions. Or movement from shot to shot can make time seem to stand still or can extend time by repeating an action or parts of it in any of a number of effective variations. Brief shots may be used to under-line increased activity or to build suspense, and these may be interspersed with longer shots to convey relative calm.

By splicing together shots, the film maker can achieve not only great mobility and emphasis through repitition and variation, but also effective comparisons and contrasts through juxtaposition in time. Whereas juxtaposition in space places details side by side for examination in a still photo or a single movie shot, juxtaposition in time suggests relationships between details in shots which occur near to each other in time. If, for example, we see a shot of a group of women gossiping and see immediately or shortly afterward a shot of hens in a farmyard, the comparison is clear. Of, if we see a shot of a murder being com-mitted in a woods and then see shots of people picnicking nearby or of a quiet stream flowing past, the murder seems all the more brutal because of the peace-ful contrasting shots. Juxtaposition in time can be used also to impart informa-tion by suggestion or to build suspense. If we see a shot of a young woman sitting on a park bench looking periodically at her watch, then see a shot of a young man hurrying through the park, and see finally a shot of two pigeons on a park path cooing to each other, we can infer that the man is hurrying to meet the woman in the park because they are in love. Or, if we see shots of a thief robbing a house intermixed with shots of a man walking toward the house, climbing the steps, and turning a key in the front door, the tension mounts be-cause we anticipate a confrontation.

The process of selecting movie shots, determining their length, and assem-bling them is generally called "editing" and is performed by a film editor working with the movie director or by the director himself. The action of any film, there-fore, is most strongly influenced by three sources: the screenwriter who sug-gests the action in his script, the director who controls the action as it is being filmed, and the editor (sometimes the director himself) who selects, cuts, and combines the shots after they are photographed.

In continental Europe, the term "montage" is used almost synonymously with editing, but in the United States montage refers to a more specific technique in which a sequence of short, rapid shots is used to represent a passage of time usually involving much activity. If, for example, in a film about prizefighting, a young boxer is working his way up to a championship fight over a period of three years, we may see many very brief shots of the boxer in training, the boxer pounding opponents, trains racing between cities, pages being torn off calen-dars, and newspaper headlines proclaiming greater and greater victories. Thus, in a minute or two, we are aware of three years' activity and progress. Montage can be used also to build excitement, as with a representation of a horse race in which we see many brief shots—featuring a variety of visual angles and rela-tive scales of size—of horses' hooves biting the turf, jockeys urging on their mounts, graceful forms racing by a fence, and excited viewers screaming in the grandstand.

In editing or montage, the commonest transition between shots is made by splicing one shot directly to another so that we see one bit of detail or action replaced immediately by another. This instantaneous change is called a "cut." Other transitional methods besides the direct cut are sometimes used to achieve special effects. The "fade-out–fade-in," for instance, is the transition in which the picture dims out to black and the new picture grows gradually brighter out of the darkness. This technique is generally used to suggest a passage of time or a major change of place. The "mix," or "dissolve," is the transition in which the old and new pictures blend for a moment as the old picture disappears and the new picture takes its place. The dissolve can suggest a change in time or place and often suggests a movement into the past or into the not-immediate future, usually through memory or dreams. The variety of other transitional methods in films includes the "wipe," the "iris-out–iris-in," the "turnover," and the "blur-out–blur-in." In the wipe, an invisible line passes across the screen removing the old picture and replacing it with the new one. In an iris-out–iris-in, the old picture grows dark from the edges to the center, and the new picture appears from the darkness, growing brighter from the center to the edges. In a turnover, the whole picture seems to flip, and the new picture appears on the back of the old. These last three devices occur most often in comedies. The blur-out–blur-in is like the dissolve except that the picture grows wavy or slips out of focus during the transition. Like the dissolve, this often ushers in memories or dreams. With the growing sophistication of filmgoers over the years, the special transition method has steadily decreased and has been replaced by the direct cut. Today's film audiences are so used to flashbacks, flash forwards, and quick changes in time and space that they seldom require technical cues.

The ability to use movement effectively within shots and between and among shots characterizes the good film maker. He regulates time to dramatic advantage, utilizes imaginative movement of subject and camera within shots, and edits skillfully between and among shots—creating forceful juxtaposition in time and employing smooth transition—to achieve maximum expression through his art.

POINTS TO CONSIDER

Fredric Rissover: Basic Visual Elements of the Photograph and the Motion Picture

Still Photography

1. In what ways is photography creative in the same sense that painting or poetry is creative? What is meant by a "good eye"? Why is this quality more essential to a photographer than to a painter?

2. What is framing? What are some of the effects that the use of framing can have on a picture? What is meant by the composition of a photograph? How

is it related to framing? Why is a diagonal line more exciting than a vertical or horizontal line? What is meant by the term "juxtaposition in space"? How is it different from composition? How is it affected by framing?

3. How can the photographer alter the relative sizes of objects within a photograph? How can this help to express his feelings about the objects?

4. What is meant by the term "visual angle"? What effects can be achieved through the variations of its use? By a downward angle? By an upward angle?

5. What effects can be achieved through the use of special lighting techniques and variations in focus and exposure?

Motion Pictures

1. What dimension does the motion picture add to the photograph? How does this affect such considerations of still photography as framing, visual angle, relative size, and juxtaposition?

2. What are the three basic components of movement within an individual movie shot? What general effects are achieved through the use of horizontal motion? Vertical motion? Diagonal motion? What is panning? Zooming in? Zooming out? What effect is achieved by speeding up these techniques?

3. What effect is achieved through slow motion? Through fast motion? How does the moviemaker create slow motion and fast motion?

4. How can the moviemaker expand or compress time? What sort of events would most likely be compressed? Why? What sort of events would most likely be expanded? Why? Can you think of any examples of the use of these techniques in recent movies?

5. What is meant by the term "editing?" How can an editor build suspense? How can he convey a feeling of calm? What is montage? What is juxtaposition in time? How are these also a part of editing?

6. What is meant by the term "transition"? How does it relate to editing? What is the cut? the dissolve? the fade-out–fade-in? What effects do they achieve? What are some of the less common transitional devices, and what effects do they achieve?

By permission of Richards Rosen Press.

Photograph by Ralph Crane. Life *Magazine,* © *Time Inc.*

Photograph by James Foote. Photo Researchers, Inc.

Photograph by Harry Benson.

Photograph by Harry Benson.

Photography and Motion Pictures

Wide World Photos.

Photograph by Gilles Caron. Pix Inc.

Photography and Motion Pictures

Photograph by Co Rentmeester. Life *Magazine,* © *Time Inc.*

SPORTS ILLUSTRATED *photograph by Herb Scharfman.* © *Time, Inc.*

▨ POINTS TO CONSIDER ▨

Photojournalism

1. What is the principal effect which each of the photos makes upon you? Can you observe some examples of the photographers' having employed any of the artistic means discussed in the preceding article to heighten the effects?

2. Some people feel that good examples of photojournalism really require no captions. Do you think that the preceding photos make their "messages" sufficiently clear without captions or explanations?

3. What kinds of news items are best presented in photos, and what kinds are best presented in words? What can photos "say" that words cannot? What can words say that photos cannot?

4. Under what circumstances do you feel that film can present a news item better than a still photo can? When can a still photo be more effective than film?

Love, Death, Sacrifice, And So Forth

William Saroyan

The Daring Young Man on the Flying Trapeze,
1962

Tom Garner, in the movie, on the screen, a big broad-shouldered man, a builder of railroads, President of the Chicago & Southwestern, staggers, does not walk, into his room, and closes the door.

You know he is going to commit suicide because he has staggered, and it is a movie, and already a long while has passed since the picture began, and something's got to happen real soon, something big, gigantic, as they say in Hollywood, a suicide or a kiss.

You are sitting in the theatre waiting for what you know is going to happen.

Poor Tom has just learned that the male offspring of his second wife is the product of his grown son by his first wife. Tom's first wife committed suicide when she learned that Tom had fallen in love with the young woman who finally became his second wife. This young woman was the daughter of the President of the Santa Clara Railroad. She made Tom fall in love with her so that her father would go on being President of the Santa Clara. Tom had bought the Santa Clara for nine million dollars. Tom's first wife threw herself beneath a streetcar when she found out about Tom's infatuation. She did it by acting, with her face, her eyes, and lips and the way she walked. You didn't get to see anything sickening, you saw only the motorman's frantic expression while he tried to bring the car to a stop. You heard and saw the steel wheel grinding, the wheel that killed her. You heard people screaming the way they do about violent things, and you got the idea. The worst had happened. Tom's wife Sally had gone to her Maker.

Sally met Tom when he was a trackwalker and she a teacher in a small country school. Tom confessed to her one day that he did not know how to read, write or do arithmetic. Sally taught Tom to read, write, add, subtract, divide and multiply. One evening after they were married she asked him if he wanted to be a trackwalker all his life, and he said that he did. Sally asked him if he didn't have at least a little ambition, and Tom said he was satisfied, trackwalking was easy work, they had their little home, and Tom got in a lot of fishing on the side. This hurt Sally, and she began to act. Tom saw that it would mean a lot to Sally if he became ambitious. Sitting at the supper table, he said that he would. A strange look came into his eyes, his face acquired great character. You could almost see him forging ahead in life.

Sally sent Tom to school in Chicago, and she did Tom's work as a trackwalker in order to have money with which to pay for his tuition, a great woman, an heroic wife. You saw her one winter night walking along a railroad track, packing tools and oil cans, snow and desolation all around her. It was sad. It was meant to be sad. She was doing it for Tom, so that he would be able to become a great man. The day Tom announced that he had been made foreman of the construction of the Missouri Bridge, Sally announced she was with child, and Tom said now they could never stop him. With Sally and his baby to inspire him Tom would reach the heights.

Sally gave birth to a son, and while Tom was walking to her bedside you heard symphonic music, and you knew that this was a great moment in Tom's life. You saw Tom enter the dimly lighted room and kneel beside his wife and baby son, and you heard him pray. You heard him say, Our father which art in heaven, thine the glory and the power, forever and forever. You heard two people in the theatre blowing their noses.

Sally made Tom. She took him from the track and sent him to the president's chair. Then Tom became infatuated with this younger and lovelier woman, and Sally threw herself beneath the streetcar. It was because of what she had done for Tom that the suicide was so touching. It was because of this that tears came to the eyes of so many people in the theatre when Sally destroyed herself.

But Sally's suicide did not have any affect on Tom's infatuation for the younger woman, and after a short while he married the girl, being a practical man part of the time, being practical as long as Hollywood wanted him to be practical. Tom's son, a young man just expelled from college for drunkenness, moved into Tom's house, and had an affair with Tom's second wife.

The result was the baby, a good healthy baby, born of the son instead of the father. Tom's son Tommy is an irresponsible but serious and well-dressed young man, and he really didn't mean to do it. Nature did it. You know how nature is, even in the movies. Tom had been away from home so much, attending to business, and his second wife had been so lonely that she had turned to her husband's son, and he had become her dancing partner.

You saw her holding her hand out to the young irresponsible boy, and you heard her ask him significantly if he would like to dance with her. It took him so long to take her hand that you understand the frightening implication instantly. And she was so maddeningly beautiful, extending her hand to him, that you knew you yourself would never have been able to resist her challenge, even under similar circumstances. There was something irresistible about the perfection of her face and figure, lips so kissable, stance so elegant, body so lovely, soul so needful.

It simply had to happen. Man is flesh, and all that.

So the big railroad builder, the man who always had his way, the man who broke the strike and had forty of his men killed in a riot, and a fire, has staggered into his room and closed the door.

And you know the picture is about to end.

The atmosphere of the theatre is becoming electrical with the apprehension of middle-aged ladies who have spent the better parts of their lives in the movies, loving, dying, sacrificing themselves to noble ideals, etc. They've come again to the dark theatre, and a moment of great living is again upon them.

You can feel the spiritual tenseness of all of these ladies, and if you are listening carefully you can actually hear them living fully.

Poor Tom is in there with a terrific problem and a ghastly obligation.

For his honor's sake, for the sake of Hollywood ethics, for the sake of the industry (the third largest in America, I understand), for God's sake, for your sake and my sake, Tom has got to commit suicide. If he doesn't, it will simply mean we have been deceiving ourselves all these years, Shakespeare and the rest of us. We know he'll be man enough to do it, but for an instant we hope he won't, just to see what will happen, just to see if the world we have made will actually smash.

A long while back we made the rules, and now, after all these years, we wonder if they are the genuine ones, or if, maybe, we didn't make a mistake at the outset. We know it's art, and it even looks a little like life, but we know it isn't life, being much too precise.

We would like to know if our greatness must necessarily go on forever being melodramatic.

The camera rests on the bewildered face of Tom's old and faithful secretary, a man who knew Tom as a boy. This is to give you the full implication of Tom's predicament and to create a powerful suspense in your mind.

Then, at a trot, with the same object in view, time hurrying, culminations, ultimates, inevitabilities, Tom's son Tommy comes to the old and faithful secretary and exclaims that he has heard Tom, his father, is ill. He does not know that his father knows. It is a Hollywood moment. You hear appropriate music.

He rushes to the door, to go to his father, this boy who upset the natural order of the universe by having a sexual affair with his father's young wife, and then, bang, the pistol shot.

You know it is all over with the President of the Chicago & Southwestern. His honor is saved. He remains a great man. Once again the industry triumphs. The dignity of life is preserved. Everything is hotsytotsy. It will be possible for Hollywood to go on making pictures for the public for another century.

Everything is precise, for effect. Halt. Symphonic music, Tommy's hand frozen on the door-knob.

The old and faithful secretary knows what has happened, Tommy knows, you know and I know, but there is nothing like seeing. The old and faithful secretary allows the stark reality of the pistol shot to penetrate his old, faithful and orderly mind. Then, since Tommy is too frightened to do so, he forces himself to open the door.

All of us are waiting to see how it happened.

The door opens and we go in, fifty million of us in America and millions more all over the earth.

Poor Tom. He is sinking to his knees, and somehow, even though it is happening swiftly, it seems that this little action, being the last one of a great man, will go on forever, this sinking to the knees. The room is dim, the music eloquent. There is no blood, no disorder. Tom is sinking to his knees, dying nobly. I myself hear two ladies weeping. They know it's a movie, they know it must be fake, still, they are weeping. Tom is man. He is life. It makes them weep to see life sinking to its knees. The movie will be over in a minute and they will get up and go home, and get down to the regular business of their lives, but now, in the pious darkness of the theatre, they are weeping.

All I know is this: that a suicide is not an orderly occurrence with symphonic music. There was a man once who lived in the house next door to my house when I was a boy of nine or ten. One afternoon he committed suicide, but it took him over an hour to do it. He shot himself through the chest, missed his heart, then shot himself through the stomach. I heard both shots. There was an interval of about forty seconds between the shots. I thought afterwards that during the interval he was probably trying to decide if he ought to go on wanting to be dead or if he ought to try to get well.

Then he started to holler. The whole thing was a mess, materially and spiritually, this man hollering, people running, shouting, wanting to do something and not knowing what to do. He hollered so loud half the town heard him.

This is all I know about regular suicides. I haven't seen a woman throw herself under a streetcar, so I can't say about that. This is the only suicide I have any definite information about. The way this man hollered wouldn't please anyone in a movie. It wouldn't make anyone weep with joy.

I think it comes to this: we've got to stop committing suicide in the movies.

▧ POINTS TO CONSIDER ▧

William Saroyan: Love, Death, Sacrifice, and So Forth

1. How do you know Tom Garner is going to commit suicide? Is it often possible to sense what is going to happen simply by being aware of the amount of time lapsed since the beginning of a movie?

2. What does Saroyan imply by his use of the words "act" and "acting" ("This hurt Sally, and she began to act.")? What does this tell us of Saroyan's attitude toward most movies?

3. What conventions or cliches of movie acting, situations, camera work or editing, music, and the like does Saroyan point out?

4. Just how many clues can you find in this article that reveal Saroyan's attitude toward his subject (don't neglect the title)?

5. Why are the people in the theater weeping? Why is this a "great moment of living for them"?

6. How does the actual suicide Saroyan remembers from his childhood contrast

with the movie suicide? Why do you think Saroyan describes the man as "hollering" rather than using a more serious term? Does Tom holler?

7. In what ways is Saroyan's criticism of sentimental movies similar to Pauline Kael's in her review of *The Sound of Music* (p. 203)? To what elements do Saroyan and Mrs. Kael object? Would Saroyan agree with Rick DuBrow's premise in his article "Is There Really Any Violence on TV?" (p. 152)?

8. What does Saroyan mean when he says, "We've got to stop committing suicide in the movies"? Who does he suggest is actually committing suicide? In what sense is he correct?

A Hollywood Premier

Nathanael West
Miss Lonely-Hearts and The Day of the Locust,
1939

When Tod reached the street, he saw a dozen great violet shafts of light moving across the evening sky in wide crazy sweeps. Whenever one of the fiery columns reached the lowest point of its arc, it lit for a moment the rose-colored domes and delicate minarets of Kahn's Persian Palace Theatre. The purpose of this display was to signal the world premiere of a new picture.

Turning his back on the searchlights, he started in the opposite direction, toward Homer's place. Before he had gone very far, he saw a clock that read a quarter past six and changed his mind about going back just yet. He might as well let the poor fellow sleep for another hour and kill some time by looking at the crowds.

When still a block from the theatre, he saw an enormous electric sign that hung over the middle of the street. In letters ten feet high he read that—

MR. KAHN A PLEASURE DOME DECREED

Although it was still several hours before the celebrities would arrive, thousands of people had already gathered. They stood facing the theatre with their backs toward the gutter in a thick line hundreds of feet long. A big squad of policemen was trying to keep a lane open between the front rank of the crowd and the facade of the theatre.

Tod entered the lane while the policeman guarding it was busy with a woman whose parcel had torn open, dropping oranges all over the place. Another policeman shouted for him to get the hell across the street, but he took a chance and kept going. They had enough to do without chasing him. He noticed how worried they looked and how careful they tried to be. If they had to arrest someone, they joked good-naturedly with the culprit, making light of it until they got him around the corner, then they whaled him with their clubs. Only so long as the man was actually part of the crowd did they have to be gentle.

Tod had walked only a short distance along the narrow lane when he began to get frightened. People shouted, commenting on his hat, his carriage, and his clothing. There was a continuous roar of catcalls, laughter and yells, pierced occasionally by a scream. The scream was usually followed by a sudden movement in the dense mass and part of it would surge forward wherever the police line was weakest. As soon as that part was rammed back, the bulge would pop out somewhere else.

The police force would have to be doubled when the stars started to arrive. At the sight of their heroes and heroines, the crowd would turn demoniac. Some little gesture, either too pleasing or too offensive, would start it moving and then nothing but machine guns would stop it. Individually the purpose of its members might simply be to get a souvenir, but collectively it would grab and rend.

A young man with a portable microphone was describing the scene. His rapid, hysterical voice was like that of a revivalist preacher whipping his congregation toward the ecstasy of fits.

"What a crowd, folks! What a crowd! There must be ten thousand excited, screaming fans outside Kahn's Persian tonight. The police can't hold them. Here, listen to them roar."

He held the microphone out and those near it obligingly roared for him.

"Did you hear it? It's a bedlam, folks. A veritable bedlam! What excitement! Of all the premieres I've attended, this is the most . . . the most . . . stupendous, folks. Can the police hold them? Can they? It doesn't look so, folks . . ."

Another squad of police came charging up. The sergeant pleaded with the announcer to stand further back so the people couldn't hear him. His men threw themselves at the crowd. It allowed itself to be hustled and shoved out of habit and because it lacked an objective. It tolerated the police, just as a bull elephant does when he allows a small boy to drive him with a light stick.

Tod could see very few people who looked tough, nor could he see any working men. The crowd was made up of the lower middle classes, every other person one of his torchbearers.

Just as he came near the end of the lane, it closed in front of him with a heave, and he had to fight his way through. Someone knocked his hat off and when he stooped to pick it up, someone kicked him. He whirled around angrily and found himself surrounded by people who were laughing at him. He knew enough to laugh with them. The crowd became sympathetic. A stout woman slapped him on the back, while a man handed him his hat, first brushing it carefully with his sleeve. Still another man shouted for a way to be cleared.

By a great deal of pushing and squirming, always trying to look as though he were enjoying himself, Tod finally managed to break into the open. After rearranging his clothes, he went over to a parking lot and sat down on the low retaining wall that ran along the front of it.

New groups, whole families, kept arriving. He could see a change come over them as soon as they had become part of the crowd. Until they reached the line, they looked difficult, almost furtive, but the moment they had become part of it, they turned arrogant and pugnacious. It was a mistake to think them harmless curiosity seekers. They were savage and bitter, especially the middle-aged and the old, and had been made so by boredom and disappointment.

All their lives they had slaved at some kind of dull, heavy labor, behind desks and counters, in the fields and at tedious machines of all sorts, saving their pennies and dreaming of the leisure that would be theirs when they had enough. Finally that day came. They could draw a weekly income of ten or fifteen dollars. Where else should they go but California, the land of sunshine and oranges?

Once there, they discover that sunshine isn't enough. They get tired of oranges, even of avocado pears and passion fruit. Nothing happens. They don't know what to do with their time. They haven't the mental equipment for leisure, the money nor the physical equipment for pleasure. Did they slave so long just to go to an occasional Iowa picnic? What else is there? They watch the waves come in at Venice. There wasn't any ocean where most of them came from, but after you've seen one wave, you've seen them all. The same is true of the airplanes at Glendale. If only a plane would crash once in a while so that they could watch the passengers being consumed in a "holocaust of flame," as the newspapers put it. But the planes never crash.

Their boredom becomes more and more terrible. They realize that they've been tricked and burn with resentment. Every day of their lives they read the newspapers and went to the movies. Both fed them on lynchings, murder, sex crimes, explosions, wrecks, love nests, fires, miracles, revolutions, war. This daily diet made sophisticates of them. The sun is a joke. Oranges can't titillate their jaded palates. Nothing can ever be violent enough to make taut their slack minds and bodies. They have been cheated and betrayed. They have slaved and saved for nothing.

Tod stood up. During the ten minutes he had been sitting on the wall, the crowd had grown thirty feet and he was afraid that his escape might be cut off if he loitered much longer. He crossed to the other side of the street and started back.

POINTS TO CONSIDER

Nathanael West: A Hollywood Premier

1. What is the difference between the ways individuals act and the ways mobs act?

2. The crowd at the Hollywood premier is compared with crowds at what other activities?

3. What different mass communications media are referred to in this selection?

4. What is the relationship between mob behavior and the effects of mass media?

5. How does life as depicted in movies compare with real life? How does life as reported in newspapers compare with real life?

6. How do the mass media cause people to become restless and dissatisfied?

7. Compare this selection with the "Smith and the Telly" selection from Alan Sillitoe's *The Loneliness of the Long Distance Runner* (p. 154) and John Gregory Dunne's "A Riot on TV" (p. 148). What similar comments do they make about the effects of the mass media upon the public?

8. What is the "California dream"? To what extent does it exist today? Why do you think that the politics and culture of California reflect such extremes of both conservatism and radicalism?

"Lights! Camera! Love!"

●   ●

On *The Sound of Music*

Pauline Kael
Kiss, Kiss, Bang, Bang, 1968

The success of a movie like *The Sound of Music* makes it even more difficult for anyone to try to do anything worth doing, anything relevant to the modern world, anything inventive or expressive. The banks, the studios, the producers will want to give the public what it seems to crave. The more money these "whole-some" movies make, the less wholesome will the state of American movies be. "The opium of the audience," Luis Bunuel, the Spanish director, once said, "is conformity." And nothing is more degrading and ultimately destructive to artists than supplying the narcotic.

What is it that makes millions of people buy and like *The Sound of Music*— a tribute to "freshness" that is so mechanically engineered, so shrewdly calcu-lated that the background music rises, the already soft focus blurs and melts, and, upon the instant, you can hear all those noses blowing in the theater? Of course, it's well done for what it is: that is to say, those who made it are experts at manipulating responses. They're the Pavlovs[1] of moviemaking: they turn us into dogs that salivate on signal. When the cruel father sees the light and says, "You've brought music back into the house," who can resist the pull at the emotions? It's that same tug at the heartstrings we feel when Lassie comes home or when the blind heroine sees for the first time; it is a simple variant of that surge of warmth we feel when a child is reunited with his parents. It's basic, and there are probably few of us who don't respond. But it is the easiest and perhaps the most primitive kind of emotion that we are made to feel. The worst despots in history, the most cynical purveyors of mass culture respond at *this* level and may feel pleased at how tenderhearted they *really* are because they do. This kind of response has as little to do with generosity of feeling as being stirred when you hear a band has to do with patriotism.

I think it is not going too far to say that when an expensive product of modern technology like *The Sound of Music* uses this sort of "universal" appeal, it is because nothing could be safer, nothing could be surer. Whom could it offend? Only those of us who, *despite the fact that we may respond,* loathe being manip-ulated in this way and are aware of how self-indulgent and cheap and ready-made are the responses we are made to feel. And we may become even more aware of the way we have been *used* and turned into emotional and esthetic

[1] Ivan Pavlov (1849–1936) was a Russian biologist whose experiments showed that animals can be conditioned to respond to a signal as well as to the experience for which it stands. He had a group of dogs which heard the sound of a bell whenever they were fed; after a while, they began to salivate whenever they heard the sound of a bell.

imbeciles when we hear ourselves humming those sickly, goody-goody songs. The audience for a movie of this kind becomes the lowest common denominator of feeling: a sponge. The heroine leaves the nuns at the fence as she enters the cathedral to be married. Squeezed again, and the moisture comes out of thousands—millions—of eyes and noses.

And the phenomenon at the center of the monetary phenomenon? Julie Andrews, with the clean, scrubbed look and the unyieldingly high spirits; the good sport who makes the best of everything; the girl who's so unquestionably good that she carries this one dimension like a shield. The perfect, perky schoolgirl, the adorable tomboy, the gawky colt. Sexless, inhumanly happy, the sparkling maid, a mind as clean and well brushed as her teeth. What is she? Merely the ideal heroine for the best of all possible worlds. And that's what *The Sound of Music* pretends we live in.

Audiences are transported into a world of operetta cheerfulness and calendar art. You begin to feel as if you've never got out of school. Up there on the screen, they're all in their places with bright, shining faces. Wasn't there perhaps one little Von Trapp who didn't want to sing his head off, or who screamed that he wouldn't act out little glockenspiel routines for Papa's party guests, or who got nervous and threw up if he had to get on a stage? No, nothing that mars this celebration of togetherness. Not only does this family sing together; they play ball together. This is the world teachers used to pretend (and maybe still pretend?) was the real world. It's the world in which the governess conquers all. It's the big lie, the sugarcoated lie that people seem to want to eat. They even seem to think they should feed it to their kids, that it's healthy, wonderful "family entertainment."

And this is the sort of attitude that makes a critic feel that maybe it's all hopeless. Why not just send the director, Robert Wise, a wire: "You win, I give up," or, rather, "We both lose, we all lose."

POINTS TO CONSIDER

Pauline Kael: On *The Sound of Music*

1. To what characteristics does Pauline Kael attribute the great commercial success of *The Sound of Music?* What other examples of successful popular art do you know that share these characteristics?

2. Why does Mrs. Kael feel such dismay at the success of *The Sound of Music?* What does she feel is wrong with such a pleasant movie? Whom does she feel is most to blame? Do you agree?

3. What does Mrs. Kael mean at the end when she says, "We both lose, we all lose"?

But Don't Knock *The Sound of Music*

Lawrence DeVine
The Miami Herald, May 24, 1966

The job security of a critic is generally somewhat less than beginning bomb demolition students, parachute testers or Balkan kings, if better than certain sheriffs, Gabor husbands or left-handed third-basemen.

In some places, the only thing that will displace a critic—for better or worse —is the earth opening up and swallowing him whole, or a successful assassination plot carried out stealthily in a darkened theater.

In less estimable situations, however, it takes but a little mail and the hapless critic is out of his attuned ear. Such a case reached prominence last week in that worthy organ devoted to the molding and shaping of the public taste, McCall's magazine.

McCall's was paying legal tender to one Pauline Kael to write its film reviews. This she did to the best, it is presumed, of her ability. Then it happened. Mrs. Kael, a wife and homemaker herself, wrote that the wholesome and lovable movie *The Sound of Music,* was really sort of icky.

That did it. Call Dr. Spock a Bolshevik, condemn The Pill, but do not tread lightly on *The Sound of Music.* Mrs. Kael was instantly deprived of her salary check and her place on the masthead as the letters poured in in defense of the Trapp family film.

Now Mrs. Kael is a published author (of *I Lost It at the Movies,* a book of film criticism) and former reviewer for Film Quarterly and Sight and Sound magazine. It seems safe to speculate she perhaps knew more about whether *The Sound of Music* was purest marshmallow than did the folks back at the office writing about prettier feet, the teenager and the telephone and timely warnings about Captain Kangaroo.

That, of course, is secondary. Primarily, it seems that grounds for cashiering one of your troops, company pride aside, ought to be something stronger than letters from Julie Andrews fans.

About mail: H. L. Mencken used to inscribe his angry mail with the words "You may be right"—and sent it back from whence it came. A sensible and altogether gentlemanly approach.

Mrs. Kael, however, may be better off looking for work elsewhere. Plato phrased it as succinctly as anyone: "If men should order their counselors to pander to their wishes . . . I should consider as unmanly one who accepts the duty of giving such forms of advice and one who refused it to be a true man" Or, in this case, a true woman.

Oh well, McCall's, back to the recipes and foot care.

Lawrence DeVine: But Don't Knock *The Sound of Music*

1. What does Lawrence DeVine think are the qualities of a good critic? How, then, does he feel about Pauline Kael as a critic?

2. How does DeVine feel about *McCall's* magazine? How does he express his feeling?

3. What characteristics of mass media in general is DeVine criticizing?

From "The Sound of Money": A *Mad* Magazine Parody

Mort Drucker
Stan Hart

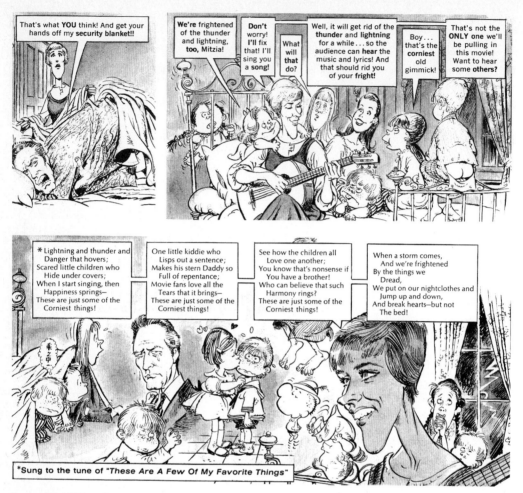

*Sung to the tune of "These Are A Few Of My Favorite Things"

POINTS TO CONSIDER

Mort Drucker and Stan Hart: "The Sound of Money"

1. What qualities of *The Sound of Music* are Drucker and Hart criticizing in their cartoon parody? Do they criticize any of the same things that Pauline Kael did in her review of the movie (p. 203)?

2. What qualities of sentimental movies in general do Drucker and Hart satirize? To what other movies that you have seen could this parody be applied? To what TV shows?

3. What kinds of humor can Drucker and Hart achieve in their cartoon that would be difficult to achieve with words alone?

The *Other* Side of the Mountain

Edward Arthur

St. Louis Post-Dispatch, April 18, 1969

A statement by the president of Arthur Enterprises, a chain of popular movie theaters in St. Louis, Missouri.

Three weeks ago 50,249 St. Louisans poured out en masse to four of our 23 theatres to see a charming film entitled "My Side of the Mountain."

On Sunday of the week "My Side of the Mountain" was appearing, all four theatres were filled to capacity for all four performances.

How did this all come about? It came about because some organizations and many individuals had expressed the opinion that nothing but "dirty" pictures are shown.

We arranged to show three consecutive family programs, in four of our most important theatres in convenient locations and at prices to fit the family budget.

"My Side of the Mountain" received intense advance publicity. The reasons for showing it and the subsequent films received wide news coverage.

The overwhelming response to "My Side of the Mountain" indicated the community's wish to substantiate its pleas for family movies by supporting them at the box office.

The second film, "Angel in My Pocket," was shown a week later in the same theatres and at the same prices.

But a peculiar thing happened. Instead of 50,249 people attending, 22,428 came. The third week, a Walt Disney program—"Smith" and "Incredible Journey," presently showing, has an attendance to date of 14,712.

It is the unusual that attracts interest. And it was the unusual conditions surrounding "My Side of the Mountain" that produced the exaggerated response.

Hollywood makes the finest motion pictures in the world. We believe that the motion pictures available today are those that the public supports and indicates it wants. No producer makes the tremendous investment necessary to make a picture that he does not believe is in keeping with the public's taste. Producers try to gauge months, sometimes years, in advance what will please you and us.

This applied successfully with "The Sound of Music," "My Fair Lady," "Who's Afraid of Virginia Woolf," "Funny Girl," "The Odd Couple," "The Lion in Winter," "Guess Who's Coming to Dinner," "Oliver" and "Rosemary's Baby."

On the other hand . . . such films as the "The Bible," "The Shoes of the Fisherman," "Doctor Doolittle," "Hellfighters," "Half a Sixpence," and "Far from the Madding Crowd" proved unsuccessful.

We do not make motion pictures. We have no control over what will be made. Our advice is neither sought nor heeded.

No one forces us to take or show any particular picture. We use our own judgment as businessmen and members of the community. The only pressures exerted on us are economic.

We do not believe that all films are suitable for all ages all of the time or all together. Neither are books or plays . . . or dinner parties. We do not believe in "quick buck" pictures, or in pornographic, perverted, "sex-for-sex' sake" entertainment . . . though much of this depends upon degree.

We believe in the responsibility of the producer, the theatre-owner, and the public.

We do not believe in censorship. We will fight it wherever it appears. We have fought for democracy and for freedom of the individual. We will fight to keep unto ourselves that freedom, just as we will fight to preserve your freedom as an individual to make your own choices.

We believe there should be a selection of films available to the public. There will be, and there should be, mature movies. There will be, and there should be, family movies. The availability of these to you, our patrons, will be our concern.

We will encourage producers, and so should you, to deliver along with films they feel should be produced from a standpoint of entertainment, culture, and social comment, groups of family pictures so that you can have the choice you want. We shall try to balance the scale in our theatres.

We believe that what is supported will be delivered. If we patronize the best and stay away from the worst, it will produce a result. If we patronize the worst, and stay away from the best, this too will produce a result.

Sex, perversion, brutality . . . all receive attention. Why? Because they concern the unusual. The so-called "good" is often ignored.

Many good family pictures have been shown in our theatres during the past two years. They have, for the most part, gone unsung, unnoticed and *unseen.*

We sincerely thank all who attended, wrote, and telephoned to express their thanks for "My Side of the Mountain," "Angel in My Pocket," "Smith," and "Incredible Journey."

We sincerely thank the producer of "My Side of the Mountain" . . . Mr. Robert Radnitz . . . for consistently delivering wholesome family entertainment. "Mountain" has been his greatest success—thanks to you.

[Signed]

Edward B. Arthur

Edward B. Arthur

P. S. We know we cannot please all of the people all of the time. But we try.

Edward Arthur: The *Other* Side of the Mountain

1. Why was the movie *My Side of the Mountain* so well attended when it was shown in St. Louis? Why were the subsequent "family type" films less well attended?

2. What conclusions does Arthur draw about the relationship between the types of films made and shown and the types of films widely attended? What conclusion can be drawn about the relationship between what movies the public says it wants and what movies it pays to see?

3. What observations does Arthur make about sexy or violent films and about censorship? To what extent do you agree with him? In what way can the general public influence most effectively the types of movies made and shown?

The New Film Audience

Larry Cohen

Saturday Review, December 27, 1969

According to the headline of an article that appeared late last May in *The New York Times,* buried with the film advertisements on page 36, "Young Writers Say They Don't Read." The five interviewed authors, all of whom were respectably under thirty, announced that they rarely if ever opened a book. "It's just easier to go to a movie and let it all wash over you," one of them said.

There were, of course, prominent exceptions to this impatient rule. Hermann Hesse and J. R. R. Tolkien both have large youthful followings. So does Kurt Vonnegut, Jr., who was singled out because "he writes cinematically." But most authors met a grimmer, much less cordial fate. Reading was regarded as an academic pastime, and most books were relegated to the level and enthusiasm of a chore. The article came to an abrupt close with one of those statements that must have chilled the warmest hardbound heart. One of the young writers, Sally Grimes, who had previously spent some time composing obituary notices for the *Philadelphia Bulletin,* committed her own cool piece of manslaughter by concluding: "I find I'm reading less and less. I really don't know why."

It occurs to me that the content of such a remark is less important than the tone with which it appears to have been said. Just think about what she's announcing. The death of literature? Hardly. The temporary disaffection of a substantial cross section of young writers (and young readers) with books? Maybe, despite the fact that the paperback market place is currently a veritable gold mine and new soft-cover publications such as *New American Review* and *US* have whopping, young readerships.

But listen to the statement rather than just its meaning. What resounds is something casual and half-shaded, something innocent and perhaps even unconscious. The remark sounds like an afterthought, as if the speaker was deaf to any echo. There is nothing guilty about such a confession, no sense that the Furies of Literature are about to swoop down upon her for heresy. It is the nonchalance that says everything, the pronouncement itself relatively little. For the mood to which Miss Grimes and the other young writers are subscribing may well be an accurate expression of a *new* sensibility, one which is defined in part by its very lack of guilt about not being well-read and, on the other hand, by its overtly positive enthusiasm about film. In its openness and bluntness, "I really don't know why" reflects 1969 and a large new audience.

These changes in emphasis are so recent that it's extremely difficult to pin down their source with any real exactitude. There are clues, however, and a quick personal flashback to four years ago, around the time I graduated from high school, brings to mind a different picture. The kids with whom I grew up were avid readers; some of them even lay awake late at night and sweated out plans for writing the Great American Novel. Vietnam and a pervasive drug scene were not substantial issues yet; like us, they were in their pubescent[1] stages, and the day they would be taken for granted as realities seemed a long way off. Literature still had its grip on us and we on it. For, McLuhan and television notwithstanding, the primary frame of reference from which we derived our formal tastes and plans for the future was still verbal. Our own Great Expectations used writers like Ken Kesey, Thomas Pynchon, J. D. Salinger, and Nathanael West as models and sources of passionate discussion.

Significantly mitigating this classical orientation was a film course I took in my senior year with about thirty other kids. We spent the first part of a fall semester staring at supposedly familiar objects—a leaf or our thumb, for example—and discovered the hard way what Joseph Conrad meant when he argued that his purpose was to make us *see.* With our thumbs out of our mouths, we then began looking at films by Griffith, Chaplin, Eisenstein, and Welles. *Potemkin* and *Citizen Kane* served as textbooks; we dissected their sequences frame by frame and assimilated a new vocabulary, learning how a movie was put together and why it still worked decades later. While most of our friends were surrendering themselves to term papers on Milton or even to diagraming the perennial sentence, we were reading the late James Agee's movie criticism and screenplays, using Arthur Knight's *The Liveliest Art* to gain a historical context, and worrying about montage and nonlinear structures. In retrospect, we already were taking films personally and seriously.

By 1969, what has happened is simply this: the young audience for books has not so much shrunk as the young audience for motion pictures has appreciably grown and become more vocal. As a breed, the kids of the late Fifties and early Sixties—the ones who had avidly attended university creative writing courses or earnestly imagined themselves as editors for a New York publishing house—were now generally anachronistic.[2] For that matter, almost no one I knew at college read anything beyond the required classroom texts. Students were now crowding and overfilling smoky lecture halls to see and "rap" about films—their theory and history—and in more than a few instances this new breed was also making 8 and 16 mm movies despite the cost of equipment.

One crucial difference between movies and the other arts was simple accessibility. Even in the cultural provinces of the Middle West, it was possible to see as many as a half-dozen films a week. (Francis Ford Coppola, the thirty-year-old director of *You're a Big Boy Now* and *The Rain People,* predicts that "movies will be sold like soup in the future," that "you'll be able to buy it in cartridges for $3 and play it as you would a record, at home.") In addition to sheer

---

[1] Pubescent means adolescent.

[2] Anachronistic means inappropriate to the time.

availability, films were answering the lusting college cry for "relevance," taking both their raw celluloid material and subject matters from today rather than the day before yesterday.

In this regard, *Blow-Up* functioned as the pivotal film; it radicalized the way in which many college students responded to film. More than three years after it first appeared, it remains a significant milestone in this country's awareness of motion pictures. Antonioni's tour of mod London was one of the first movies young people saw more than once. Its ambiguities, its mysteries, and its technological break-throughs brought them back to the theater again and again, converting them to the language of film. (Curiously and ironically, it even inspired some kids to become photographers.) Rather than just being one more foreign film, *Blow-Up* was a primer in technique.

In the process of this shift of focus off the writer and onto the film-maker, the literary gods lost many of their aspiring novices to a medium that was itself in a state of relative infancy. There was and is, of course, a set of both happy and notorious exceptions. Nabokov's *Ada* and John Fowles's *The French Lieutenant's Woman*—works of genius in my opinion—would be quickly purchased in spite of their prohibitive costs in hardbound editions. Similarly, there would be large campus audiences for such national best sellers as *Portnoy's Complaint, Myra Breckinridge,* and *Couples.* The big money and larger audience, however, now belonged to film and it is not surprising that all of these novels (with the understandable exception of *Ada*) are headed for the screen.

One key sign of film's evolution as the form that matters for young people today is the number of campus literary successes now being made into motion pictures. We already have witnessed several: Peter Brook's grainy 1963 adaptation of William Golding's book *Lord of the Flies;* Larry Peerce's pushy but humorous Sixties transplant of Phillip Roth's 1959 novella, *Goodbye Columbus;* and the soon-to-be-released film version of John Barth's *The End of the Road.* Even the indomitable classroom Shakespeare found himself ruthlessly pruned and feverishly revitalized for a young audience as the literally teen-age Leonard Whiting and Olivia Hussey became Romeo and Juliet. If the results in this latter case were a trifle goofy, seeing the star-crossed lovers played by kids against the background of director Franco Zeffirelli's lush visual imagery almost justified any irreverence.

As we enter a new decade, the possible list of properties based on collegiate favorites increases. A new company, United Screen Arts, has optioned Hesse's *Steppenwolf,* and Conrad Rooks, whose hallucinatory film-nightmare on drugs, *Chappaqua,* was released several years ago, is rumored to be preparing the same author's *Siddhartha* for the screen. Hillard Elkins, the producer of *Oh! Calcutta!,* is readying a movie version of *Cat's Cradle,* and other works by Vonnegut— including *Player Piano* and *Sirens of Titan*—are also scheduled. Some of these are tentative projects and may never make it to the screen. Their mere presence on the boards, however, suggests a different contextual base for American films in the future. With Tolkien's *Lord of the Rings* soon to go into production, can Richard Fariña's *Been Down So Long It Looks Like Up to Me* be far behind?

One industry journal recently estimated that "at least 70 per cent of box-office revenue comes from young people between 16 and 29," a statistic that indicates that the economy of motion pictures is quantitatively a matter of age. Thought of five years ago *only* as an entertainment form—with a separately delineated category for "art" house imports—movies are now *in* and regarded as a legitimate pursuit in America. In contrast, the more traditional arts such as theater and opera are shaky if not altogether ready to enter an old age home. The lines at the box office are a proof of sorts that film and film alone is attracting kids. Just as it is inconceivable that anyone would stand in line for two hours to see a play or purchase a book, it is taken for granted that one will wait this long to see *Midnight Cowboy* in a city like New York. Legitimate theater, with the exception of such youth-geared musicals as *Hair* and *Salvation,* exerts little if any appeal. And the one-week performance by the Who of their rock-media opera *Tommy* at the Fillmore East is the closest anyone under thirty will get to a tier at the Metropolitan.

If *Blow-Up* was instrumental in attracting young people to film, the equivalent American landmark was Mike Nichols's *The Graduate.* Holden Caulfield,[3] his worried future, identity-crisis, and traumas fairly intact, found a close screen ally in the person of Benjamin Braddock as played by Dustin Hoffman. Both characters assert the same basic appeal, a nervy and youthful cry against hypocrisy and false values that are captured lucidly by one word: *plastics.* What seems to me to be vital about the movie is that is signifies a phenomenon of rapport rather than a purely esthetic triumph; that it functions as a sociological replacement for Salinger despite its own confusions and impurities of self-conscious camerawork; that its score is by Simon and Garfunkel rather than Max Steiner.

The pair of films that I think genuinely reflect the end of this decade and the start of another are *Easy Rider* and *Alice's Restaurant.* As companion pieces of styles, attitudes, and approaches, they form a composite blow-up of what is happening in this country. They both take drugs for granted as a part of the grass ethic, and they are both possessed with a sense that we are becoming our own films. They are also intrinsically interesting in what they tell us about the interaction between audiences and movies, in the way the former sees itself on the screen.

Of the two, *Rider* works more obviously and is the more immediate film, applying the lyrics of Paul Kantner's song "We Can Be Together" by visually demonstrating that "we are all outlaws in the eyes of America." More than any film in recent memory, it generates its own pulse into the heartbeats of its predominantly under-thirty audience. The spirit of the movie is personal, even conversational. It says yes, it has been to this wave length of the United States

---

[3] Holden Caulfield is the hero of J. D. Salinger's novel *The Catcher in the Rye.*

before, and to prove that its age is ours, the soundtrack makes intensive use of contemporary rock—Steppenwolf, the Band, and Jimi Hendrix, among others. When Roger McGuinn sings "It's Alright Ma (I'm Only Bleeding)" near the end of the film, the audience and the movie have a viselike grip on each other. They go back a long way together, and I'm not altogether certain that anyone who wasn't weaned on Bob Dylan—whether three or thirty—can share the journey. Sometimes, the film says about itself, you just have to be there to understand.

Alice also utilizes music as its integral base, but directs it toward a more complicated, trickier, and eventually subtler end. Some of the soundtrack is simply music, like the appropriate and evocative "Songs to Aging Children Come," by Joni Mitchell. It is used as a quiet, melancholic background for a funeral sequence in the snow, a scene that owes a formal and emotional debt to the final part of Francois Truffaut's *Fahrenheit 451*. There are other songs including Pete Seeger's renditions of "Pastures of Plenty" and "The Car Song." The traditional hymn "Amazing Grace" becomes a generational link between a revival meeting and a youthful and communal Thanksgiving Day at Ray and Alice's church. And then there is the title song itself, the best expression of what the movie is really about. It articulates a cartooned life-and-death style, a giving and a taking, the good and bad times of a country in its logical but paradoxical youth. "You can get anything you want," says the song, "*excepting* Alice," suggesting the peculiar light and dark moods of an America and a film whose final shot will literally mimic this tension between lament and celebration.

The two films are similar in other ways. Both use nonprofessionals as well as trained actors; both are framed by the geography of late-Sixties America. *Rider* goes cross country on its fateful cycle journey to a whorish New Orleans, and along the harrowing way shows us places where the word police has a long "o," a vowel stretched out so far that it almost whistles like a rubber band. It is a land of motels with quickly turned on No Vacancy signs as soon as its turned-on, long-haired riders arrive. And inevitably, it is a mental landscape full of crewcut goons with murderous aim if not intent.

Alice documents a lighter but hardly less scary America: a country of induction boards in which a young black veteran of the war has a hook instead of a hand; in which Arlo is violently abused for his hair and called a "hippie perversion"; in which Vietnam is pronounced Veetnam; and in which a solitary billboard from the Johnson administration still says "Keep America Beautiful! Cut Your Hair."

The crucial differences between the two films are not raw material but age and tone. For all intensive purposes, *Rider* is the first work of a young man (although Dennis Hopper is thirty-three and goes back to the days of James Dean in the Fifties), and *Alice* is the sixth movie by a middle-aged man sincerely trying to bridge the considerable Great Divide. Hopper's vision is obsessed with death and prostitution from its very first minute on the screen; it senses persecution all around it, and it invites us to join in with our personal nightmares and experiences, our collective paranoia.[4] It says that this is the way this country is, and, cleverly, it shows us the devastating fire and explosions in advance of their actual, sequential appearance that ends the film.

Undeniably, the movie is horribly effective; its own confusions even add a terrifying and inescapable logic. When the lawyer George Hanson (played brilliantly by Jack Nicholson) is killed, the loss is acute. The movie misses him; it came alive when he appeared, and in a curious way it seems to die when he does. Fonda's and Hopper's destruction elicits a strong response by virtue of the brutality of the act rather than by feelings for the individuals. Ours is a purely visceral reaction[5] to murder, a response we even indulge in. But we have no time to think, no time to sort out the differences between the deaths. Despite whatever Hopper claims were his intentions, the film lurches out of control and so does the audience. There is a distinction that demands time to be thought out: namely, that Hanson was worth more alive than dead, and Wyatt and Billy become emotionally more valuable to us precisely *because* they die. It is a distinction few if any of us are able to make while still in the theater.

Alice also has its share of deaths: the passing of Woody Guthrie, of Shelley, of a whole way of life personified by the reconsecrated church. But unlike the brutal murders of *Rider,* both the man and boy die off-screen here. Their deaths are presented as a part of life rather than an end to it. Penn's film is vitally and compassionately interested in life and in a sense of humor as a style for coping, for living in Moratorium America without paranoia. Arlo's songs and manner are those of mild ridicule despite the disasters that shroud the film; the music and the style seem healthy, and they wear well.

In effectively suggesting these youthful but polar responses to domestic life, the two films are expressive landmarks for a medium and a country that are suffering growing pains. Hopper's seems more important right now because it slams in the gut, it is frequently right by sheer instinct, *because* it lacks subtlety. Penn's complex work—with its neat geometrical triangles, both religious and secular—strikes me as the more masterful and enduring motion picture. In its own way, *Alice* is a remake of the fifteen-year-old *Rebel Without a Cause* by Nicholas Ray. Yes, Arlo's hair is longer than James Dean's: he doesn't wear white socks, and the girls aren't as heavily lip-sticked as Natalie Wood. But what Penn is attempting is a translation into a late-Sixties style of the earlier film's anguish, vulnerability, and groping search for a surrogate family. And in linking Arlo with Dean's different but nonetheless similarly transcendent sort of articulateness, *Alice* suggests not only a way of being young in America, but also a possible way of being older. . . .

[4] Paranoia is an abnormally intense fear of persecution.
[5] A visceral reaction is a reaction at gut level.

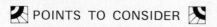

POINTS TO CONSIDER

Larry Cohen: The New Film Audience

1. What influences do you think are behind the fact that the young people of today are interested in and involved with films the way the young people of the 1950s and earlier decades were interested in and involved with literature and writing? Consider social, educational, and technological influences.

2. What recently popular and currently popular stories and novels have been made and are about to be made into films? What percentage of them seem to be works particularly popular among young readers aged sixteen to thirty?

3. Which particular films does Cohen think were especially influential in interesting the young people of the late 1960s in film as a relevant and creative art form? Why? What films since *Easy Rider* and *Alice's Restaurant* have been especially popular with young film audiences? Why?

4. In what ways have folk and rock music and films developed simultaneously as art forms that are socially relevant to young people?

5. To what extent has the fact that many young people today are making their own films influenced the making of commercial films? Give some examples.

6. Look at the entertainment page of a newspaper and try to determine which films are particularly aimed at "the new film audience." What are the characteristic qualities of these films? Which films are clearly aimed at an older audience? How can you tell?

Ideas for Investigation, Discussion, and Writing

Photography and Motion Pictures

1. Why do some people believe that photography is not as "artistic" a form of expression as is painting? To what extent do you agree? What limitations does photography have in comparison to painting? What can photography do that painting cannot?

2. To what extent do you feel that photography is as "artistic" a form of expression as is painting? What evidence can you cite that others feel as you do? Who are some of our country's best-known photographers? Can you use some examples of their work to help you prove your point?

3. How does news photography differ from "the more artistic kinds" of photography? To what extent do they overlap? Can you find some examples of "artistic" news photography to prove this point? What well-known news photographers are admired for the artistic qualities of their work?

4. To what extent has photography changed the way in which we learn about or understand the world about us? Compare photography to print as a way of learning. To what extent has photography taken some of the glamor out of our lives?

5. To what extent do current motion pictures portray life as you believe it really is, and to what extent do you think they portray life as we would like it to be or as we prefer to think it is? How is the view of reality in the movies affected by the prejudices and taboos of society? Do you believe the movies have changed much in the ways that they portray reality over the past fifty or so years?

6. How great an effect do you feel that the film—as both "artistic" and "informative" medium—has upon the attitudes and behavior of our society? Why does it not have a greater effect?

7. What effects—in terms of both content and techniques—has the great popularity of television had upon the kinds of movies being produced today? To what degree do you think the effects have been favorable? To what degree do you think they have been unfavorable?

8. Compare the technical devices used for achieving effects in early movies with the technical devices used for achieving effects in current movies. Which of the early movie techniques do we still use frequently and which have we largely abandoned? Why? Which recently introduced film techniques seem particularly effective in terms of contemporary interests and tastes? Why?

9. Some film critics have felt that color and sound detracted from rather than enhanced the artistic qualities of movies. Why? To what extent do you agree or disagree? Why?

10. Read a variety of newspaper and magazine reviews of a particular motion picture. What elements of the movie do the critics pay most attention to? How does the emphasis vary among different critics? To what extent do they agree or disagree about the movie? How much emphasis do they place on the social relevance of the movie? How many of the seven questions about popular art listed in the introduction to this anthology, on page 3, do the critics attempt to answer? If you see the movie, compare your view with the critics'.

11. Read a best seller that has been made into a movie, and then see the movie. What additions, deletions, and changes in emphasis have been made in the movie version? To what extent is the movie version more complex or less complex than the book version? What explanations can you offer for these changes? To what extent are the changes essential because of the change in medium, and to what extent were the changes made for other reasons? Which version do you prefer? Why? Do you think your opinion of the movie would be different if you had not read the book?

12. Try to write a scenario or a shooting script for a silent movie based upon a story you have read or upon an original idea. How will you communicate the ideas and emotions in purely visual terms? How will time serve as an important consideration in helping you to achieve your effects? Assuming you will actually make the movie, how will your limitations of time, money, and technical equipment affect your movie? Why do you think that movie-making has become such a popular hobby of late?

13. How does the experience of watching a movie in a theatre differ from the experience of watching live theatre or of watching television? What do these other media offer that film cannot? Do you think that the musical play *Hair* could be made into an effective movie?

PART SIX

POPULAR LITERATURE

Popular literature, both fiction and nonfiction, comes to us in a variety of publications. Magazines and newspapers publish poems and short stories as well as longer novels and nonfiction in serialized or condensed form. The availability of paperback books allows readers to build up personal libraries at relatively low cost, and book clubs encourage us to buy hardcover selections while they are still current topics of conversation.

Fiction provides a kind of intimate entertainment which neither movies nor television can entirely supplant. Indeed, movies and television often encourage the sale of books when novels are made into films or when they are publicized on television talk shows. Like movies and TV series, popular fiction provides us with emotional outlets and both reflects and influences our feelings about who and what is heroic or romantic, dangerous or absurd.

Nonfiction has grown tremendously in popularity in the past twenty years, probably because more people have received better and more advanced formal educations; because journalism and television has informed us of a wider scope of fascinating subjects; and because we feel subconsciously that our age of technological advance and rapid accumulation of knowledge demands that we seek "fact" rather than "fiction." Recent nonfiction best sellers have covered a broad range of subjects from always popular biographies and histories to more recently popular studies in psychology, sociology and anthropology, medicine, ecology, big business, and education.

There is also an intriguing area between fiction and nonfiction which a number of contemporary writers are developing. The report of current events presented with the structure and emotional overtones of a novel represents one such experiment. Another is current science fiction; unlike science fiction of the past which looked forward to the wonders and terrors of the future, it presents as its substance the scientific realities and potentials of our own time.

The Best-seller List

From "The Talk of the Town," in *The New Yorker*
December 8, 1962

A recent *Times* best-seller list included a coloring book for adults, a journal kept by a child, a pamphlet of newspaper photographs with humorous captions, the autobiography of a baseball manager, the reminiscences of a lawyer who had appeared for the defense in a sensational Hollywood trial, a discussion of dieting, and a study of the sexual activities of unmarried women. These seven works, filling nearly half the slots in the nonfiction section of the list, had appeared there a combined total of a hundred and twenty-two weeks, and would presumably remain there until other books—of similar quality—were published to replace them. Fortunately, the list is meaningless; indeed, the only redeeming quality of best-seller charts in general is their inaccuracy. They are based on slim and unreliable evidence, they disagree among themselves, and as indicators of what is actually being bought and read they are almost worthless. Few bookstores are consulted, fewer report, and there is nothing to prevent the ones that do report from falsifying their records to suit their inventories. Moreover, the provincial storekeeper, like the rural citizen, has more than his share of the vote. A book that sells a hundred copies at the Brentano's on Fifth Avenue is given no greater weight in the surveys than one that sells nine copies at Scrantom's, in Rochester. The most popular books in any store are the ones that count; the margin and the region of their popularity are considered irrelevant. For the issue of November 25th, for example, the *Herald Tribune* survey was compiled on the basis of reports from only thirty-four stores; Vroman's, of Pasadena, was side by side with the Scribner Book Store, in New York. The *Times,* usually so scrupulous in supplying sources for its news articles, does not list the number, size, or location of reporting booksellers at all. An ambiguous paragraph in italics tells us that the *Times* survey is based on reports from "leading booksellers in 41 cities showing the sales rating of 16 leading fiction and general titles over the last 3 weeks." Which the 41 cities are, how many bookstores report in each, why the unlikely numbers of 41 and 16 were chosen (the *Tribune* has an equally inexplicable, though not nameless, 34 and 10), and what the meaning of the word "leading" is—these questions are unanswered. The reader is left with the list, to make of it what he will. Meanwhile, the inaccurate ratings perform a major disservice to serious writings, the sales of which are often damaged by omission from the list.

Even if the chart meant something, even if it were based on reliable records of national sales volume (records that publishers are particularly reluctant to issue), one wonders what value the best-seller list could have for the reading public. Most industries release such itemized sales figures only to trade journals, where the producer finds out what he may expect to sell—not the consumer what he ought to buy. The book chart, on the other hand, presumably tries to show the conformist how the literary herd is running—and encourages him to run away from literature with the herd. If manufacturers ordinarily refrain from publishing statistics to show what everyone else is wearing and eating, surely the literary journals need not insist on telling us what everyone else is reading— and telling it inaccurately besides. Since sales in the arts have never been an index to value ("Moby Dick" was not a best-seller in its time, nor were any of Henry James' novels after "The Portrait of a Lady"), it is hard to imagine what serious purpose the charts can have. If the list is intended merely as a helpful guide to the anxious semiliterate, the *Times* would perform a greater service by listing the exact stores and regions to which it applies. Most readers, after all, are not required to participate in literary discussions across the nation; each is ordinarily confined to his own geographical area, and a chart that showed which books were selling well at the *local* bookstore would save readers the embarrassment of being competent to discuss at a cocktail party in Pasadena only those books that were deemed best-sellers in Vermont.

POINTS TO CONSIDER

The New Yorker : The Best-seller List

1. What are some of the reasons why the best-seller list is not an accurate indication of what books people are reading?

2. What does *The New Yorker* feel is the function of the best-seller list? What might be some of the beneficial functions of an accurate best-seller list? What are some of the detrimental effects of a best-seller list, accurate or not?

Ambushing a Best-Seller

Edmund Wilson

Classics and Commercials, 1946

This magazine has not always shown foresight in recognizing future successes, and it has sometimes ignored or dismissed in a note novels that were destined to sell hundreds of thousands and to go on selling for years. I have, therefore, lately been watching the publishers' lists in the hope of catching one of these books before it started on its triumphant progress; and, difficult though it seems to be to distinguish the coming best-seller from other specimens of inferior fiction, I have decided—from the amount and kind of advertising that the book is being given by the publisher and from the appearance of a picture of the heroine on the cover of *Publisher's Weekly*—that *The Turquoise,* by Anya Seton, has a good chance of landing in the upper brackets. I may be wrong, but I am going to report on it on the assumption that it will be widely read.

The heroine of *The Turquoise,* then, is, as I hardly need to say, a Cinderella. The child of the younger son of a Scottish baronet and of the daughter of a Spanish hidalgo resident in the American Southwest, she is early left a penniless orphan and grows up among the illiterate natives, part Indian, part Spanish, of New Mexico. "Her mouth, always wide, lost its childish innocence, and the lips revealed a passionate curve. Her skin grew moister and more glowing; beneath the dirt and tan shone the velvety whiteness of her Castilian heritage. She was still a thin, ugly child, her gray eyes were still too big for the small face and gave her a goblin look, but she now sometimes showed the first indications of the sex magnetism which was later to give her an illusion of beauty more seductive than actual symmetry." Her natural high breeding and dignity also asserted themselves in the sordid milieux[1] of her early years, so that people instinctively deferred to her quality.

She had been named Santa Fe, after the place where she was born, but her father had been shy of the name for its association with her mother's death. "'Santa Fe—' said Andrew bitterly, and at the sound of his voice the baby suddenly smiled. 'Aye, 'tis a daft name for ye, small wonder ye smile.' He repeated the name, and this time the last syllable echoed in his mind with a peculiar relevance. 'Fey! There's a true Scottish word will fit you, for ye're fated—doomed to die as we all are, poor bairnie.'" She was doomed, yet she was also chosen, for she had inherited from a Scottish grandmother a gift of mind-reading and second sight, which enabled her not only, by a little concentration, accurately to predict the future but also to know what other people were thinking and to

[1] Sordid milieux means squalid surroundings.

tell them what they had in their pockets. "You are born to great vision, little one," said an old Indian shaman[2] in a "deep, singing tone." "For you they have made thin the curtain which hides the real. But there is danger. You must listen to the voice of the spirit, or your body and its passions will betray you." And he gave her a turquoise pendant, "the color of the Great Spirit's dwelling," in order that she should always remember that her power derives from the Spirit.

She ran away, at the age of seventeen, with a travelling Irish adventurer who had a one-man medicine show. She amazed him by divining at once the ingredients of the "Elixir" he was selling. "There came the sensation of light and a swift impression which she translated into words. 'In this bottle, there is river water—' She paused, then amplified, 'Water from the Rio Grande where you filled it.' Terry made an exclamation and uncrossed his legs. Fey continued calmly, 'There is also whiskey, a little sugar and—chile powder. No more.' She put the bottle on the floor beside her stool, and raised her eyes." He was impressed by her possible usefulness as a feature for his medicine show, a dependable mind-reading act which required no confederate or code; and she, on her side, was attracted to him strongly. "He was twenty-three and of that dashing Irish type which rouses many a woman's imagination. . . . The chin was pugnacious, the mouth, warmly sensual, also showed humor, while the greenish eyes, ill-tempered now, as they often were, seldom produced that impression on women because of their romantic setting of thick dark lashes. He was vivid and very male. Fey, unaccustomed to height and breadth of shoulder, gazed at the ripple of muscles beneath his white silk shirt, and thought him miraculous."

They took to the road together, got married. But her gift, when she debased it, failed her: she could no longer tell prostitutes their original names or inventory the contents of pocketbooks. Dashing Terry—who sincerely admires her but who has to be got out of the way— is rather implausibly made to desert her in a cheap lodging-house in New York. She had been pregnant, though he had not known it, but for a time she was able to earn a living at the Arcadia Concert Saloon. "While she sang, wandering from table to table strumming her guitar and smiling, she diffused sex magnetism, and she titivated the goggling out-of-towners who comprised three-quarters of the Arcadia's patronage." (The proper meaning of "titivate"—here, as often, used for titillate—seems hopelessly to have suffered the fate of "jejune" and "disinterested.") Then she goes to have her baby in a hospital, where a Quaker woman doctor befriends her and tries to persuade her to study medicine. Here she is nursing her baby: "The girl was beautiful; she [the woman doctor] had never realized it before. Or if not exactly beautiful, something far more disturbing. She was alluring, every line of her body, partly unclothed as it now was, pointed to seductive allure."

But the hospital is repellent to Fey: "I loathe sick people and poor people," she tells herself. "I want nothing now of life but luxury and refinement." She

---

[2] An Indian shaman is a medicine man.

has conceived an audacious design on a certain Simeon Tower, the son of a Jewish peddler, who has become one of New York's richest men by dint of his native shrewdness and by "throwing plums to Big Bill Tweed as he rose to power by means of the most corrupt politics ever known in New York." She goes straight to his office in Wall Street and forces her way into his presence. "I think we would like each other," she says. "'That is a trifle crude,' he said coldly. 'Will you kindly state your business?' His blunt, well-manicured hand made a slight gesture, the prelude to dismissal." But he looks "at the full high outline of her breasts under the leaf-brown silk, at the wide coral-tinted mouth," and succumbs to her seductive allure. He soon gets her a divorce and marries her, and there begins one of those period pageants which, with the recent patriotic exploitation of the American historical legend, have become a cheap and routine feature of so many of our books, plays and films. There is an "at home" at Phoebe and Alice Cary's, at which the visitor is "drawn over to a red settee where Susan B. Anthony and Elizabeth Cady Stanton are discussing . . . the advent of the bustle." (Fey has of course recognized early the greatness of Walt Whitman. Opening *Leaves of Grass* in a book store, "'This is for me,' she said at once, her eyes shining. 'This man understands.' Mr. Tibbins had flushed a dull red. 'That's not a proper book for a young woman to read!' 'Oh, but it is!' said Fey, hardly conscious of him. 'It's true and good. It makes me strong.' And her rapt eyes reread a page.") Simeon is shocked and alarmed by the fact that "on January sixth, Jim Fisk had been shot and killed by Josie Mansfield's paramour, Edward Stokes," and he has a life-or-death struggle with Jay Gould, as "The Mephisto of Wall Street sits like a small black spider silently enmeshing enterprise after enterprise." Simeon Tower has hitherto been excluded from the social Four Hundred, the custodian of which is Ward McAllister; but Fey, with her usual directness—which Simeon "dimly recognized as the product of generations of breeding"—goes to McAllister and asks to be taken in. "It is," he tells her, "my privilege to help guard the—may I say—inner sanctum from pollution"; but "I'll see what I can do," he ends, bowing.

At the first great ball that the Towers give, with Mrs. Astor present, Fey's rascally ex-husband turns up, having impudently crashed the gate. Fey yields again to his Irish charm and spends a night in a raffish hotel with him. But Terry has conceived the idea of blackmailing Simeon Tower and, "sunk in an amorous drowsiness," he murmurs, "'The old boy's an easy mark.' 'Why do you say that?' She pulled the light chain and the gas flared up, while she contemplated Terry with steady narrowed eyes." "Listen then, Terry," she announces, when she has grasped the situation. "It is finished at last, and I feel for myself a loathing. I was always a—an incident to you, as I have been now. I knew this. I even told myself this over and over, but I—Oh, what's the use! Perhaps it was necessary that by yielding to my body I might become free of it and you."

Unfortunately, Fey's second sight was still in abeyance at this time, so she could not prepare herself for what was about to happen. With the connivance of a villainous secretary, Terry launches his campaign of blackmail, and one day, when he has thrown it in Simeon's teeth that Fey has been unfaithful to him, Simeon takes out a revolver and shoots him. Simeon is sent to the Tombs, and we are led to believe that Fey is going to marry a Scottish relation who has been sent over by her grandfather to find her. But, on a visit to her husband in prison, her power of clairvoyance dramatically comes back (though it is now, it seems, moral insight rather than mind-reading or knowledge of the future). The words of the old Indian return; the past reveals itself to her in a series of blinding flash-backs. She knows she has been to blame. Her consciousness is penetrated "with annihilating truth": *"You are responsible, you!"* She tells her suitor that she can never be his and makes him return to Scotland; she trains herself in hospital work; she goes on the stand at her husband's trial and, by confessing her in-fidelity, obtains the acquittal of Simeon. Then she takes him away to New Mexi-co, where they live for the rest of their years in a four-room adobe house, while she ministers to the natives, who "regard her with semi-superstitious reverence." "She had much medical knowledge and she had an almost miraculous intuition as to what ailed the sick bodies or souls which came to her." After her death, she was known as "La Santa."

The Turquoise thus follows a familiar line. It is a typical American novel written by a woman for women. The great thing about this kind of fiction is that the heroine must combine, in one lifetime, as many enjoyable kinds of roles as possible: she must be sexually desirable and successful, yet a competent pro-fessional woman; she must pass through picaresque adventures,[1] yet attain the highest social position; she must be able to break men's hearts, yet be capable of prodigies of fidelity; she must have every kind of worldly success, yet rise at moments to the self-sacrifice of the saint. She must, in fact, have every pos-sible kind of cake and manage to eat it, too. A bait is laid for masculine readers, also, by periodically disrobing the heroine and writing emphatically of her sexual appetite. And the whole book is written in that tone and prose of the women's magazines which is now so much a standard commodity that it is probably possible for the novelist to pick it up at the corner drugstore with her deodorant and her cold cream.

Yet *The Turquoise* sticks below the level of the more compelling specimens of this fiction by reason of the lack in it of any real feeling of even the feminine daydreaming kind that does sometimes enliven these books. There is not even a crude human motivation of either the woman or the men. The heroine, who is supposed to be intuitive, full of warm emotions and eager desires, is as incredible in her relations with her husbands as they are in their relations with her. She is made, for example, to lay siege to Simeon simply because she craves money and position, but the stigma of calculation is eliminated by showing her later

---

[1] Picaresque adventures are those of a wandering rogue. (I don't know the feminine form of the word rogue.)

as passionately in love with her husband—yet not so passionately, it appears still later, that she will not be tempted to slip with Terry. The whole thing is as synthetic, as arbitrary, as basically cold and dead, as a scenario for a film. And now the question presents itself: Will real men and women, in large numbers, as the publishers obviously hope, really buy and read this arid rubbish, which has not even the rankness of the juicier trash? Or have I been using up all this space merely to warn you against a dud? Watch the best-seller lists for the answer.

Several people who read this article imagined that it was a burlesque; they assumed, from the absurdity of the story, that I must have made the whole thing up. But *The Turquoise* was perfectly real, and it has justified my worst apprehensions by selling more than nine hundred thousand copies.

POINTS TO CONSIDER

Edmund Wilson: Ambushing a Best-Seller

1. What characteristics of best-selling historical and romantic fiction are exemplified in the novel *The Turquoise?* Do you know of other popular novels or other popular art forms which have any of these characteristics?

2. What are Edmund Wilson's feelings about such novels? How does he express his feelings?

3. To whom do such novels as *The Turquoise* usually appeal? Why? What other forms of popular art often appeal in similar ways to these same people?

"While it does call for the total destruction of our social system, it does so in such a witty and entertaining way as not to give offense to the average reader."

The Dirty Blockbuster as 'Roman à Clef':
A review of *The Love Machine* by Jacqueline Susann

Calvin Trillin
Life, May 30, 1969

The genre of novel known as The Dirty Blockbuster is founded on what scholars of the field call The Bernie Geis Device. A novel about an Italian-American pop singer who becomes the king of Hollywood, for example, employs the device which, at one stroke, gives the reader the illusion of having a peek into the bedrooms of the mighty and saves the author the necessity of thinking up a character of his own. The point is to follow some celebrity's life so closely that the voice from under every hairdryer can ring with authority in discussing what the book is *really* supposed to be about. In *The Love Machine,* for instance, the title character is an icy hypersexual who becomes the ruthless president of a television network and then, amidst exotic rumors about his private and professional life, is toppled—an obvious allusion, of course, to my brief career as coeditor of *Beautiful Spot, A Magazine of Parking.* I'm not angry; everybody has to make a living. I was even rather amused at how little the author, Jacqueline Susann, bothered to change the details of my life. Robin Stone, the Love Machine, went to Harvard rather than Yale, was a fighter pilot in the Second World War rather than a public-information Specialist Fourth Class during peacetime, comes from New England rather than the Midwest, is single instead of married. I have never been known as the Love Machine, at least not to my knowledge, though once, at a Spanish-language summer school, I knew a girl named *La Maquina*—but only by reputation.

Naturally, Miss Susann has tried to spice things up a bit. For instance, in *The Love Machine* Robin Stone finally lost his job by becoming involved in a brawl with the parent corporation's president's aging but style-setting wife—who, in her desire for him, was enraged when he delayed leaving a Hollywood party with her so he could talk for a while to the Italian Homosexual who had been the last companion of his mother (or at least the woman he thought was his mother) and in her rage took the gold bracelet that the Italian Homosexual had had Robin's name engraved on, a bracelet that could have been embarrassing not only to Robin, who happened to have been secure enough in those matters to have had a pleasant platonic relationship with the Italian Homosexual but also to the Italian Homosexual and to the Italian Homosexual's beau, an English Homosexual who was a film star and who, becoming particularly upset after the parent corporation's president's wife struck the Italian Homosexual on the head with an Academy Award, slapped her around and recovered the bracelet, which she had placed between her breasts, recently tightened by surgery. Actually, that's not quite the way it happened at *Beautiful Spot, A Magazine of Parking.* I lost my position as coeditor because I tried to impress a girl I met with one of those "I can get you in the movies, baby" lines—telling her confidently, "I can get you an editorial position on *Beautiful Spot, A Magazine of Parking.*" She seemed completely unimpressed. So the next day I decided to offer her the editorship. My coeditor and I both stepped down, but then I couldn't remember the girl's name or how to reach her, and I never saw her again. There were no homosexuals, foreign or domestic.

There are times, naturally, when I become irritated at the effects of having my persona used by a complete stranger. My wife's sarcasm has begun to wear thin—"Hey, Machine, maybe you could plug yourself in long enough to empty the garbage." That sort of thing. There is, of course, a potential for personal embarrassment in having readers connect some of Robin Stone's sexual exploits with me. Fortunately for me, Miss Susann has not included any explicit descriptions of the sexual act. Her approach to writing about sex is reminiscent of those quaint Historical Blockbusters in which two people's lips met and the next thing the reader knew it was the following morning—the only difference being that Miss Susann's characters manage to get out a dirty word or two before their lips meet. With the act described discreetly if at all, the only possible area of embarrassment for me is the type and number of people involved. I want to make it clear, for instance, that I have never been to bed with an altered transsexual— an experience that, in Miss Susann's account, turns out to be not as interesting as it sounds. Otherwise, I have tried to be big enough to say that the whole thing is harmless.

POINTS TO CONSIDER

Calvin Trillin: *The Dirty Blockbuster* as "Roman à Clef"

1. What characteristics of the best-seller hero or heroine does Robin Stone, the Love Machine, possess? Compare Stone with the heroine of *The Turquoise* ("Ambushing a Best-Seller," p. 225), with Tom Garner ("Love, Death, Sacrifice, and So Forth," p. 211), or with the hero of any other best seller or movie you know.

2. Why does Trillin claim that *The Love Machine* is modeled on his life? Explain how different the hero is from him.

3. How is Trillin's method of criticizing *The Love Machine* similar to Ira Wallach's criticism of Mickey Spillane's violent detective novels in "Me, the Judge," page 253? Do you think the method is effective?

Me, the Judge

Ira Wallach

Hopalong Freud Rides Again and Other Parodies, 1952

PUBLISHER'S PREFACE

"I'm going to cut valentines out of your large intestine!"

Pete Rivet[1] believed in justice. When the killer struck, Pete swore he'd shoot him down, right through the gut, with a slug as big as a 14-ounce sinker. Then, when the killer was lying there with a slug in his belly, Pete swore he'd kick in his teeth. Then he'd jump on his face. Then he'd get a hacksaw and saw the body into parts.

Then he'd jump on the parts. Then he'd smash the teeth on the hacksaw. Then he'd work over that louse of a hardware dealer who sold him a hacksaw with smashed teeth.

When the suspects piled up, including passionate Martha Emery, passionate Louise Higgleston, and passionate Natalie Wallace, Pete knew this wasn't for mouthpieces and judges and juries. It was up to Pete to keep law and order.

Of *Me, the Judge*, the *Houston Blade* commented, "At last! A writer who knows how to fill in the gaps between blood and sex with blood and sex!" Echoing this praise, a reviewer in the *Chicago Times-Union* wrote, "Pete Rivet is something new in detectives. He is a sadistic, degenerate idiot." These, and other enthusiastic comments, have made *Me, the Judge* a favorite with discriminating readers everywhere.

MODERN CLASSICS, INC.

1.

I walked into the room. The body lay in the closet, feet sticking out. Matt Abel looked at me. Matt is a smart cop. "An .88," Matt said.

On the couch sat a girl. Even with her shoulders heaving with sobs I could see she was beautiful.

"Martha Emery," Matt explained. "They were going to get married."

"Poor kid," I murmured. Then I suddenly felt like I was burning up with hate. God, how I hated that killer! Nick Jenkins was my pal, my buddy. Straightest guy that ever lived. I'd grown up with Nick. Together we'd planned to smash some guy's teeth down his throat. It was Nick who taught me how to shove a knife in a mug up and sideways instead of down and straight. Everybody loved Nick.

---

[1] Pete Rivet is modeled most closely after Mike Hammer, the hero of a series of detective novels by Mickey Spillane. One of the most popular (and violent) Mike Hammer adventures is titled *I, the Jury*.

I stood there looking at what was left of him. "Nick," I said, "It's too late for you to do anything about this. The reason for this is because you are dead, Nick. But listen to me anyway, Nick. I'm going to make you a promise, Nick. I'm going to find the killer, Nick. And when I find him I'm going to let him have it. Right in the belly button, Nick."

I bowed my head out of respect for the dead.

"Take it easy, Pete." It was Matt Abel's voice.

"I'm tired of taking it easy."

"I want the killer," Matt said.

"Nothing doing, Matt. No judge and jury this time. Sometimes those trials drag on three weeks. Sometimes they even let the guy go because he's innocent. But that isn't going to happen this time. I'm going to get the killer, innocent or guilty, and when I do, I'm going to saw off his head, crack his ribs, jump on his neck, smash his Adam's apple, beat in his nose, tear off his ears, pull out his hair, bend back his fingers, twist off his toenails, and shatter his kneecap. But before I do this I'm going to work him over with a rusty knife. I'm like that, Matt. I want a clean and decent America, a place where our kids can grow and sniff the good fresh air."

Matt sighed. He knew when he was licked.

2.

Matt and the other cops left. I stayed to look around. Martha, poor kid, was still crying. She said, "Excuse me," and she went into the next room. When she came back she was wearing a cheesecloth negligee that buttoned down the front. I could see the womanly rippling muscles underneath and the fine wide breasts that fought the negligee to be free. She sat down on the couch and cut off the buttons. The negligee fell open. She didn't bother to close it. Huba huba.

I went over to her. In a moment I felt her soft wet mouth against mine. She held me so tight it hurt. She was trying to get closer, closer. "Did Nick have any enemies?" I asked.

"Not that I know of," she said. God, she was beautiful.

"Anything strike you as unusual about him last week?"

"Nothing," she moaned, "except that he said he had to spend the weekend at the Higglestons in Long Island."

I pushed her away from me and straightened my tie. "Got to go to Long Island," I said.

She held her arms toward me.

"Not now, baby," I said. "I want it to be beautiful. This would spoil everything."

I left. Behind me I heard Martha beating her head against the wall in rage and exasperation. I chuckled.

3.

Jane Higgleston was society. She was in her sixties, and she gave some of the real swank shindigs on the Island. Only I knew that Jane Higgleston ran a string of whore houses and also had her finger in the dope trade and the numbers racket.

The Higgleston estate was the flashiest thing on the Island. I drove up at 80 m.p.h., braked the wreck in front of the door, and jumped out. The butler opened the door. I pulled out my .45 and laid open his cheek with the butt end. You could see his molars with his mouth closed. "Now can I come in?" I asked.

I found Jane Higgleston sitting in her wheel chair. I flashed my badge.

"Well, Mr. Rivet, what can I do for you?" she asked.

"Tell me how you first met Nick Jenkins."

"I never met Nick Jenkins," she said. She was a cool one, all right. But I knew how to handle that. When she wasn't looking I came up with my fist and it landed in her midriff right up to the wrist. She slipped to the floor with a groan. I took the old biddy's cane and beat her across the nape of the neck. "Now maybe you'll talk," I said.

"All right," she groaned. "How do you want me to have met Nick Jenkins?"

"You met Nick Jenkins three years ago at the community bake in Scarsdale. He entered his cocaine muffins. They won the prize over your opium dumplings. You hated him ever since, but you didn't kill him. Now snarl."

She snarled, and I let her have one in the eye for good measure.

When I turned something stopped me short. It was a woman. But when I say a woman, I don't say anything. She was a fine shade of tan, and under her dress I could see the light delicate muscles ripple. She had fine wide shoulders and handsome breasts that struck out against the jacket of her smart suit. Huba Huba.

"I am Louise Higgleston," she said. "Pardon me one moment." She left the room. When she returned she was dressed only in a pair of peach-fuzz panties. She lay down on the couch and beckoned.

I went over, my blood on fire. In a moment I felt her lips against mine, her body pressing hard. I could hardly breathe. The blood was hammering in my head. "Take me now," she gasped.

"Where was Martha Emery the night before Nick Jenkins met his death?"

"She was at a cock fight with the Governor and Natalie Wallace," she murmured, fighting to get closer.

I stood up and straightened my tie. There's a time for everything.

"Don't go," she begged.

"I want you," I said, "But it's got to be beautiful. Let's not spoil everything."

I rushed out, pausing only long enough to shoot the butler.

4.

A bullet *zinged* by me as I started driving out. I dashed out of the wreck and charged back. In a moment I saw what had happened. Louise Higgleston lay on the floor, a bullet in her gut. I turned the corpse over with my toe.

I looked around. There was no exit except for the front door and the side doors. The window ledge was too narrow for the killer to have escaped that way. I tested the chandelier. I couldn't swing from the chandelier to the kitchen. The fireplace was blocked. There was no room between the dining room table and the wall. How did the killer leave? Why did Natalie Higgleston conceal her visit to the cock fight from her mother? Was the Governor involved with the Breslin gang? What did Nick do that year he spent in Bryn Mawr? Why did the Dean ask him to leave? Somewhere a link was missing. I had to get hold of that link.

I drove to a luncheonette to have a bite and think. The waitress came over. She was wearing a smock with no buttons. It hung open. She had nothing on underneath. Huba huba. "Tunafish on white," I said.

"Butter and lettuce?"

I grabbed her by the collar of the smock and twisted till her face turned blue. She slumped to the floor, gasping, "Take me now!" I broke a pitcher of water over her head. She came to. I yanked her up by the ear and let her have it over the side of the head with my .45. "Did I say butter and lettuce?" I snarled.

The sandwich didn't help. I hopped back into the wreck and drove to the Park Avenue apartment of Natalie Wallace.

A maid answered the door. I garroted her. Inside I found Natalie Wallace. She had just come in and she was still wearing her overcoat which hung open. She had delicate rippling muscles, emerald eyes, and hair you wanted to sink your face into and sob because it was so damn beautiful I could hardly speak for a moment. Her breasts, free and unsupported, fought against her lingerie and against her blouse.

"Pete Rivet?" she asked, looking me over.

I nodded.

"I was expecting you," she said, undressing. She lay down on the couch and held out her arms. Huba huba. The next thing I know I was in paradise, or what ought to be paradise if it isn't. "When did you last see the Governor?" I asked.

"Three weeks ago, at Danny Devine's," she said, gasping for breath.

I rubbed the lipstick off my shoes and arose. "Don't go now," she pleaded.

"I have to. If I stay I may lose control of myself," I admitted. I tore out.

5.

Danny Devine was sitting at the bar in the Cafe de Sade. I went up to him from behind and put one hand on his shoulders, grabbing his wrist with my free hand. I bent slowly. Finally the bone cracked with a little cackle. Bits of it stuck out. Devine groaned. I started to work on the other arm when a voice said, "Hold it, Pete."

Matt Abel was standing next to me. "Just one arm, Pete," he cautioned. "The guy's a taxpayer."

"Matt," I said, "I hate killers. I'm going to keep on killing so that America can stay a sweet and decent place for our kids. You can understand that, can't you, Matt?"

I could see in Matt's eyes that he understood. Matt was a good cop.

I turned back to Devine. "Go on, Devine," I said.

"Well," he sputtered, "after Ted Corio hocked his maribou gown, he had enough for the pay-off. But he knew that Nick Jenkins was on to him through Martha Emery. That's why the killer killed Martha and the Higgleston woman."

"His name?" I demanded.

Danny Devine never had a chance to answer. An .88 caught him before he could open his mouth. I turned to Matt. "Matt," I said, "we got to get the killer. He's dangerous."

6.

Back at home I sat down with a few bottles of beer to think. Was Danny Devine connected with Jane Higgleston's call houses? That would explain the little ruckus at the Cafe de Sade—and it would give Louise Higgleston a motive for getting shot. But there was no other exit from the Higgleston estate.

Then I brought the beer bottle down with a crash. I felt a chill run through me. Rising, I put the new clip in my .45 and walked slowly, soberly out the door.

I drove to the apartment. No one was home. I jimmied open the door, sat down in an arm chair, and released the safety on the .45.

In a few minutes she came in. She was cool, all right. I'll have to hand her that. She started to speak.

"It's no use, Natalie," I said. "I didn't realize it was you till I found the one little link. There was no exit from the Higgleston place. That means you didn't leave."

(She was coming toward me now, her nostrils flaring, her beautiful breasts scrimmaging with a nylon blouse.)

"If you didn't leave, that means you were there. And if you were there, that means you shot Louise Higgleston because she knew of your connections with Danny Devine."

(Her lips were open now, and they were flaring, too. I couldn't look. I had to go on talking.)

"Then I realized that you had cooked Nick's cocaine muffins, enabling him to receive first prize. Then you shot him. Why? So you could get in good with Martha Emery and run the racket from her end."

(Slowly she walked toward me, undulating rapidly. I felt my heart pounding. I knew I'd never see anything as undulant again in my life.)

"A jury wouldn't convict you on my evidence. I know that. But I convict you. Now."

(She was fumbling with the zipper on her blouse. The zipper made the soft enticing zippy sound that passionate women make when they zip their zippers. Huba huba.)

"It's no use, Natalie," I said, levelling my .45 at her belly.

"Wait," she murmured. "You can't shoot me yet."

The roar and smoke of the .45 cut her off. She grabbed her gut and looked at me in amazement. Then she sank to the floor.

"Pete," she gasped, "you shot me! Fully dressed!"

I started out. In the hall I met my publisher. "Pete," he said in his cultured accents, "you shot her fully dressed?"

"Yes," I said. "I was in a hurry. I want a clean decent America."

"Pete," he said, "go back in, undress her, and shoot her again."

After I did it, I saw Matt Abel standing in the doorway. "Some day, Pete," he said, "you're going to overreach yourself. She was a taxpayer."

POINTS TO CONSIDER

Ira Wallach: Me, the Judge

1. What characteristics of the violent detective story does Wallach parody in "Me, the Judge"? How effective do you think the parody is?

2. What qualities does Pete Rivet, or Mike Hammer, share with other popular fiction or movie heroes you know? What does he have in common with more recent fictional heroes such as James Bond?

3. What weaknesses or distortions of values in our society does Wallach satirize along with his tough detective?

4. How are Wallach's observations on popular art similar to Saroyan's in "Love, Death, Sacrifice, and So Forth," page 195, or Calvin Trillin's *The Dirty Blockbuster* as "Roman à Clef," p. 231?

Everybody's Protest Novel

James Baldwin

Notes of a Native Son, 1955

In *Uncle Tom's Cabin,* that cornerstone of American social protest fiction, St. Clare, the kindly master, remarks to his coldly disapproving Yankee cousin, Miss Ophelia, that, so far as he is able to tell, the blacks have been turned over to the devil for the benefit of the whites in this world—however, he adds thoughtfully, it may turn out in the next. Miss Ophelia's reaction is, at least, vehemently right-minded: "This is perfectly horrible!" she exclaims. "You ought to be ashamed of yourselves!"

Miss Ophelia, as we may suppose, was speaking for the author; her exclamation is the moral, neatly framed, and incontestable like those improving mottoes sometimes found hanging on the walls of furnished rooms. And, like these mottoes, before which one invariably flinches, recognizing an insupportable, almost an indecent glibness,[1] she and St. Clare are terribly in earnest. Neither of them questions the medieval morality from which their dialogue springs: black, white, the devil, the next world—posing its alternatives between heaven and the flames—were realities for them as, of course, they were for their creator. They spurned and were terrified of the darkness, striving mightily for the light; and considered from this aspect, Miss Ophelia's exclamation, like Mrs. Stowe's novel, achieves a bright, almost a lurid significance, like the light from a fire which consumes a witch. This is the more striking as one considers the novels of Negro oppression written in our own, more enlightened day, all of which say only: "This is perfectly horrible! You ought to be ashamed of yourselves!" (Let us ignore, for the moment, those novels of oppression written by Negroes, which add only a raging, near-paranoiac[2] postscript to this statement and actually reinforce, as I hope to make clear later, the principles which activate the oppression they decry.)

Uncle Tom's Cabin is a very bad novel, having, in its self-righteous, virtuous sentimentality, much in common with *Little Women.* Sentimentality, the ostentatious parading of excessive and spurious emotion, is the mark of dishonesty, the inability to feel; the wet eyes of the sentimentalist betray his aversion to experience, his fear of life, his arid heart; and it is always, therefore, the signal of secret and violent inhumanity, the mask of cruelty. *Uncle Tom's Cabin*—like its multitudinous, hard-boiled descendants—is a catalog of violence. This is

---

[1] Glibness is a smoothness of speech often covering a shallowness of personality or an incomplete understanding.

[2] Near-paranoiac means characterized by an emotion close to obsessive fear.

explained by the nature of Mrs. Stowe's subject matter, her laudable determination to flinch from nothing in presenting the complete picture; an explanation which falters only if we pause to ask whether or not her picture is indeed complete; and what constriction or failure of perception forced her to so depend on the description of brutality—unmotivated, senseless—and to leave unanswered and unnoticed the only important question: what it was, after all, that moved her people to such deeds.

But this, let us say, was beyond Mrs. Stowe's powers; she was not so much a novelist as an impassioned pamphleteer;[3] her book was not intended to do anything more than prove that slavery was wrong; was, in fact, perfectly horrible. This makes material for a pamphlet but it is hardly enough for a novel; and the only question left to ask is why we are bound still within the same constriction. How is it that we are so loath to make a further journey than that made by Mrs. Stowe, to discover and reveal something a little closer to the truth?

But that battered word, truth, having made its appearance here, confronts one immediately with a series of riddles and has, moreover, since so many gospels are preached, the unfortunate tendency to make one belligerent. Let us say, then, that truth, as used here, is meant to imply a devotion to the human being, his freedom and fulfillment; freedom which cannot be legislated, fulfillment which cannot be charted. This is the prime concern, the frame of reference; it is not to be confused with a devotion to Humanity which is too easily equated with a devotion to a Cause; and Causes, as we know, are notoriously bloodthirsty. We have, as it seems to me, in this most mechanical and interlocking of civilizations, attempted to lop this creature down to the status of a time-saving invention. He is not, after all, merely a member of a Society or a Group or a deplorable conundrum[4] to be explained by Science. He is—and how old-fashioned the words sound!—something more than that, something resolutely indefinable, unpredictable. In overlooking, denying, evading his complexity—which is nothing more than the disquieting complexity of ourselves—we are diminished and we perish; only within this web of ambiguity, paradox,[5] this hunger, danger, darkness, can we find at once ourselves and the power that will free us from ourselves. It is this power of revelation which is the business of the novelist, this journey toward a more vast reality which must take precedence over all other claims. What is today parroted as his Responsibility—which seems to mean that he must make formal declaration that he is involved in, and affected by, the lives of other people and to say something improving about this some-

[3] A pamphleteer is a writer of pamphlets often characterized by violent religious or political propaganda.

[4] A conundrum is a riddle or puzzle.

[5] An ambiguity is something which can be understood or interpreted in more than one way; a paradox is a set of contradictory conditions which exist together, for example the fact that most people are impatient for the future but regretful that time seems to pass so quickly.

what self-evident fact—is, when he believes it, his corruption and our loss; moreover, it is rooted in, interlocked with and intensifies this same mechanization. Both *Gentleman's Agreement* and *The Postman Always Rings Twice*[6] exemplify this terror of the human being, the determination to cut him down to size. And in *Uncle Tom's Cabin* we may find foreshadowing of both: the formula created by the necessity to find a lie more palatable than the truth has been handed down and memorized and persists yet with a terrible power.

It is interesting to consider one more aspect of Mrs. Stowe's novel, the method she used to solve the problem of writing about a black man at all. Apart from her lively procession of field hands, house niggers, Chloe, Topsy, and so forth—who are the stock, lovable figures presenting no problem—she has only three other Negroes in the book. These are the important ones and two of them may be dismissed immediately, since we have only the author's word that they are Negro and they are, in all other respects, as white as she can make them. The two are George and Eliza, a married couple with a wholly adorable child—whose quaintness, incidentally, and whose charm, rather put one in mind of a darky bootblack doing a buck and wing to the clatter of condescending coins. Eliza is a beautiful, pious hybrid, light enough to pass—the heroine of *Quality* might, indeed, be her reincarnation—differing from the genteel mistress who has overseered her education only in the respect that she is a servant. George is darker, but makes up for it by being a mechanical genius, and is, moreover, sufficiently un-Negroid to pass through town, a fugitive from his master, disguised as a Spanish gentlemen, attracting no attention whatever beyond admiration. They are a race apart from Topsy. It transpires by the end of the novel, through one of those energetic, last-minute convolutions of the plot, that Eliza has some connection with French gentility. The figure from whom the novel takes its name, Uncle Tom, who is a figure of controversy yet, is jet-black, wooly-haired, illiterate; and he is phenomenally forbearing. He has to be; he is black; only through this forbearance can he survive or triumph. (*Cf.* Faulkner's preface to *The Sound and the Fury:* These others were not Compsons. They were black: —They endured.) His triumph is metaphysical,[7] unearthly; since he is black, born without the light, it is only through humility, the incessant mortification of the flesh, that he can enter into communion with God or man. The virtuous rage of Mrs. Stowe is motivated by nothing so temporal as a concern for the relationship of men to one another—or, even, as she would have claimed, by a concern for their relationship to God—but merely by a panic of being hurled into the flames,

---

[6] *Gentleman's Agreement* is a novel and a movie about the ways that people have expressed their prejudices against Jews by excluding them from certain neighborhoods, hotels, and organizations. *The Postman Always Rings Twice* is a novel and a movie about a woman who falls in love with a poor laborer who is passing through town and plots with him to kill her husband. The wife and her lover are eventually found out and punished.

[7] Metaphysical means abstract or detached.

of being caught in traffic with the devil. She embraced this merciless doctrine with all her heart, bargaining shamelessly before the throne of grace: God and salvation becoming her personal property, purchased with the coin of her virtue. Here, black equates with evil and white with grace; if, being mindful of the necessity of good works, she could not cast out the blacks—a wretched, huddled mass, apparently, claiming, like an obsession, her inner eye—she could not embrace them either without purifying them of sin. She must cover their intimidating nakedness, robe them in white, the garments of salvation; only thus could she herself be delivered from ever-present sin, only thus could she bury, as St. Paul demanded, "the carnal man, the man of the flesh." Tom, therefore, her only black man, has been robbed of his humanity and divested of his sex. It is the price for that darkness with which he has been branded.

Uncle Tom's Cabin, then, is activated by what might be called a theological terror, the terror of damnation; and the spirit that breathes in this book, hot, self-righteous, fearful, is not different from that spirit of medieval times which sought to exorcize evil by burning witches; and is not different from that terror which activates a lynch mob.[8] One need not, indeed, search for examples so historic or so gaudy; this is a warfare waged daily in the heart, a warfare so vast, so relentless and so powerful, that the interracial handshake or the interracial marriage can be as crucifying as the public hanging or the secret rape. This panic motivates our cruelty, this fear of the dark makes it impossible that our lives shall be other than superficial; this, interlocked with and feeding our glittering, mechanical, inescapable civilization which has put to death our freedom.

This, notwithstanding that the avowed aim of the American protest novel is to bring greater freedom to the oppressed. They are forgiven, on the strength of these good intentions, whatever violence they do to language, whatever excessive demands they make of credibility. It is, indeed, considered the sign of a frivolity so intense as to approach decadence[9] to suggest that these books are both badly written and wildly improbable. One is told to put first things first, the good of society coming before niceties of style or characterization. Even if this were incontestable—for what exactly is the "good" of society?—it argues an insuperable confusion,[10] since literature and sociology are not one and the same; it is impossible to discuss them as if they were. Our passion for categorization, life neatly fitted into pegs, has led to an unforeseen, paradoxical distress; confusion, a breakdown of meaning. Those categories which were meant to define and control the world for us have boomeranged us into chaos; in which limbo we whirl, clutching the straws of our definitions. The "protest" novel,

[8] A theological terror is terror based upon a religious belief. To exorcise is to drive something away through religious or magical incantations and ceremonies.

[9] Decadence here is the lack of concern about anything but one's own pleasures.

[10] An insuperable confusion is one which can't be overcome.

so far from being disturbing, is an accepted and comforting aspect of the American scene, ramifying[11] that framework we believe to be so necessary. Whatever unsettling questions are raised are evanescent, titillating;[12] remote, for this has nothing to do with us, it is safely ensconced in the social arena, where, indeed, it has nothing to do with anyone, so that finally we receive a very definite thrill of virtue from the fact that we are reading such a book at all. This report from the pit reassures us of its reality and its darkness and of our own salvation; and "As long as such books are being published," an American liberal once said to me, "everything will be all right."

But unless one's ideal of society is a race of neatly analyzed, hardworking ciphers, one can hardly claim for the protest novels the lofty purpose they claim for themselves or share the present optimism concerning them. They emerge for what they are: a mirror of our confusion, dishonesty, panic, trapped and immobilized in the sunlit prison of the American dream. They are fantasies, connecting nowhere with reality, sentimental; in exactly the same sense that such movies as *The Best Years of Our Lives*[13] or the works of Mr. James M. Cain are fantasies. Beneath the dazzling pyrotechnics of these current operas one may still discern, as the controlling force, the intense theological preoccupations of Mrs. Stowe, the sick vacuities of *The Rover Boys*.[14] Finally, the aim of the protest novel becomes something very closely resembling the zeal of those alabaster missionaries to Africa to cover the nakedness of the natives, to hurry them into the pallid arms of Jesus and thence into slavery. The aim has now become to reduce all Americans to the compulsive, bloodless dimensions of a guy named Joe.

It is the peculiar triumph of society—and its loss—that it is able to convince those people to whom it has given inferior status of the reality of this decree; it has the force and the weapons to translate its dictum into fact, so that the allegedly inferior are actually made so, insofar as the societal realities are concerned. This is a more hidden phenomenon now than it was in the days of serfdom, but it is no less implacable.[15] Now, as then, we find ourselves bound, first without, then within, by the nature of our categorization. And escape is not effected through a bitter railing against this trap; it is as though this very striving

---

[11] Ramifying means branching out.

[12] Something which is evanescent is insubstantial and tends to fade quickly. Titillating is exciting pleasurably, often by suggesting something that may be considered immoral or improper.

[13] *The Best Years of Our Lives* is a novel and a movie about an injured soldier who must readjust to society after the war.

[14] Pyrotechnics are fireworks, meaning here an excessively elaborate display. "The sick vacuities of *The Rover Boys*" refers to the shallowness of a series of adventure books for boys.

[15] Serfdom is a form of slavery. Implacable means relentless or impossible to appease, as in the expression "an implacable enemy."

were the only motion needed to spring the trap upon us. We take our shape, it is true, within and against that cage of reality bequeathed us at our birth; and yet it is precisely through our dependence on this reality that we are most endlessly betrayed. Society is held together by our need; we bind it together with legend, myth, coercion, fearing that without it we will be hurled into that void, within which, like the earth before the Word was spoken, the foundations of society are hidden. From this void—ourselves—it is the function of society to protect us; but it is only this void, our unknown selves, demanding, forever, a new act of creation, which can save us—"from the evil that is in the world." With the same motion, at the same motion, at the same time, it is this toward which we endlessly struggle and from which, endlessly, we struggle to escape.

It must be remembered that the oppressed and the oppressor are bound together within the same society; they accept the same criteria, they share the same beliefs, they both alike depend on the same reality. Within this cage it is romantic, more, meaningless, to speak of a "new" society as the desire of the oppressed, for that shivering dependence on the props of reality which he shares with the *Herrenvolk*[16] makes a truly "new" society impossible to conceive. What is meant by a new society is one in which inequalities will disappear, in which vengeance will be exacted; either there will be no oppressed at all, or the oppressed and the oppressor will change places. But, finally, as it seems to me, what the rejected desire is, is an elevation of status, acceptance within the present community. Thus, the African, exile, pagan, hurried off the auction block and into the fields, fell on his knees before that God in Whom he must now believe; and who had made him, but not in His image. This tableau, this impossibility, is the heritage of the Negro in America: *Wash me,* cried the slave to his Maker, *and I shall be whiter, whiter than snow!* For black is the color of evil; only the robes of the saved are white. It is this cry, implacable on the air and in the skull, that he must live with. Beneath the widely published catalog of brutality —bringing to mind, somehow, an image, a memory of church-bells burdening the air—is this reality which, in the same nightmare notion, he both flees and rushes to embrace. In America, now, this country devoted to the death of the paradox— which may, therefore, be put to death by one—his lot is as ambiguous as a tableau by Kafka.[18] To flee or not, to move or not, it is all the same; his doom is written on his forehead, it is carried in his heart. In *Native Son,* Bigger Thomas stands on a Chicago street corner watching airplanes flown by white men racing against the sun and "Goddamn" he says, the bitterness bubbling up like blood, remembering a million indignities, the terrible, rat-infested house, the humiliation of home-relief, the intense, aimless, ugly bickering, hating it; hatred smoulders through these pages like sulphur fire. All of Bigger's life is controlled,

[16] *Herrenvolk* are members of a master race.

[17] Franz Kafka (1883–1924) was an Austrian writer of tales in which people become mysteriously caught up in nightmare situations.

[18] *Native Son* is a novel by the black American author Richard Wright.

defined by his hatred and his fear. And later, his fear drives him to murder and his hatred to rape; he dies, having come, through this violence, we are told, for the first time, to a kind of life, having for the first time redeemed his manhood. Below the surface of this novel there lies, as it seems to me, a continuation, a complement of that monstrous legend it was written to destroy. Bigger is Uncle Tom's descendant, flesh of his flesh, so exactly opposite a portrait that, when the books are placed together, it seems that the contemporary Negro novelist and the dead New England woman are locked together in a deadly, timeless battle; the one uttering merciless exhortations,[19] the other shouting curses. And, indeed, within this web of lust and fury, black and white can only thrust and counter-thrust, long for each other's slow, exquisite death; death by torture, acid, knives, and burning; the thrust, the counter-thrust, the longing making the heavier that cloud which blinds and suffocates them both, so that they go down into the pit together. Thus has the cage betrayed us all, this moment, our life, turned to nothing through our terrible attempts to insure it. For Bigger's tragedy is not that he is cold or black or hungry, not even that he is American, black; but that he has accepted a theology that denies him life, that he admits the possibility of his being sub-human and feels constrained, therefore, to battle for his humanity according to those brutal criteria bequeathed him at his birth. But our humanity is our burden, our life; we need not battle for it; we need only to do what is infinitely more difficult—that is, accept it. The failure of the protest novel lies in its rejection of life, the human being, the denial of his beauty, dread, power, in its insistence that it is his categorization alone which is real and which cannot be transcended.

POINTS TO CONSIDER

James Baldwin: Everybody's Protest Novel

1. Who is James Baldwin? For what is he well known?

2. Why does Baldwin consider sentimentality an evil? Compare Baldwin's views with Pauline Kael's in her review of *The Sound of Music* (p. 203).

3. What kind of "panic" does Baldwin think motivates our superficial acts of charity? How does this panic relate superficial charity to cruelty? What is the difference in understanding between the truly charitable man and the superficially charitable man who acts out of panic?

4. What is the relationship between complexity and reality both in life and in art?

5. In what way are protest novels reassuring rather than disturbing to the average reader? Do you think this applies also to protest songs and movies?

6. What does Baldwin feel has become the aim of the sterile modern "protest novel"? Do you think this is true of protest songs and movies as well?

[19] Exhortations are urgings or pleadings.

Drawing by Shirvanian. By
permission of Look magazine.

The Rise of Non-Fiction

John Fischer

St. Louis Post-Dispatch, December 5, 1965

Aside from its literary merits (which seem to me considerable), Truman Capote's "In Cold Blood" may turn out to be a milestone in the history of American writing. For it is likely to force the critics, and the mandarins of the university English faculties, to recognize that a new kind of "creative writing" has arrived on the literary landscape, full grown, vigorous, and self-confident. In fact, it already is shouldering aside the traditional forms of creative writing—usually defined as fiction, poetry, play writing, and sometimes criticism.

The new form is, of course, non-fiction. For at least 20 years it has been growing in importance, and during the last decade it has (in my view, at least) become the dominant type of American writing. So far, however, it has attracted little critical attention. This isn't surprising, since the critical establishment— especially that wing entrenched in the universities—is one of the most conservative of institutions, normally lagging two or three decades behind the really live currents in American intellectual life. Now the new Capote book seems likely to compel this establishment to acknowledge that something fresh and significant is happening, worthy of serious critical appraisal. For reasons to be noted in a moment, I am not at all sure this is a good thing.

It can be argued that every period produces its characteristic literary form. In Homer's time it was the epic, designed for recitation at palace banquets before warriors, well-primed with wine, who wanted to hear about their heroic deeds and those of their forefathers. In Shakespeare's day it was the poetic drama. Byron and Tennyson found that their contemporaries had an almost bottomless appetite for semi-lyrical narrative poems. During the last half of the nineteenth century and the early decades of this one, the novel became dominant. And in our own lifetime, the novel has gradually but inexorably yielded to non-fiction, in the guise of the magazine article and the reportorial book.

In any period the characteristic literary form can be recognized by certain earmarks. It is always the most popular. Its practitioners, therefore, are relatively well paid; Shakespeare probably was the most prosperous writer of his century, for example, while Byron and Tennyson both made substantial fortunes from their poetry. Throughout the glory years of fiction, many a novelist—Mark Twain, Galsworthy, Harold Bell Wright, and Hemingway, to mention a few of widely-varied merits—got comfortably rich. Nevertheless, while any particular literary form is at its peak, its practitioners are considered low fellows, undeserving of critical or academic reverence. Only after it has passed its flowering, and is well on the way toward being replaced by its successor, does the new mode become fully respectable. Consequently, the Elizabethan playwrights, the glory of their age, had to do their drinking in raffish taverns rather than ducal palaces. Again, all through the Victorian period the novel was considered something slightly improper, more suitable for the servants' quarters than the parlor. Now, of course, the novel has been officially enshrined, so that thousands of Ph.D. candidates worship it like acolytes, turning out endless analyses of Henry James and Herman Melville with the repetitive piety of Talmudic scholars.[1]

Meanwhile, fiction has long since lost its once-dominant place in the esteem of mere readers. Back in the Twenties, Americans bought roughly two novels, in their original editions, for every work of non-fiction; by 1950 the reverse was true—and the popular trend toward non-fiction has been gathering speed ever since. For instance the AVERAGE sale of Harold Bell Wright's 19 novels was more than a half million copies each, while one of them reached 1,650,000. Nowadays a sale of only 50,000 copies is almost certain to put a book at the top of the fiction best-seller list; and the author's next book can by no means be sure of an eager, automatic audience of the kind that Wright (and scores of better novelists) once commanded.

Some reasons for the shift are fairly obvious. For one thing, millions of people who once turned to fiction for amusement, fantasy, and escape now get much the same commodities from television, easier and at less cost. Moreover, the real world has become more interesting—indeed, more fantastic—than the world of fiction. When men are exploring sunken cities beneath the seas, walking in space, building mega-death weapons, cruising under the polar ice cap, starting rebellions every other weekend, and making espionage a mass industry, it is hard for a novelist—short of genius—to keep up with them. As Philip Roth said recently: "The actuality is continually outdoing our talents, and the culture tosses up figures daily that are the envy of any novelist. . . ."

At the same time (and perhaps for this same reason) most novelists have abandoned any effort to interest the great public; indeed, they (and most of the critics who make "serious" literary reputations) now regard story-telling as disreputable, and a place on the best seller list as a badge of shame. Instead they concern themselves with sensibility, with the inner drama of the psyche, disregarding the large events of the outside world. Often they are accomplished craftsmen. Their style is luminously burnished; they write on two levels, or even three; their work contains more symbols than a Chinese band; it plumbs the depths of the human soul; it may be (in Felicia Lamport's phrase) as deeply felt as a Borsalino hat. But usually, alas, it just isn't much fun to read. If such exercises in occupational therapy don't sell very well, the author has small grounds for complaint.

A more fundamental reason for the drift away from fiction, I believe, is that the best writers of our time are finding that non-fiction forms—notably the ar-

[1] Acolytes are attendants or assistants at a religious service. The Talmud is a collection of writings on Jewish civil and religious law.

ticle and its book-length equivalent—are more flexible, more suitable for expressing the significant ideas and emotions of our time. Witness John Hersey, whose "Hiroshima" clearly is a better book than any of his novels. Theodore White, an eminently successful novelist, has now turned to reporting the making of presidents, a kind of narrative all the more moving because it is true. Norman Mailer has not yet made a complete conversion; but his disastrous last novel demonstrates the superiority of his non-fiction work, such as "Advertisements for Myself" and "The Presidential Papers."[2] Much the same thing could be said of James Baldwin, and a dozen other novelists.

Capote's new book is perhaps the most convincing illustration of all. In it he has reported the true story of a multiple murder on a Kansas farm, using all of the most subtle techniques of the novelist and yet sticking meticulously to hard, recorded fact. He explores the character and motivation of the two murderers with as much insight as he has brought to any of the people in his novels. And the very actuality of his story endows it (in my opinion, at least) with a stature, and a relevance to our time, which far surpass anything in his fiction. In the quality of its writing, it may well be the best of the new type of reportorial book—so good that even the academic critics will find it hard to ignore.

I am not of course suggesting that the novel is finished. Undoubtedly it will linger on indefinitely as a subordinate literary mode, much like poetry, which is being written these days in greater volume than ever, even though a book of verse seldom sells more than 500 copies. What I am suggesting is that non-fiction writing, which has been attracting both our best writers and our largest audiences for a good many years, is now—at long last—likely to achieve recognition for what it is: the characteristic literary medium of our time.

POINTS TO CONSIDER

John Fischer: The Rise of Non-Fiction

1. What are the indications that the novel is growing less popular as a popular art form and that nonfiction is growing more popular?

2. Why does Fischer feel that nonfiction has gained such popularity in the past twenty-five years? Can you think of other reasons?

3. What popular nonfiction narratives have been written since *In Cold Blood?* Have you read any of them? Which do you currently read more of for pleasure—fiction or nonfiction? Why?

4. Why do you think that respectability or critical acceptance for an art form usually comes later than its popularity? Can you think of some art forms that have been popular for a while but that are just recently becoming "respectable"—that is, being seriously reviewed and taught in schools?

[2] More recently, Norman Mailer has written *Miami and the Siege of Chicago* about the 1968 political conventions.

Ideas for Investigation, Discussion, and Writing

Popular Fiction

1. Compare, in an essay, a representative sample or samples of contemporary popular fiction with popular fiction of the past. What similarities are there? What differences? Did the popular fiction of the past use basically the same appeals as that of our time? What are these techniques? (An example of an interesting comparison: The adventures of James Bond versus the Arthurian legends of The Knights of the Round Table.)

2. Write an essay comparing a popular novel with a more sophisticated literary treatment of the same topic. Examples might be a James Bond compared with Graham Greene's *Our Man in Havana* or with John Le Carré's *The Spy Who Came in From the Cold* or a detective novel compared with Dostoevsky's *Brothers Karamazov*. What similarities can you find? Are they important? Why? What differences can you find in such things as character development, depth of ideas, complexity of plot. What would happen to the literary work if its author followed the same rules as the author of the popular work?

3. Analyze several examples of a particular type of popular fiction, such as science fiction, westerns, historical novels, or detective stories. What is the particular appeal of this kind of fiction? How does the novel achieve this particular appeal? Cite quotations and incidents from the books that illustrate your point. Does this type of fiction appeal to a certain specialized audience? How?

4. Using examples from several popular novels by different authors discuss the characteristics of the hero or heroine of popular fiction. What quality or qualities seem to be necessary to the protagonists of popular novels? How do different authors approach the problem of creating an acceptable protagonist? Why are these qualities important to the success of the book?

5. With reference to one or more appropriately sentimental popular novels, discuss James Baldwin's statement that "Sentimentality, the ostentatious parading of excessive and spurious emotion, is the mark of dishonesty, the inability to feel; the wet eyes of the sentimentalist betray his aversion to experience, his fear of life, his arid heart; and it is always, therefore, the signal of secret and violent inhumanity, the mask of cruelty."

6. Analyze a particular popular novel for narrative techniques. What tricks does the author use to keep you reading? What hints does he drop to tickle your interests? What tensions, questions, apprehensions does he manufacture

so that you will keep turning the pages? What promise does he make? Does he disappoint you? If so, how?

7. In a comparative analysis of several popular novels or in an intensive analysis of a single popular novel, show how the author lets his protagonist—and thus the reader as well—have, in Edmund Wilson's words, "every possible kind of cake and manage to eat it too."

8. Compare a popular movie with its subsequent novelization. How does the nature of the printed medium affect the various elements of the movie, such as plot, character, theme? What is lost; what is gained? How do these changes reflect the inherent superiorities or inferiorities of the novel as a popular medium?

9. Using Edmund Wilson's technique of summary and occasional quotation, "write" a novel designed to be a best seller. Employ in this novel as many devices and appeals of the popular novel as are applicable. Add an afterword explaining your devices and appeals and how you expect them to make your novel appeal to a large audience.

PART SEVEN

POPULAR MUSIC

Popular music serves as a good barometer of the general concerns and emotions of its time. The temperament of twentieth-century America has developed from "The Good Ol' Summertime," to "Over There," to "Yes We Have No Bananas," to "The World Is Waiting for the Sunrise," to "I Could Have Danced All Night," to the age of "Aquarius."

Reflecting the "melting pot" theory of our country's development, American popular music has been enriched greatly by the folk and dance music of other countries—especially Mexico and the rest of Latin America—as well as by cultural minority groups within the country, especially the Jews and the blacks—the former in big bands, show music, and current folk protest music, the latter in religious music and jazz, now popular in the forms of soul and rock. The recent rapid growth of a black cultural identity in this country has been a major contribution to current pop music in this country. So has the culture of our country's young people with its tremendous energy and its intense concern for the state of society.

Expanding technology has also contributed greatly to contemporary popular music. The radio and the record player have shaped, widened, and disseminated our musical tastes both in this country and around the world for the past fifty years. The common use of electronic musical instruments and sophisticated recording studio equipment also reflects the influence of technology.

Big business—the force which determines what music and musicians will be popular, when they will be popular, and how long their popularity will last—has also been a major shaper of modern pop music. Although all of the popular art forms transmitted via the mass media are greatly influenced in this country by big business, none, with the possible exception of television, is so controlled by the sources of its financial support as popular music.

The Music of Protest

Burt Korall

Saturday Review, December 16, 1968

Youth damns the past, defines the diseased present, and demands change. Their outrage and defiance takes various forms—from direct confrontation and protest, satire, love in the face of hate, to drugs and dropping out. What remains constant is a flood of commentary—youth taking the world's pulse and their own, using music to purge themselves, while increasingly irritating and provoking the forces of reaction. In essence, they function as an alarm clock for the country and march to the tune of their aspirations, hoping to attain sanity, reason, physical and mental mobility, love and, most important, realistic appraisal on a mass level.

Having overrun popular music and realized its power as a tool, they are cementing a link with an increasingly large audience through the country and the world. It is a matter of record that music representative of the tidal wave of youth sells more heavily than any other kind—and not only to youngsters. Cultural lag doesn't seem a problem in this era of multiple communication, even in more provincial areas.

The music of youth, like their clothes and hair styles, simultaneously singularizes and isolates them, while lending tribal strength.[1] Nothing new; swing music of the 1930s and be-bop ten years later spawned analogous figures which, for simplicity's sake, we will call hipsters. They, too, had their own folkways, manner of dressing, language, and lived on the periphery of the establishment.

One major difference, however, separates today's rag-tagger from the hipster of old. Living away from the illness of the establishment is primary to today's young—at least until they can motivate some radical changes. The old-time hipster, on the other hand, put down the world as unbearably square but still was part of it. Politics and the expression of the need for radical metamorphosis were not his bag. Comfortable in his own orbit, where everything was familiar and relaxed, the hipster dismissed the square as funny and unfeeling. They couldn't dig him; they didn't know how. Proudly, but with a hint of finger-popping hositility, he ambled down Main Street in big town and small, flaunting his difference and his cool.

The rag-tag generation finds no humor in the mistakes and cop-outs of the conforming armies. Sleeping, easily fooled, bigoted people are a travesty, they say, and are responsible for the relative chaos in which we live. Anything

---

[1] The popular show *Hair* is advertised as "the American tribal love-rock musical."

but cool, youth senses what is wrong and how things should be. They find muscle in their growing numbers and the possibilities implicit in grouping for attack on the status quo, and in the attack itself. As for a sharply definitive sense of identity—that's another matter. The search continues. For the moment, the method, culminating in revelation, has not been found. The young of earlier generations fostered the idea that they knew who they were. "Today's youth have no such delusion," critic Albert Goldman declares. "But lacking any clear-cut sense of identity has only made them more keenly aware of everyone else's."

Cross-ventilation of ideas and techniques combined with the inner and outer ferment in the country have produced a radical change in popular music —now a fascinating, if sometimes troubled mixture of elements, which truly reflects our present position. What Goldman has deemed the "Rock Age"—the period in which we live—indeed has been a time of assimilation. Musically it has "assimilated everything in sight, commencing with the whole of American music: urban and country blues, gospel, hillbilly, Western, 'good-time' (the ricky-tick of the Twenties), and Tin Pan Alley. It has reached across the oceans for the sounds and rhythms of Africa, the Middle East, and India. It has reached back in time for the baroque trumpet, the madrigal, and the Gregorian Chant; and forward into the future for electronic music and the noise collages of *musique concrète*.[2] By virtue of its cultural alliances, the Beat has also become the pulse of pop culture."

It remains to be determined whether music-song is a powerful, provocative instrument, which aids the cause of change. Does our contemporary musical amalgam,[3] itself implicit protest against the limited popular music of the past, make its point?

There is widespread disparity of opinion concerning the cogency of musical protest. Critic John Cohen states that "topical songs are like newspapers; pertinent to the latest developments, bearing the latest ideas, and ending up in the garbage can." It is his contention that "for young people in the cities, the topical songs have become abstract emotional substitutes for what is going on in the world; and although this can be a good factor when it stimulates people to action, more often it is a delusion." By making such connections, he explains, "topical songs blind young people into believing they are accomplishing something in their own protest, when, in fact, they are doing nothing but going to concerts, record stores, and parties at home."

Admittedly, protest music diminishes in impact once the crisis in question

---

[2] *Musique concrète,* or concrete music, begins with already existing sounds—recorded music, recorded noises, electronic noises—and arranges them, often with alterations and distortions, into a new art form. It has been employed for ballet and for movie soundtracks. Some popular rock musicians (such as the Beatles, The Mothers of Invention, and Pink Floyd) have produced similar music on their albums.

[3] An amalgam is a fusion or a blending.

is past. It does, however, serve as a source of strength, unification, and expression when the battle is raging. Music's depth of importance within the civil rights movement earlier in this decade is a matter of history. It converted many to the cause in a manner that signs, demonstrations, and other means did not. Even more important, the songs solidified the chain of commitment among the followers. Northern writers, including the ever present Pete Seegar, Phil Ochs, Tom Paxton, and Len Chandler, among others, personalized the struggle, giving their own reactions to various situations. They spoke of injustices and what had to be done. The Southern freedom singers and writers, working within the Afro-American tradition, using gospel and rhythm and blues forms and songs, with lyrics to fit each occasion, also cut deeply and made their point, leaving an eduring mark. One has only to refer back to the tremendous effect of "We Shall Overcome."

At the base of today's musical protest, casting a giant shadow that sometimes goes unnoticed by current practitioners, are generations of black blues singers and players—disenfranchised,[4] alienated, and imprisoned, who had their say, if sometimes obliquely, and broke through using the only medium at their disposal, music. Equally influential in casting the current shapes and forms for contemporary comment were individuals of conscience and compassion who sang of injustice and helped people find answers to pressing questions in their songs.

The prototypical figure[5] in the latter category is the late Woody Guthrie, a truth-teller about whom Tom Paxton had said: "The most important thing Woody gave us was courage to stand up and say the things we believe." A ramblin' man who wandered through his beloved land, he was devoted to causes—some deemed radical; however, with time on our side, it is plain to see that all Guthrie wanted to do was make us aware of the country's good points and bad, while bringing us closer to it. His thoughts, generally couched in simple, human terms, are accessible to all. Through more than 1,000 songs, he strung the history of the America he knew—from the deprivations of the Depression through the first post-World War II years, until his illness began to take hold of him and prove prohibitive on his talent.

Those who register complaint and desperation today are not far removed in spirit from Guthrie and other bards of yesterday, like black artists Big Bill Broonzy and Leadbelly, who spoke out of their experience and tried to bring mass focus to inequality and the number of sicknesses in the land. Today, however, the voices of dissent are louder, for cause; we cannot wait any longer for the rapport to develop whereby we can live with one another. It is either pass down an inheritance of absurd reality or change direction.

Amidst the hurt, disappointment, and hopelessness, there seems reason for

---

[4] Disenfranchised means deprived of rights and powers.

[5] A prototypical figure is a model or a pattern which others copy or reflect.

limited optimism. The 1960s have been crucial years in the journey to a new reality. An extended period of silence, repression, and resultant welling up of feeling came to an end. A revolution broke out in music—and the other arts as well—paralleling the turmoil throughout the national and international structure. Folk artists in America again began speaking openly, following years of black lists and red channels. With the coming of Ornette Coleman and the emergence and development of John Coltrane, jazz again became a maverick. On the heels of an era concerned with consolidation and progressive rediscovery of roots, after the death of Charlie Parker in 1955, the ground breakers reached out, touching new bases. They provoked the young to look to their feelings. The music, though unfinished in many of its aspects and chaotic to the uninitiated, motivated a complete re-examination of existing guidelines, and challenges us to think about our lives and what the future will offer.

Some sage, for lack of a more ornate description, deemed it "The New Thing." An oversimplification, but appropriate for a sudden turning in the road. Bringing into play a variety of techniques from diverse musical and extra-musical sources, the practitioners mutate and revamp the jazz we know playing havoc on its identity. Exactly what will emerge remains to be heard; it's certain that jazz, by nature an evolving form, can never be the same. The revolution continues. To accept it wholly, completely discarding yesterdays, seems out of the question. To open one's self to its positive aspects and prospects is a necessity. A highly contemporary manifestation, it certainly has been instrumental in shaking jazz loose from a progressive case of nostalgia, a malaise which could envelop and incapacitate the music and its players.[6]

It comes clear that it is no longer possible to separate music and life as it really is. Politics, sexuality, racial pride, deep and true feelings have entered popular music to stay. Our youth is central to this metamorphosis.[7]

Bob Dylan has been *the* standard-bearer of the 1960s. A stylistic son of Woody Guthrie at the beginning of his career, he stepped forward in 1961 and initiated a stream of comment that continues to this day. Particularly at the outset he noted in no uncertain terms the hypocrisy of this country and the need for vigorous change. Using the narrative form, in the tradition of Guthrie, his first records echoed with the meaninglessness of life, the impossiblity of racial inequality, the imminence of death, as man moved further and further from himself. It was time to take hold, NOW.

Deemed a poet by some, a prophet by others, a self-propelled mediocrity by still others, Dylan caught the tenor of the times in his songs. Innocence was a thing of the past. No longer was it possible to live with soda shoppe morality

---

[6] A contemporary manifestation is something which has recently taken shape. A malaise is an uneasiness or illness.

[7] A metamorphosis is a change in form.

and answers which had nothing to do with pressing questions. He realized that isolation from true reality was as unbearable as the reality itself. Yet this did not prohibit him from immersing himself in surrealistic pessimism. After clearly indicting the world in his "Blowin' in the Wind," he turned to an inverted mode of writing, couching his point of view within a rush of words and images, oblique and abstract, often approaching hallucination: dreams more frightening than reality. This is the subterranean Dylan, living in song in a demimonde[8] of "haunted, frightened trees"; dwarfs; clowns who seem blind; intransigent policemen. On occasion he surfaced to sing of love relationships (often unfulfilling) and to express youth's alienation from the older, reactionary generation who simply won't understand what it's all about, as on "It's Alright, Ma, I'm Only Bleeding." Dylan the observer, would make things right if he could, but the governing forces block renewal of effort.

With the release early this year of *John Wesley Harding* (Columbia CS 9604), his first album after a silence of a year and a half, he gives evidence of having thrown aside the recent past in favor of rebirth and a new maturity. The electrified accompaniment that served his purposes prior to his near-fatal accident has been unplugged. His songs are concise rather than sprawling. The imagery, if still opaque,[9] is not as dreamlike, nor just for him alone. His morality, accessible at every turn and almost religious in aspect, guides him in sharply defining good as opposed to that which is intrinsically evil. The nature of his songs and delivery are devoid of obvious artifice and the false "cool" and stances of the public person. Placing a heavy emphasis on country simplicity in vocally and instrumentally projecting his feelings, the songwriter-singer again acoustic-guitarist is back in the world. A new Dylan? Hardly. He's just a bit more direct, relaxed, open. His means and manner may change but he retains a unity of image. He is the questioning and needling voice of the 1960s.

Dylan's colleagues in the pop realm, like him, are the products of many influences and pressures. With few exceptions, their comment and mode of vocal and instrumental performances bear the marks of the black man—his inflections, mannerisms, and accents. But taken as a whole, popular music, 1968, reflects urban and provincial attitudes, sounds, and rhythms native to black and white, a spillover of techniques from traditional and contemporary classical music and foreign cultures. It is a democracy in sound—as free and flexible as the world we yearn for. It logically follows that the lyrics for this universal popular music would be as emancipated, outspoken, and diverse as the music itself.

This is very much the case. We have moved into wide-ranging application of words since swinging around the corner into the 1960s, with contexts running

---

[8] Demimonde here means a world half real and half unreal.
[9] Something which is opaque will not allow light to pass through it: Dylan's lyrics are sometimes difficult to interpret.

from the decisively concrete to abstraction. This is a considerable distance from the nonsense syllables and one-dimensional lyrics which characterized much of the song produce of the Fifties. The songsmiths aspire to be equal to the times.

Whatever the degree of accessibility of the wordage, the creator's need to link up with his audience is strongly sensed. Often, however, he will make the listeners work to achieve communion, benevolently allowing multiple interpretations of his message or lack of one, intimating that in life everyone doesn't see everything the same way. At their ultimate in surrealism and ambiguity,[10] Dylan, the Beatles, and the acid rock groups—i.e., Jefferson Airplane—might initially cloud the mind with a crazy quilt of images. But they do draw you to them within the maelstrom[11] and engage your capacities in a search that frequently is as exciting and fulfilling as the revelation that sometimes lies at the end of the trip. Observers have paralleled the experience with the drug turn on—an analogue not without basis in fact. The drug phenomenon *is* very much with us and figures in the music of youth. The maze and confusion out of which we try to make sense also structures the music and is part of its structure. Therefore, the music is singularly relevant, because it contains in its own form what's happening in and around us. If anything is true of contemporary popular music, it is the intent of its makers to set life to music.

Surprisingly, the prime movers are white—surprising only in that their black brethren have far more reason to build bandwagons. But there is reason for this. White people are freer and have less to lose. The black man generally remains repressed and is less inclined to show his true face—musically, anyway. Make no mistake, however, his protest is there for all who will take time to reach and find his soul. One has only to pay special heed to the sound and words of the blues. And sometimes the mask slips, as on this old-time entry:

> Well, I drink to keep from worrying and I laugh to keep from crying, (twice)
> I keep a smile on my face so the public won't know my mind.
> Some people think I am happy but they sho' don't know my mind, (twice)
> They see this smile on my face, but my heart is bleeding all the time.*

Admittedly, the turn of events in this decade has motivated the black man to speak more directly in his music, and to abandon to some extent the protective code and inside terminology of the past. Race pride and anger is felt in some of his songs, as well as the need to throw off strictured yesterdays. Lou Rawls, a modern black singer, with roots in gospel and the blues, gives urgent voice to

---

*"Bleeding Heart Blues," by Amos Castor. Used by permission of Northern Music Co., a division of MCA Entertainment, Inc. All rights reserved.

[10] Surrealism is the dreamlike state in which reality is oddly distorted; ambiguity is the possibility of multiple interpretations.

[11] A maelstrom is a cyclone or hurricane.

these feelings in "They Don't Give Medals (to Yesterday's Heroes)"—a song by two white writers, Burt Bacharach and Hal David, which serves black aspiration well.

> They don't give medals to yesterday's heroes,
> Yesterday's over and I got to live for today,
> I'm goin' places and nothing can stand in my way.*

Songs of burning inquiry, confrontation, and accusation are now written and performed by black people . . . and heard more and more often. Billy Taylor's "I Wish I Knew How It Would Feel to Be Free" has extraordinary currency and is increasingly performed and recorded. The musing, black folk artist-songwriter Richie Havens screams out the query, "Why must we wait until morning to wake up and BE?" in his scalding song, "No Opportunity Necessary, No Experience Needed." Otis Redding bemoans the lack of change in his hit, "Dock of Bay." James Brown, Soul Brother Number 1, raises his voice in the cause of black pride on his "Say It Loud—I'm Black and I'm Proud." Julius Lester, the literate and deeply expressive black songsmith and artist, takes a militant stance, espousing a strong front against the oppressor and the death of sterotypes: "Gonna get me a gun and shoot Aunt Jemima dead." Nina Simone often casts a skewering glance at bedridden society. Her record of Martha Holme's "Turning Point," an eye-opening comment on the existing distance between the races, is a recommended experience. Perhaps the most touching song, rendering with rare clarity the situation in the black ghetto, is the relatively unheralded "Crackerbox Livin'," by Howlett Smith, as interpreted by singer Ernie Andrews in his Dot album, *Soul Proprietor.*

> Crackerbox livin'—ain't no kind of livin',
> What is this hole you charge for?
> What is this hole we're much too large for?
> Lord of the land, won't you understand,
> We'll trade you places just for the day,
> Maybe your kids can chase the rats away,
> Maybe your kids don't need some place to play.†

Inhibition on a really major scale, however, has not been broken. Black song, drenched in blues, with the throb and sob of the church at its core, remains a reflection of ephemeral Saturday night freedom—an act of love and despair, a flash of energy in a long darkness. Centering on black people's major source of strength—the love relationship, physically solidified—it soothes hurt and repairs

*"They Don't Give Medals (to Yesterday's Heroes)," by Burt Bacharach and Hal David. © Copyright 1966 Blue Seas Music, Inc./Jack Music Co., Inc. Permission granted by publisher.
†"Crackerbox Livin'," by Howlett Smith, Hilkert Music.

dwindling dignity. "Baby, baby, baby," cries prototypical Aretha Franklin, echoing black men and women through their painful past in America. "Don't send me no doctor fillin' me up with all those pills/Got me a man named Dr. Feelgood/ That man takes care of all my pains and ills."*

The young, rebellious white, unlike his black counterpart, is unfettered. For him, however, this freedom is but part of an overall delusion. He feels trapped by the traditions and legacies of the past.

Confusion reigns. Truth and honesty are at a premium. A valid way of life is sought. To this end, the young explorer rolls across a wide spectrum of subject matter and musical means and mannerisms. He experiments with ideology and sounds, often shaping answers in the process. But they always are open to change; flexibility is part of the concept. Though his protest and comment is less centralized than his soul brother's, his objective is essentially the same. Hope is implicit in the negation of past and present mistakes—the hope for an apocalypse, which will make the blind see, the intractable feel, the world's fearful face change.[12]

Fear is the underlying feeling motivating the young. It's everywhere, openly shared. "What's becoming of the children?" people ask in a Simon and Garfunkel song. "What has become of the world?" would be a more pertinent question. Moreover, if things go on the way they have, will it be here at all? Turmoil and violence, at every turn. A heavily theatrical and ritualistic rock group called The Doors, featuring lead singer Jim Morrison, is archtypical in its bold statement of the existing situation. Mounting a saturation bombardment attack in words, lights, and amplified sound, leveling listeners into submissiveness, the unit projects the fear embedded in the young, and all of us for that matter. Listen to "When the Music's Over."

> . . . For the music is your special friend,
> Dance on fire as it intends,
> Music is your only friend,
> Until the end,
> Until the end,
> Until
> THE END.†

Threading one's way through the mountains of recent recordings, the temper of the times and the matters of concern are multiply revealed. The Vietnam war is a primary subject. A yearning for peace is predominant. "Honor is without profit

*"Dr. Feelgood," by Aretha Franklin and Ted White Publishers: Fourteenth Hour Music 1721 Field Street, Detroit, Michigan.
†"When The Music's Over," words and music by The Doors. © Copyright 1967 by Nipper Music Company, Inc.
[12] The apocalypse is the destruction of this world to make way for a better one.

in its own country," declare The Split Level in the song, "Speculator," included in the group's recent Dot album. Kenny Rankin, a Mercury artist, singing Fred Neil's song, "The Dolphin," underscores the crucial fact: "Peace gonna come only when hate is gone." It seems indicated that songs will continue to pour from the cauldron until the situation in Southeast Asia is eased. Joan Baez inevitably will lead the voices of nonviolence and peace—just as inevitably as songs taking the opposite stance, like Barry Sadler's "The Ballad of the Green Berets," will be created.

The gap in understanding between young and not so young consistently is mirrored in music. Razor-sharp satirists, who laugh to keep from crying, like Frank Zappa's Mothers of Invention, define the situation with a sneering smile, lending it dimensions it would not otherwise have. In a song called "Mom & Dad," Zappa goes for the heart, querying parents: "Ever take a minute just to show a real emotion? . . . Ever tell your kids you're glad that they think?" Country Joe and The Fish, a San Francisco group deeply involved in today's swirl, also waves the ammonia bottle under the collective nose of America. Though its material has a comedic exterior and unit treatment deepens the satiric quality, these fellows aren't fooling around.

Loneliness also is a frequent song subject. "All the lonely people/Where do they all come from," the Beatles wonder. Confusion and the bureaucracy of life also crops up often, as on Arlo Guthrie's "Alice's Restaurant." The positive power of love to turn people away from their destructive proclivities is still another notable theme. ". . . plant them now, never a better time," Buffy Sainte-Marie says in her song, "The Seeds of Brotherhood." Record after record reveals the inner plight and acute sensitivity of today's youth and the world in which they live. The warnings are there to be understood.

In recent months, however, pop music of protest has taken on a much more affirmative tone. Songs define what might be, as opposed to expressing a condition. The recent assassinations of Martin Luther King and Robert Kennedy certainly contributed to this reversal. Seemingly artists and the industry as a whole have realized that there is no other alternative and concluded, exclusive of one another, to use music affirmatively, hopefully for a positive result.

Within a short space of time over a dozen items have been released—all statements of hope and faith in the underlying strength and possibility of the country. Included in this number are Laura Nyro's "Save the Country," James Brown's "America is My Home," a rash of inspirational songs—notably treatments of "The Impossible Dream" from *Man of La Mancha*—and the Kim Weston album, *This is America.*

Whatever the plight of America, its music indicates that the people are reaching out to find it and themselves. Some want revolution; others desire yesterday. Certainly things cannot stay the same. Take a look around. Listen to today's music. It's all there.

◤ POINTS TO CONSIDER ◥

Burt Korall: The Music of Protest

1. What are some of the types of folk and popular music which have been assimilated into modern rock music?

2. What comparison is made between topical protest songs and newspapers? Do you agree with the comparison?

3. Do you feel that protest songs share some of the faults of protest novels described by James Baldwin in "Everybody's Protest Novel," page 239?

4. What positive effects have protest songs had upon the young people and upon our society as a whole? Give some examples.

5. Who were some of the first musicians to develop protest songs in this country in the 1930s and 1940s? Who were the most influential singers of protest music in the 1960s? Which songs became particularly well known?

6. What are some of the various kinds of protest songs, both in subject and in style? (See the lyrics of five protest songs, pp. 266–271.) Which performers represent each style?

"So you see, young man, instead of singing always of kings and knights and maidens fair, you would do well to include in your repertory songs dealing with a broader cross-section of the entire community."

▨ FIVE PROTEST SONGS

Little Boxes

Malvina Reynolds

Little boxes on the hillside
Little boxes made of ticky tacky,
Little boxes on the hillside,
Little boxes all the same.
There's a green one and a pink one
And a blue one and a yellow one,
And they're all made out of ticky tacky
And they all look just the same.

And the people in the houses
All went to the university,
Where they all were put in boxes,
Little boxes all the same.
And there's doctors and lawyers
And business executives,
And they're all made out of ticky tacky
And they all look just the same.

And they all play on the golf course
And drink their martinis dry,
And they all have pretty children
And the children go to school,
And the children go to summer camp
And then to the university,
Where they all get put in boxes
And they come out all the same.

And the boys go into business
And marry and raise a family,
And they all live in boxes
Little boxes all the same.
There's a green one and a pink one
And a blue one and a yellow one,
And they're all made out of ticky tacky
And they all look just the same.

Rollin' Home

Eric Anderson

Truth, with all its far out schemes, lets time decide what it should mean;
It's not the time but just the dreams that die.
And sometimes when the room is still, time with so much truth to kill
Leaves you by the window sill so tied.
Without a wing to take you high, without a clue to tell you why.
I just want to keep my name, not bother anybody's game,
Without ideas of gold, or fame, or insane heights.
I don't need a lot of money, I don't want a playboy bunny,
Just a love to call my honey, late at night, in my arms,
By my side, in my arms, late at night.

But I don't know, I ain't been told,
Ev'rybody wants a hand to hold, they're so afraid of being old,
So scared of dying, so unknown, and so alone—rollin' home.

I see the ones who crawl like moles, who for a front would trade their souls,
A broken mirror's the only hole for them.
And for you who'd exchange yourselves, just to be somebody else,
Pretending things you never felt or meant;
You don't live what you defend, you can't give, so you just bend.
Now if you care what people think, like they supplied some missing link,
They'll just stand back and watch you sink so slow.
They'll never help you to decide, they'll only take you for a ride,
After which they'll try and hide the fact that they don't know
What you should do, where you should go,
What you should do, where you should go.

But I don't know, I ain't been told,
Ev'rybody wants a hand to hold, they're so afraid of being old,
So scared of dying, so unknown, and so alone—rollin' home.

There's nothing big I want to prove, no mountains that I need to move,
Or even claim what's right or true for you.
My sights, my songs, are slightly charred, you might think they miss their mark,
But things are only what they are and nothing new.
For me, I think they'll do, but for me I think they'll do.
Well, I can see a king and queen, a beggar falling at my feet,
They all must see the same sad dreams at night;
Futility and senseless war, pit the rich against the poor,
While cause is buried long before the fight
For what was wrong, for what was right,
It's just the strong who ever says what's right.

But I don't know, I ain't been told,
Ev'rybody wants a hand to hold, they're so afraid of being old,
So scared of dying, so unknown, and so alone—rollin' home.

The Sound of Silence

Paul Simon (as sung by Simon & Garfunkel)

Hello darkness, my old friend,
I've come to talk with you again,
Because a vision softly creeping
Left its seeds while I was sleeping,
And the vision that was planted in my brain still remains
Within the sounds of silence.

In restless dreams I walked alone
Narrow streets of cobblestone
'Neath the halo of a street lamp
I turned my collar to the cold and damp,
When my eyes were stabbed by the flash of a neon light that split the night
And touched the sounds of silence.

And in the naked light I saw
Ten thousand people, maybe more,
People talking without speaking,
People hearing without listening,
People writing songs that voices never shared, no one dared
Disturb the sound of silence.

"Fools," said I, "you don't know
Silence like a cancer grows.
Hear my words that I might teach you.
Take my arms that I might reach you."
But my words like silent raindrops fell,
Echoes in the wells of silence.

And the people bowed and prayed
To the neon god they made
And the sign flashed out its warning
In the words that it was forming;
And the sign said:
"The words of the prophets are written on the subway walls and tenement halls
And whispered in the sounds of silence."

Birmingham Sunday

Richard Fariña (as sung by Joan Baez)

Come round by my side, and I'll sing you a song,
I'll sing it so softly, it'll do no one wrong.
On Birmingham Sunday the blood ran like wine
And the choir kept singing of freedom.

That cold Autumn morning no eyes saw the sun,
And Dady Mae Columns, her number was one.
In an old Baptist church there was no need to run
And the choir kept singing of freedom.

The clouds they were dark and the Autumn wind blew,
And Dannies McNair brought the number to two.
The falcon of death was a creature they knew,
And the choir kept singing of freedom.

The church it was crowded, and no one could see
That Cynthia Weldly's dark number was three.
Her prayers and her feelings would shame you and me
And the choir kept singing of freedom.

Young Carol Roberts had entered the door,
And the number her killers had given was four.
She asked for a blessing and asked for no more
And the choir kept singing of freedom.

On Birmingham Sunday a noise shook the ground
And people all over the earth turned around.
For no one recalled their cowardly sound
And the choir kept singing of freedom.

The men in the forest they want us to leave.
How many black things grow in the blue sea?
I asked them right off with a tear in my eye,
How many dark shapes in the forest?

The Sunday has come and the Sunday has gone,
And I can't do much more than to sing you a song.
I'll sing it so softly it'll do no one wrong
And the choir kept singing of freedom.

All My Children of the Sun

Pete Seeger

The navigator said to the engineer,
"I think our radio's dead;
I can hear but I can't send
And there's bad weather ahead."
The pilot said to the copilot,
"Our right engine's gone,
But if I can make it over these mountains
Perhaps I can set her down."
All my children of the sun.

Five hundred miles from nowhere
We bellylanded on a river.
We bid a quick goodbye to that ship of silver.
Twenty-five piled out the window;
Twenty reached the shore,
Turned to see our metal bird
Sink to rise no more.
All my children of the sun.

We found some floating logs,
We found some sharp stones;
We cut some vines and made a raft—
It was our only hope.
The navigator said he thought
There was a town somewhere down stream,
So now each man tried to do his best
To paddle as a team.
All my children of the sun.

All except one young guy
Who kept arguing with the navigator.
He said he'd read about a waterfall
We would come to sooner or later.
At a river's bend he persuaded us
To bring our raft to beach,
But a search party found the river smooth
As far as eye could reach.
All my children of the sun.

Once again he persuaded us to stop,
We cursed at the delay;
Once again we found the river
Flowing on the same old way.
We said, "Shut up your arguing,

You give us all a pain.
Why don't you pitch in and do your part?
Be constructive for a change."
All my children of the sun.

Still Egghead kept on talking
In that same longwinded way.
We said, "If you won't paddle,
Get the hell out of our way."
We told him to go sit far back at the stern,
Then we strained the paddle harder,
And then the river made a turn.
All my children of the sun.

One paddler heard the sound of tapping;
What he saw when he did turn
Was Egghead with a sharp stone
Cutting the vines that bound the stern.
With a cry of rage the paddler
Leapt up to his feet
He swung his long pole
And knocked Egghead into the deep.
But now the logs were splaying out,
The raft had come unbound;
Like mad we paddled for the shore
Before we all were drowned.
All my children of the sun.

The search party went out to find more vines
To tie the raft up tight;
In twenty minutes they returned
Their faces pale with fright.
They said, "A quarter mile down river
We found a waterfall,
It's over a hundred feet in height,
We'd none of us have lived at all."
All my children of the sun.

And that is why on the banks
Of a far off wilderness stream
Which none of us, none of us,
Will ever see again,
There stands a cross for someone
Hardly older than a boy
Who, we thought,
Was only trying to destroy.
All my children of the sun.

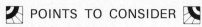

POINTS TO CONSIDER

Five Protest Songs

1. What faults or weaknesses in personal relationships or in society are being protested by each of these five songs? Do you notice any overlapping in the kinds of protests made by these songs?

2. What is the chorus or refrain in each of these songs? What purpose or effect does it achieve in each song?

3. Which of these songs involve dramatic situations? What larger issue is represented by each of the limited dramatic situations?

4. What images or symbols in these songs do you feel are particularly striking or effective? Why?

5. Some details are purposely puzzling or indefinite. Why do you suppose they were written this way?

6. What is the significance of the title of each of these songs?

7. How does the music in each case contribute to the idea or mood of the song?

Soul is selling. Ahmet Ertegun and Jerry Wexler of Atlantic Records, who began selling rhythm and blues (La Vern, Joe Turner, The Drifters) to a limited white audience in the mid-Fifties, now find their organization (which includes Atco and the distribution of Stax, Volt, and Dial) leading the Top 100 charts. The previous champion was the Motown group of Berry Gordy, whose Detroit Sound is also Negro, hence soulful, but much slicker—dance music. The endless succession of artists in the Atlantic stable (Otis Redding, Aretha Franklin, Sam & Dave, and on and on) are rawer, grittier, more bluesy, three adjectives that suggest what soul is without getting down to it.

There is a difference between the soulful performer—nearly any Negro, an occasional white—and soul music, which more or less began with Ray Charles a dozen years ago. Charles added gospel elements (typical progressions, an amenohyeah chorus) to the blues (which had the same roots as gospel anyway), retained his funky jazz piano (same roots) and brought it all together with a frantic stage style, more histrionic than the straighforward presentation of bluesmen like Muddy Waters and B. B. King. Soul music is a combination of surface elements. It is less subtle and poetic than older blues forms, more complex than the R&B of the Fifties, more meaningful lyrically than the Motown stuff. It is remarkably close to the blues, but both races buy it.

Defining soul itself is more difficult and presumptuous. The concept is guarded jealously by the members, who, like the faithful everywhere, prefer to regard it as beyond verbalization. In truth, "soulful" is a lot closer to "black" than anyone wants to admit, especially as understood by black people, who after all should know, and one approach to the subject is through the few white singers who get play on soul stations. What sets them apart? The Righteous Brothers, two white Southern Californians, made the first breakthrough with their near-perfect rendition of gospel-rock counterpoint. More recently, The Young Rascals have done exceptionally well in Negro markets, and other American singers— Mitch Ryder, even Johnny Rivers—have made some inroads. In addition, those great, hoarse old pros, Frank Sinatra and Tony Bennett, are usually admitted into the canon by performers if not radio stations. (As a curiosity, all these latter are Italian-American. Of course, so was Frankie Avalon. And so is Al Martino.)

But although all the English singers found their major inspiration in one form or another of American Negro music, only Tom Jones and Stevie Winwood (of The Spencer Davis Group and Traffic) make it. WWRL, Soul Radio in New York, was swamped with complaints when it tried to broaden programming with The

Rolling Stones. A white jazz critic has called Eric Burdon and The Animals "a blackface act," which seems an unexceptional opinion. The Beatles? Forget it.

Why? First, many English groups are rooted in blues that predate soul, and are therefore considered unhip. Second, the English sound is dominated by loud guitars, while soul emphasizes the emotive solo voice. But there has always been something missing in addition, and I think it was precisely what was missing that made the English groups click in the first place. The Frankie Avalons always did their music straight—"sincere" was Ricky Nelson's favorite word—but, for the usual anthroposociosexual reasons, their sincerity was gutless. In one way or another, the English groups injected a sense of self-consciousness into their music deliberately—as parody or self-parody or just plain fun. Even The Stones have a sardonic edge: "I am an Englishman singing this black music."

Soul music can be happy, but it can't be fun. It has two essential ingredients—wildness, controlled (Anthony and the Imperials) or indulged (James Brown), and faith in itself, a religious virtue after all. It can be horribly mawkish—Danny Boy, with that great high note, is a favorite on Amateur Night at the Apollo—but it always projects honest emotional effort. The Beatles and The Stones are wonderful partly because they're never that sincere. Even if they were, though, they probably wouldn't get soul-station play—a lot of soulful white music is ignored now—because the soul market is still a race market and demands fervid imitation. (Similarly, the Country-Western market remains all-white.[1]) The very few Negro groups who sound white—most notably The 5th Dimension (on the Soul City label), which crosses The Mama's and The Papa's with The Swingle Singers—get no play either.

And the old racism is still with us. Although such frankly black music has never before been so popular with whites, their range of response is limited. When a Harlem teen-ager (or housewife—soul is not teen music among Negroes) buys a record by Otis Redding, she most likely wants a surrogate for the show that left her screaming at the Apollo or the Brevoort[2]. Redding's white fans may like to dance to him or listen to him, but they aren't conscious of him as a sexual object. Yet the popularity of singers like Redding and Brown has made possible (and perhaps necessary) a new kind of sexual candor among white performers. . . .

POINTS TO CONSIDER

Robert Christgau: Soul is Selling

1. What are the musical roots of contemporary soul music? What are some of the characteristic qualities of soul music? Who are some of the best-known soul musicians?

[1] A notable exception is Charley Pride, a black musician who has recorded some popular albums of country and western music and is considered an expert in this area.
[2] The Apollo and the Brevoort are well-known theaters in New York's Harlem.

2. What white musicians and musical groups share some elements of soul music? What distinguishes their music from genuine soul?

3. How do black audiences respond to soul music differently from white audiences? What accounts for the differences?

4. Why is soul "selling" so well nowadays as compared with ten or fifteen years ago?

The Big Sound from the Country

Robert Shelton

The Face of Folk, 1968

Where does folk music end and commercial country music take over? We pose the question, but can offer no simple answer.

The whole body of American folk and pop music is such a thickly woven mesh that certain styles are continually crossing and recrossing other styles. Nowhere is this interweave more evident than in the music generally associated with Nashville, the music loosely called "Country and Western."

A good many performers in the forty-year history of Country and Western music began as "folk performers." Some never left the precincts of folk music, while others are continually walking both sides of the musical street, changing their choice of performing style for a given song or instrumental.

Contemporary Country and Western music has changed so much, has become so sophisticated, that it is difficult to recall that nearly all of it was born in folk-oriented style. Many white folk performers later "crossed over" into the patently more commercial style of Country and Western. Yet the majority of Bluegrass performers to be discussed here remained solidly in the center of the bridge that connects folk tradition with present-day Nashville music.

There has been an unfortunate tug-of-war between those folk fans who regard Country and Western music as an area for their study and enjoyment and those who make minute distinctions between what is pure folk and what is "corrupted" or commercial.

It is this sort of élitist approach[1] toward folk music and its peripheral expressions that has retarded the folk movement's ability to stay in touch with greater parts of the population. Ethnic snobs[2] and traditional determinists think, with much persuasive argumentation on their side, that "their" music is superior. At the same time, they are denying themselves the vast excitements and stimulations of kindred and tangential musics, which, while not "pure" have much else to commend themselves.

All this by way of introduction to the lively world of Nashville music. Nashville is the capital of an international music industry. It has become the vortex of a recording, publishing, broadcasting, and personal-appearance network that spreads around the world. Nashville is know by many nicknames: Music City, U.S.A.; Tin Pan Valley; the Capital of Country Music. Nashville is not only the world center of what has become a $100,000,000-a-year country music industry, but it is also a recording center for a lot of other pop musics, a center now rivaling the supremacy of New York and Hollywood in range of activity and number of musicians and recordings involved.

As to country music, the size of its international audience is almost impossible to calculate. If we say that there are some 35,000,000 country fans in the United States and Canada, what total can be supplied when we add Britain Ireland, Australia, Scandinavia, Germany, South Africa and Japan? To be conservative about it, let's say fifty million deep-dyed fans of country music, many of whom would be folk fans if some of the folk leaders didn't persist in keeping their music "élite" and of such arid delimitations as to allow no mass appeal.

At any rate, out of Nashville spin some 15,000 live performances annually. There are about five hundred song-writers living in the Nashville-Davidson County district, and the more than two dozen recording studios there are kept busy, often on a round-the-clock basis.

How did the industry happen to center itself in Nashville? The answer can be given in three little words: "Grand Ole Opry." This unbelievably indestructible American radio show and institution, born November 28, 1925, was to provide the nucleus for the entire country music industry. With ever-traveling performers making the rounds, it was only their return to Nashville to appear on station WSM's "Opry" that made them available for recording.

The announcer-host of the WSM "Barn Dance," the show that was to evolve into "Grand Ole Opry," was a former newspaper man named George D. Hay, who had earlier helped station WLS in Chicago start its "Barn Dance." The performers on that first WSM show were an eighty-year-old bearded fiddler named Uncle Jimmy Thompson and his niece, Eva Thompson Jones, who played piano and sang. Uncle Jimmy scraped out an hour's worth of old jigs, reels, and sentimental

---

[1] The élitist sees himself in a special limited group of people who are more knowledgeable.
[2] Ethnic snobs insist upon "cultural purity."

parlor and country songs. After only a few minutes, requests began to pour into the station from listeners by wire and telephone. The new show was a hit.

Just two years later, George Hay, known widely by his nickname, "The Solemn Old Judge," renamed the show 'Grand Ole Opry," and it has since become the grand old dinosaur of American radio. Having missed airtime only during a few of President Franklin D. Roosevelt's "Fireside Chats," the "Opry" is believed to be the oldest continuous broadcast in radio. Either directly on its clearchannel station or through subsidiary syndicated shows, the country music on the "Opry" reaches some 10,000,000 persons each week.

When the "Opry" started, country music was also in its early phases. Mostly, it was just a rural folk music, put onto early radio to fill the vacuum for entertainment for regional audiences. Folk-country music was beginning to score with the simultaneous growth of electric recording. (The first country recording *of consequence* was Fiddling John Carson's Atlanta sessions of 1923.) As ironic as it may seem, it was two electronic media, recording and radio, that were to transform a regional folk music into an international industry.

The content of a four-hour "Opry" broadcast today or the infinite variety of music recorded in Nashville reflect how comprehensive the term "country music" has become. It includes ballads, heart songs, Bluegrass, Western songs, train songs, breakdowns, fiddle and guitar tunes, hoedowns, and a lot more. Country music embraces a wide range of styles, from the strictly traditional folk-oriented to bright, urbane love ballads or novelty or sacred tunes that have a distinctly modern flavor. As in jazz and pop music, there are such a variety of styles and approaches to Country and Western music that each have their strong adherents.

As I wrote in *The Country Music Story* (Bobbs-Merrill), the soundtrack of a documentary on country music would carry a symphony of varied sounds:

"It would be the clang of an electric guitar, the subtle fretting of Merle Travis's unamplified guitar; the piercing, stirring "Gloryland March" of Wilma Lee and Stoney Cooper; the yodeling of Kenny Roberts; the devilish banjo tricks of Don Reno; the clunk of Stringbean's old banjo; Pappy McMichen's bow sliding across his 1723 Italian violin, which he has to call a fiddle; Johnny Cash pointing his guitar at an audience as if he were going to hold them up; a screaming "Howdy" from beneath Cousin Minnie Pearl's straw hat; Jimmy Wakely singing to his horse; Zeke Clements explaining how to skin a cat to make a banjo; Archie Campbell telling a racy story one minute and singing a gospel song the next; Ralph Peer telling rustic auditioners to relax and sing out in a Southern hotel room; Ernest Tubb speaking like a benign Lincoln in a ten-gallon hat; Hank Williams crying his lonesome words into a microphone; Jimmie Rodgers hearing a whistle in the night. It is a rare and exciting sound."

It would be next to impossible to compress my history of Country and Western music into one essay. . . . All that can be hinted at, for the urban folk fan, is that there is a tremendous amount of musical quality lying over the hills to Nashville. There is also a lot of junk, pap, commercial garbage. The student or fan of

Country and Western music, therefore, has a greater job of selectivity to tread between the dross and the ore. But it is worth the effort, if only to catch one of the heartfelt gospel songs of Roy Acuff, the "king of country music"; to marvel at the guitar virtuosity of Chet Atkins; to sense the beautiful part-singing of The Blue Sky Boys; to watch Cousin Emmy's dynamic manner on stage; to roar at the unhusked corn of Homer and Jethro or Grandpa Jones.

Too many thousands of performers make up the vast Breughelesque[3] canvas of America's "other popular music," Country and Western, to be touched on here. We can only urge that you try to give Country and Western another listen—to find out why Buck Owens and George Jones and their hard-driving "honky-tonk" style of singing is so popular; to sense Roger Miller's place in a continuum that places his "King of the Road" in a direct line of descent from the hobo songs of Cliff Carlisle, to see how Hank Snow and Ernest Tubb are latter-day twigs off the sturdy branch that produced Jimmie Rodgers, "the singing brakeman" and "the father of country music," way back in the mid-1920's.

One area where the folk fan seems most closely in touch with country music is that large overlapping zone called Bluegrass. Thanks to the popularizing of such city stalwarts as Mike Seeger and Ralph Rinzler, Bluegrass is widely known to nearly every folk fan. Here is a style of rural ensemble musicmaking, vocal and instrumental, that is almost an equivalent of rural string-band jazz, and an equally compelling cousin of the varied instrumental bands of European and Latin-American villages.

To tell it in its simplest outlines, Bluegrass evolved from the string bands who were active in the 1910's and 1920's. These string bands, such as Gid Tanner and The Skillet Lickers, had, in turn, evolved from earlier banjo-fiddle combinations of the nineteenth century. Even that trend can be found to have been an American variant of Irish and Scottish pipe and flute ensembles. Whatever this circuitous line of descent, Bluegrass style as we know it today, was largely set in the late 1940's by a series of seminal bands led by the great Kentucky singer and mandolin player, Bill Monroe.

Monroe's bands were to be the seed-bed of Bluegrass. Through its various formations passed nearly every major Bluegrass stylist of our time. The leading offshoot of Monroe's Bluegrass Boys were Lester Flatt and Earl Scruggs, whose own band, The Foggy Mountain Boys, have in their own time become the nation's leading "glamour" Bluegrass band. Scruggs's virtuosity on the five-string banjo is, of course, legendary and actual at the same time. He gave the instrument a fluidity and lyricism that was almost unknown before, and his style of picking has been widely imitated.

During the height of the urban folk revival, there were to be nearly as many excellent city-based Bluegrass bands as there were in the country. As with coun-

---

[3] Breughelesque refers to the style of Pieter Breughel (1520–1569), a Flemish painter known for his canvases active with scenes of peasant life.

try bands, the urban pickers generally kept the same instrumentation of guitar, banjo, mandolin, Dobro (a steel guitar fretted in the Hawaiian manner), and bass. The voices were to be as athletic and free as were the instruments, with the over-all sound adding up to a kind of whirlwind magic. Among the best of the city bands are The Greenbriar Boys and The Charles River Valley Boys, New Yorkers and Bostonians respectively, who added country-born members and went on to become important style-setters in the folk revival.

Of course, to single out just a few country and city Bluegrass bands scarcely does justice to the breadth of this important subdivision of American folk and country music. But for the person seeking an introduction to one of the more exciting musical styles of our era, the recordings of these groups would speak volumes.

The debate about whether to consider all of Country and Western music as part of the folk stream will not end overnight. What is clear is that a growing catholicity of taste[4] is happily spreading through the folk movement, beginning to embrace neighboring musical styles that have esthetic validity, if not purity. It is in this spirit that the work of the John Edwards Memorial Foundation at the University of California at Los Angeles is to be praised.

Here is a study and research center devoted generally to American folk music, but specifically to the Country and Western field. It is the hope of many of us who regard Country and Western as a viable field for study, that the Edwards Foundation will prosper and grow. It appears to be the reigning philosophy of many at the foundation that Hank Williams is as worthy of study as is The Texas Drifter, Goebel Reeves; that Johnny Cash is at least as important as some unknown folk minstrel who never made a cent commercially, but who stuck stubbornly to his own native tradition. It is such approaches as this that make one feel that the folk movement in the United States is really coming of age, beginning to understand that there are popular musics of value even though they do not measure up to the rigorous standards of a purely traditional esthetic.[5]

But while appreciating this, one must also have respect for the tireless proponents of the older music. In this regard, one can have nothing but praise for such groups as The Friends of Old-Time Music, a small and definitely non-profit organization that brought to New York and many other cities of the Northeast the very best in obscure country musicians. Working independently at first, and later cooperating with the Newport Folk Foundation, the Friends of Old-Time Music were trying to say that the folk musicians who had been passed over by Nashville had as much to say, in human and musical terms, as any star turned out by Country and Western music.

The musical-revival trio The New Lost City Ramblers was also trying to spread the wonder and magic of string-band music of the 1920's and 1930's with its own

[4] Catholicity of taste is liberality with a broad range of interest and understanding.
[5] An esthetic here is a set of artistic values.

playing. Soon, The New Lost City Ramblers were themselves losing work to the musicians they had helped rediscover from the past. The success of The Ramblers ironically worked to make the music and musicians they studied come to the fore while the group that had done this so painstakingly was actually receding quietly into oblivion. This selfless form of activity represents perhaps one of the glowing, little-known aspects of the folk revival that gave it beauty and ethics and honor.

In the face of those for whom the folk revival was either just a vehicle to peddle their own wares, their own dogma, or their own egos, the work of The Friends of Old-Time Music and The New Lost City Ramblers will help remind everyone of what the best impulses were among the city youngsters who helped produce the folk revival of yesterday, today, and tomorrow.

POINTS TO CONSIDER

Robert Shelton: The Big Sound from the Country

1. How are the mass media responsible for turning a regional art form with a limited audience into a popular art form with millions of fans?

2. How did Nashville happen to become the country music capital of the world?

3. What different kinds of music are included in the general term "country music"? Who are some of the best-known country music performers?

4. Are there any differences between "folk music" and "country music"? If so, what are they? Can you give some examples? What is "bluegrass," and how does it overlap the two? Who are some well-known "bluegrass" musicians?

5. What groups are trying to spread the popularity and encourage the serious consideration of country and western music? What other popular art forms do you know of that have recently become subjects for "serious consideration"?

Fancy Rock

Michael Zwerin

The New Republic, March 16, 1968

The music called rock is the most vital, valid and interesting music of our time. Until recently I doubted this proposition and perhaps feared the ridicule of some friends, but now the evidence is all in its favor.

The Agony of Modern Music, written in 1955 by Henry Pleasance, begins:

> Serious music is a dead art. The vein which for three hundred years offered a seemingly inexhaustible yield of beautiful music has run out. What we know as modern music is the noise made by deluded speculators picking through the slagpile.

Pleasance thought the relevant evolution was in American popular music and jazz, despite the conventional notion that "serious" music is by definition superior to all others. Since then jazz has begun to suffer many of the same communication problems. It is fast becoming just as snobbish and inbred—nothing if not serious. "Serious" music continues to be composed, performed, listened to and discussed by an element of society which refuses to recognize its own isolation. New music which cannot excite the enthusiastic response of the lay listener has no claim to his indulgence because contrary to popular belief, all music which now survives in the standard repertoire was popular in its own time. Modern "serious" music is attempting to perpetuate a European musical tradition whose technical resources are worn out. Serious musicians cannot break from this tradition without renouncing the special status they enjoy, and are therefore in serious trouble.

Paul Hindemith stated the problem:

> Our modern music, compared with the music of earlier times, has reached a very high level of complexity. An individual composer, aware of this fact, usually wants to contribute his share to the presumed progress of music, and thereupon he adds complications of his own—complications of technique which will eventually fracture the framework set up by the physical conditions of style which, in their ultimate esoteric[1] loneliness, are bound to reach the borderline of unintelligible enigmas.

Elvis Presley, the Everly Brothers and people like them brought Negro music ("soul") out from underground when their white versions hit the big charts in the fifties. Then Chuck Berry, Muddy Waters, Ray Charles and, recently, the late Otis Redding were allowed to emerge from the ranks of the invisible. The Rolling

[1] Esoteric means appreciated by only a few people with specialized interests.

Stones, the Beatles and others made no secret of their admiration for soul music; they stole from it. The old story: white kids appropriating colored kids' dances. But this was different. They added on to it; rebuilt, remodeled and repainted it to the point where the original foundation is disappearing. Now Jimi Hendrix has turned it around by taking the white electronic/psychedelic superstructure and building his own super-soul penthouse on top.

Folk rock, raga rock, baroque rock, Bach rock, jazz rock—popular music is no longer simple. A troubadour (Donovan), an Indian (Ravi Shankar), and a poet (Leonard Cohen), have all become pop stars. Very strange.

While "serious" composers sweat over their computers and "chance" music, while jazzmen pontificate about exotic time signatures and ethnic combinations, the Beatles, without artistic fanfare, make millions out of "All You Need is Love" in 7/4 time and "Good Morning, Good Morning" in 5/4, make the sitar a standard sound on radio and make it possible for someone like James Guercio to include an "electronic collage" in the teenybopper hit "Susan."

Rock is verbal, tuneful, visual, rhythmic and communicative—a combination which is putting everybody else out of business. The beat, the dancing, is the key. (In France, rock is called "beat.") Harmonic, melodic or verbal sophistication wouldn't sell without that simple-minded physical pulse on the bottom. One. One. One. One. As long as that's there, anything else goes. Put Bach, Stravinsky, John Coltrane or T. S. Eliot above it and millions listen. But with increasing sophistication, rock musicians are also getting more adventurous, more subjective and closer to that "borderline of unintelligible enigmas."

The repeated "one" is becoming four, five, seven or is even getting free of time. Drummers are playing more complicated breaks. Guitarists stretch further away from the melody and tonality. Electronic interludes are getting longer and further out. Pop music may even have given birth to a new medium: music produced solely for recording, as distinct from a live performance as a film is from a stage play. The Beatles' "Sergeant Pepper's Lonely Hearts Club Band" was not the first recording to combine the studio with extended forms and a rock beat—"Pet Sounds" by the Beach Boys has that credit—but it is the most complete and successful. So far, anyway; others are following in droves.

James William Guercio manages, produces, conducts and arranges for a schlock-rock group called the Buckinghams. Under his direction they are getting less schlock.[2] But their music is really his, excluding the hits ("Kind of a Drag," "Susan"), which are banal enough to support it. Guercio was born in Chicago twenty-two years ago. He went to DePauw University "hoping to be the leading composer of the 20th century. I always considered that was my function. But when I got into college I discovered the vocabulary wasn't there anymore. There's nothing wrong with rules—it's just a question of where they take you. When Kennedy was killed, I split from school, long hair and all. I'd been playing string

[2] Schlock is pretentious work of obviously inferior quality.

bass with the symphony—all my background was legitimate. Completely legitimate, man. I went through college teaching guitar rather than playing pop gigs. I knew nothing about pop music until I left school and went on the road with Dick Clark, backing up almost every act in show business on bass guitar.

> For awhile, I thought a lot about jazz, trying to give it some kind of commercial meaning. Sure there's Getz and Miles Davis and all the mechanicals who sell a lot of albums. But there's no center to it, no criteria.
> Let's see . . . I'm trying to give you a motive—to tell you why I'm involved, why I ended up having to be a manager and a producer. These are exciting times. I see pop music as one of the most constructive forces in our civilization. I think it was Sartre who said that movies would become an art form as soon as the equipment and facilities to make them became available to everybody, as available as pencil and paper. That's what is happening with pop music and that's why I'm involved with it—despite the rotten nature of the business.

As a specific instrument, the bass guitar has probably undergone the greatest evolution, a symptom of the substantial evolution of rock itself. First marketed by the Fender Corporation in the fifties, it was a bastard instrument guitar or bass players switched to occasionally. This isn't so easy anymore and with the top groups it is becoming completely impossible. Too much technique is required.

The breaking up of the strict, rhythmic bass line began at Motown in Detroit and Stax/Volt in Memphis when they started mixing the bass at a higher level. It became more exposed and soon more elaborate—horizontal and free. Paul McCartney synthesized it. (The Beatles are milestones in so many ways.) Guerico says: "I learned bass from Beatles' albums. McCartney was the first to really get the linear bass line in rock together. McCartney did so much; I can't tell you how much he did to change the instrument."

Bob Mosely is recognized as one of the strongest bass guitar players around. He is twenty-five, grew up around California beaches, wears beads and his blonde hair is long. Now he plays with a group called Moby Grape. I told him how I felt about the simple beat being essential, and that the loosening of the bass line, while interesting, could mean a serious loss of audience. He doesn't agree; "Have you seen the new dancing? It's coming right along with the music; getting to be really free-form or—what do you call it—interpretive dancing. As an individual you can pick what you want to follow. You can dance to the bass line, a guitar line, a drum figure or all of them together. Your hands can become the guitar, your head the bass, your feet the drums and so on. As the music gets better and more complicated, the dancing will too."

Since talking to Mosely and Guercio, I've spent a lot of time listening to rock records—particularly the Beatles—with the bass turned way up. There's a lot there, a lot I never heard before, even on records with which I'm familiar. On the slow portion of "A Day in the Life," (Sergeant Pepper) for example, McCartney's line moves tastefully, nothing spectacular but going to unexpected places with imagination. It has a lot to do with the general feeling of the piece, although he doesn't club you with it—it is a secondary line after all. In general, McCartney isn't particularly adventurous either harmonically or rhythmically, but his sound is smooth, the level is just right, the musical material perfect for the setting. I consider him artistic.

Since "Sergeant Pepper" was released last spring, other groups have been getting away with electronic collages, ambitious, sometimes pompous, instrumentation and extended forms. Bass-guitar players have taken to flying all over their Fenders, filling every available hole and some that aren't there. Excess is not unknown in rock. But the musicianship is certainly improving and the best are getting better. Rock is searching, uneven and often juvenile. But it is not stagnant and it is rarely dull.

Last week the top three albums on *Billboard* magazine's chart were "Magical Mystery Tour" by the Beatles, The Stones', "Their Satanic Majesties Request," and Bob Dylan's "John Wesley Harding." Any form, (dare I say "art" form?) in which the best is also the most popular has got to be healthy.

Where will it all lead? Probably toward a less physical music, to the concert hall, to the "borderline of unintelligible enigmas." Super stars no longer play their music for dancing and it is, in fact, fast getting less danceable. Even second echelon groups like Moby Grape mostly play concerts. No doubt, we will soon hear a concerto for rock band and symphony orchestra. And then "pop" music may no longer be popular.

POINTS TO CONSIDER

Michael Zwerin: Fancy Rock

1. What kind of music is meant by the term "serious music"? What does the article indicate is happening to serious music and especially to the composition of serious music?

2. What reason does Zwerin give for his belief that "new music which cannot excite the enthusiastic response of the lay listener has no claim to his indulgence"? What does the author mean by a "lay listener"? Is this necessarily a person who knows nothing about music?

3. How has jazz suffered from the same problems as "serious" music?

4. What does the author consider the key to all kinds of rock? What is folk rock? Raga rock? Baroque or Bach rock? What examples of these do you know?

5. What new medium has pop music helped to create?

6. According to the article, what direction is popular dancing taking?

7. Where does the author feel rock music is heading? What evidence is there to support this idea? Do you notice it heading this way?

Rock For Sale

Michael Lydon

Ramparts, June 1969

> Businessmen they drink my wine
> Plowmen dig my earth
> None of them along the line
> Know what any of it is worth
>
> BOB DYLAN, "All Along the Watchtower"*

In 1956, when rock and roll was just about a year old, Frankie Lymon, lead singer of Frankie Lymon and the Teenagers, wrote and recorded a song called "Why Do Fools Fall in Love?" It was an immediate million-selling hit and has since become a rock classic, a true golden oldie of the sweet-voiced harmonizing genre. The group followed it up with other hits, starred in a movie, appeared on the Ed Sullivan Show, toured the country with Bill Haley and the Comets, and did a tour of Europe. Frankie, a black kid from Harlem, was then thirteen years old. Last year, at twenty-six, he died of an overdose of heroin.

Despite the massive publicity accorded to rock in the past several years, Frankie's death received little attention. It got a bit more publicity than the death in a federal prison of Little Willie John, the author of "Fever," another classic, but nothing compared to that lavished on the breakup of the Cream or on Janis Joplin's split with Big Brother and the Holding Company. Nor did many connect it with the complete musical stagnation of the Doors, a group which in 1967 seemed brilliantly promising, or to the dissolution of dozens of other groups who a year or two ago were not only making beautiful music but seemed to be the vanguard of a promising "youth cultural revolution."

In fact these events are all connected, and their common denominator is hard cash. Since that wildly exciting spring of 1967, the spring of *Sgt. Pepper's Lonely Hearts Club Band,* of be-ins and love-ins and flower-power, of the discovery of psychedelia, hippies and "doing your thing"—to all of which "New Rock," as it then began to be called, was inextricably bound—one basic fact has been consistently ignored: rock is a product created, distributed and controlled for the profit of American (and international) business. "The record companies sell rock and roll records like they sell refrigerators," says Paul Kantner of the Jefferson Airplane. "They don't care about the people who make rock or what they're all about as human beings any more than they care about the people who make refrigerators."

Recently, the promoters of a sleazy Southern California enterprise known as "Teen Fair" changed its name to "Teen Expo." The purpose of the operation remains the same: to sell trash to adolescents while impressing them with the joys of consumerism. But nine years into the '60s, the backers decided that their '50s image of nice-kid teenagerism had to go. In its place, they have installed "New Rock" (with its constant companion, schlock psychedelia) as the working image of the "all new!" Teen Expo.

By the time the word gets down to the avaricious cretins[1] who run teen fairs, everybody has the message: rock and roll sells. It doesn't make money just for the entertainment industry—the record companies, radio stations, TV networks, stereo and musical instrument manufacturers, etc.—but for law firms, clothing manufacturers, the mass media, soft drink companies and car dealers (the new Opel will "light your fire!"). Rock is the surest way to the hearts and wallets of millions of Americans between eight and thirty-five—the richest, most extravagant children in the history of the world.

From the start, rock has been commercial in its very essence. An American creation on the level of the hamburger or the billboard, it was never an art form that just happened to make money, nor a commercial undertaking that sometimes became art. Its art was synonymous with its business. The movies are perhaps closest to rock in their aesthetic involvement with the demands of profitability, but even they once had an arty tradition which scorned the pleasing of the masses.

Yet paradoxically it was the unabashed commerciality of rock which gave rise to the hope that it would be a "revolutionary" cultural form of expression. For one thing, the companies that produce it and reap its profits have never understood it. Ford executives drive their company's cars but Sir Joseph Lockwood, chairman of EMI, the record company which, until Apple, released the Beatles' records, has always admitted that he doesn't like their music. The small companies like Sun and Chess Records which first discovered the early stars like Elvis Presley and Chuck Berry were run by middle-class whites who knew that kids and blacks liked this weird music, but they didn't know or really care why. As long as the music didn't offend the businessmen's sensibilities too much—they never allowed outright obscenity—and as long as it sold, they didn't care what it said. So within the commercial framework, rock has always had a certain freedom.

Moreover, rock's slavish devotion to commerciality gave it powerful aesthetic advantages. People had to like it for it to sell, so rock had to get to the things that the audience really cared about. Not only did it create a ritualized world of dances, slang, "the charts," fan magazines and "your favorite DJ coming your way" on the car radio, but it defined, reflected and glorified the listener's ordinary

[1] Avaricious cretins are greedy and mentally retarded.

world. Rock fans can date their entire lives by rock; hearing a "golden oldie" can instantaneously evoke the whole flavor and detail of a summer or a romance.

When in 1963–64, the Pop Art movement said there was beauty in what had been thought to be the crass excreta[2] of the Eisenhower Age, when the Beatles proved that shameless reveling in money could be a stone groove, and when the wistful puritanism of the protest-folk music movement came to a dead end, rock and roll, with all its unabashed carnality and worldliness, seemed a beautiful trip. Rock, the background music of growing up, was discovered as the common language of a generation. New Rock musicians could not only make the music, they could even make an aesthetic and social point by the very choice of rock as their medium.

That rock was commercial seemed only a benefit. It ensured wide distribution, the hope of a good and possibly grandiose living style, and the honesty of admitting that, yes, we are the children of affluence: don't deny it, man, dig it. As music, rock had an undeniably liberating effect; driving and sensual, it implicitly and explicitly presented an alternative to bourgeois insipidity.[3] The freedom granted to rock by society seemed sufficient to allow its adherents to express their energies without inhibition. Rock pleasure had no pain attached; the outrageousness of Elvis' gold lamé suits and John Lennon's wildly painted Rolls Royce was a gas, a big joke on adult society. Rock was a way to beat the system, to gull grown-ups into paying you while you made faces behind their backs.

Sad but true, however, the grown-ups are having the last laugh. Rock and roll is a lovely playground, and within it kids have more power than they have anywhere else in society, but the playground's walls are carefully maintained and guarded by the corporate elite that set it up in the first place. While the White Panthers talk of "total assault upon the culture by any means necessary, including rock and roll, dope and fucking in the streets," Billboard, the music trade paper, announces with pride that in 1968 the record industry became a billion-dollar business.

> Then it's time to go downtown
> Where the agent man won't let you down
> Sell your soul to the company
> Who are waiting there
> To sell plasticware
> And in a week or two
> If you make the charts
> The girls will tear you apart.

ROGER MCGUINN AND CHRIS HILLMAN,
"So You Want to be a Rock 'n' Roll Star"*

*Copyright © Tickson Music Co.

[2] Crass excreta, in one plain word, is crap.

[3] Bourgeois insipidity is the dullness of the great middle class, now commonly known as the silent majority.

Bob Dylan has described with a fiendish accuracy the pain of growing up in America, and millions have responded passionately to his vision. His song, "Maggie's Farm," contains the lines, "He gives me a nickel, he gives me a dime, he asks me with a grin if I'm having a good time, and he fines me every time I slam the door, oh, I ain't gonna work on Maggie's farm no more." But along with Walter Cronkite and the New York Yankees, Dylan works for one of Maggie's biggest farms, the Columbia Broadcasting System.

Mick Jagger, another adept and vitriolic[4] social critic, used rock to sneer at "the under assistant west coast promotion man" in his seersucker suit; but London Records used this "necessary talent for every rock and roll band" to sell that particular Rolling Stones record and all their other products. For all its liberating potential, rock is doomed to a bitter impotence by its ultimate subservience to those whom it attacks.

In fact, rock, rather than being an example of how freedom can be achieved within the capitalist structure, is an example of how capitalism can, almost without a conscious effort, deceive those whom it oppresses. Rather than being liberated heroes, rock and roll stars are captives on a leash, and their plight is but a metaphor for that of all young people and black people in America. All the talk of "rock revolution," talk that is assiduously cultivated by the rock industry, is an attempt to disguise that plight.

Despite the aura of wealth that has always surrounded the rock and roll star, and which for fans justified the high prices of records and concerts, very few stars really make much money—and for all but the stars and their backup musicians, rock is just another low-paying, insecure and very hard job. Legend says that wild spending sprees, drugs and women account for the missing loot; what legend does not say is that most artists are paid very little for their work. The artist may receive a record royalty of two and one-half per cent, but the company often levies charges for studio time, promotion and advertising. It is not uncommon for the maker of a hit record to end up in debt to the company.

Not surprisingly, it is the black artists who suffer most. In his brilliant book, *Urban Blues,* Charles Keil describes in detail how the blues artist is at the mercy of the recording company. It is virtually impossible, he states, for an unknown artist to get an honest contract, but even an "honest" contract is only an inexpensive way for a company to own an artist body and soul.

A star's wealth may be not only nonexistent, but actually a fraud, carefully perpetuated by the record company. Blues singer Bobby Bland's "clothes, limousine, valet, and plentiful pocket money," says Keil, "are image bolsterers from Duke Records (or perhaps a continual 'advance on royalties' that keeps him tied to the company) rather than real earnings." And even cash exploitation is not enough; Chess Records last year forced Muddy Waters to play his classic blues with a "psychedelic" band and called the humiliating record *Electric Mud.*

[4] Vitriolic means as biting as acid.

Until recently, only a few stars made any real money from rock; their secret was managers shrewd to the point of unscrupulousness, who kept them under tight control. Colonel Parker molded the sexual country boy Elvis into a smooth ballad singer; Brian Epstein took four scruffy Liverpool rockers and transformed them into neatly tousled boys-next-door. "We were worried that friends might think we had sold out," John Lennon said recently, "which in a way we had."

The musicians of New Rock—most of them white, educated and middle-class—are spared much of what their black and lower-class counterparts have suffered. One of the much touted "revolutions" New Rock has brought, in fact, has been a drastic increase of the power of the artist vis-à-vis[5] the record company. Contracts for New Rock bands regularly include almost complete artistic control, royalties as high as ten per cent, huge cash advances, free studio time, guaranteed amounts of company-bought promotion, and in some instances control over advertising design and placement in the media.

But such bargaining is at best a futile reformism which never challenges the essential power relationship that has contaminated rock since its inception. Sales expansion still gives the companies ample profits, and they maintain all the control they really need (even the "revolutionary" group, the MC5, agreed to remove the word "motherfucker" from an album and to record "brothers and sisters" in its place). New Rock musicians lost the battle for real freedom at the very moment they signed their contracts (whatever the clauses) and entered the big-time commercial sphere.

The Doors are a prime example. Like hundreds of New Rock musicians, the four Doors are intelligent people who in the early- and mid-'60s dropped out into the emerging drug and hip underground. In endless rehearsals and on stage in Sunset Strip rock clubs, they developed a distinctively eerie and stringent sound. The band laid down a dynamo drive behind dramatically handsome lead singer Jim Morrison, who, dressed in black leather and writhing with anguish, screamed demonic invitations to sensual madness. "Break on through," was the message, "yeah, break on, break on through to the other side!"

It was great rock and roll, and by June 1967, when their "Light My Fire" was a number-one hit, it had become very successful rock. More hits followed and the Doors became the first New Rock group to garner a huge following among the young teens and pre-teens who were traditionally the mass rock audience. Jim Morrison became rock's number-one sex idol and the teenie-boppers' delight. The group played bigger and bigger halls—the Hollywood Bowl, the garish Forum in Los Angeles and finally Madison Square Garden last winter in a concert that netted the group $52,000 for one night's work.

But the hit "Light My Fire" was a chopped-up version of the original album track, and after that castration of their art for immediate mass appeal (a castration encouraged by their "hip" company, Elektra Records), the Doors died

[5] Vis-à-vis here means in relation to.

musically. Later albums were pale imitations of the first; trying desperately to re-capture the impact of their eary days, they played louder and Morrison lost all subtlety: at a recent Miami concert he had to display his penis to make his point.

Exhausted by touring and recording demands, the Doors now seldom play or even spend much casual time together. Their latest single hit the depths; Cashbox magazine, in its profit-trained wisdom said, "The team's impact is newly channeled for even more than average young teen impact." "Maybe pretty soon we'll split, just go away to an island somewhere," Morrison said recently, fatigue and frustration in his voice, "get away by ourselves and start creating again."

But the Doors have made money, enough to be up-tight about it. "When I told them about this interview," said their manager, Bill Siddons, sitting in the office of the full-time accountant who manages the group's investments (mostly land and oil), "they said, 'Don't tell him how much we make.'" But Siddons, a person-able young man, did his best to defend them. The Doors, he said, could make a lot more money if they toured more often and took less care in preparing each hall they play in for the best possible lighting and sound; none of the Doors lives lavishly, and the group has plans for a foundation to give money to artists and students ("It'll help our tax picture, too"). But, he said, "You get started in rock and you get locked into the cycle of success. It's funny, the group out there on stage preaching a revolutionary message, but to get the message to people, you gotta do it the establishment way. And you know everybody acquires a taste for comfortable living."

> The price you paid
> For your riches and fame
> Was it a strange game
> You're a little insane
> All the money that came
> And the public acclaim—
> Don't forget who you are
> You're a rock 'n' roll star

"So You Want to be a Rock 'n' Roll Star"*

Variations on the Doors' story are everywhere. The Cream started out in 1966 as a brilliant and influential blues-rock trio and ended, after two solid years of touring, with lead guitarist Eric Clapton on the edge of a nervous breakdown. After months of bitter fighting, Big Brother and the Holding Company split up, as did Country Joe and the Fish (who have since reorganized, with several re-placements from Big Brother). The Steve Miller Band and the Quicksilver Mes-senger Service were given a total of $100,000 by Capitol Records; within a year neither one existed in its original form and the money had somehow disappeared.

Groups that manage to stay together are caught in endless conflicts about

*Copyright © Tickson Music Co.

how to make enough money to support their art and have it heard without getting entangled in the "success cycle." The Grateful Dead, who were house and bus minstrels for Ken Kesey's acid-magical crew and who have always been deeply involved in trying to create a real hip community, have been so uncommercial as to frustrate their attempts to spread the word of their joyful vision.

"The trouble is that the Grateful Dead is a more 'heard of' band than a 'heard' band," says manager Rock Scully, "and we want people to hear us. But we won't do what the system says—make single hits, take big gigs, do the success number. The summer of '67, when all the other groups were making it, we were playing free in the park, man, trying to cool the Haight-Ashbury. So we've never had enough bread to get beyond week-to-week survival, and now we're about $50,000 in debt. We won't play bad music for the bread because we decided a long time ago that money wasn't a high enough value to sacrifice anything for. But that means that not nearly enough people have heard our music."

The Jefferson Airplane have managed to take a middle route. A few early hits, a year of heavy touring (150 dates in 1967), a series of commercials for White Levis, and the hard-nosed management of entrepreneur Bill Graham gave them a solid money-making popular base. A year ago they left Graham's management, stopped touring almost entirely, bought a huge mansion in San Francisco and devoted their time to making records (all of them excellent), giving parties, and buying expensive toys like cars and color TV's. They've gone through enormous amounts of money and are now $30,000 in debt. But they're perfectly willing to go out and play a few jobs if the creditors start to press them. They resolve the commercial question by attempting not to care about it. "What I care about," says Paul Kantner, "is what I'm doing at the time. . . ."

But the Airplane also profess political radicalism, and, says Kantner, "The revolution is already happening, man. All those kids dropping out, turning on— they add up." Singer Grace Slick appeared in blackface on the Smothers Brothers show and gave the Black Panther salute; in a front window of their mansion is a sign that reads, "Eldridge Cleaver Welcome Here." But Kantner said he hadn't really thought about what that meant: would he really take Cleaver in and protect him against police attack, a very likely necessity should Cleaver accept the welcome? "I don't know, man. I'd have to wait until that happened."

Cleaver would be well-advised not to choose the Airplane's mansion for his refuge. For Kantner's mushy politics—sort of a turned-on liberalism that thinks the Panthers are "groovy" but doesn't like to come to terms with the nasty American reality—are the politics of the much touted "rock revolution." They add up to a hazy belief in the power of art to change the world, presuming that the place for the revolution to begin and end is inside individual heads. The Beatles said it nicely in "Revolution": "You say that it's the institution, we-ll, you know, you better free your mind instead."

Jac Holzman, president of Elektra Records, said it in businessman's prose: "I want to make it clear," he said, "that Elektra is not the tool of anyone's revolution. We feel that the 'revolution' will be won by poetics and not by politics—that poetics will change the structure of the world. It's reached the kids and is getting to them at the best possible level."

There is no secret boardroom conspiracy to divert antisocial youthful energy into rock and thus render it harmless while making a profit for the society it is rebelling against, but the corporate system has acted in that direction with a uniformity which a conspiracy probably could not have provided. And the aware capitalists are worried about their ability to control where kids are going: "There is something a bit spooky, from a business point of view," a Fortune issue on youth said recently, ". . . in youth's widespread rejection of middle-class life-styles ('Cheap is in'). . . . If it . . . becomes a dominant orientation, will these children of affluence grow up to be consumers on quite the economy moving scale as their parents?"

So the kids are talking revolution and smoking dope? Well, so are the companies, in massive advertising campaigns that co-opt the language of revolution so thoroughly that you'd think they were on the streets themselves. "The Man can't bust *our* music," read one Columbia ad; another urged (with a picture of a diverse group of kids apparently turning on): "Know who your friends are. And look and see and touch and be together. Then listen. *We* do." (Italics mine.)

More insidious than the ads themselves is the fact that ad money from the record companies is one of the main supports of the underground press. And the companies don't mind supporting these "revolutionary" sheets; the failure of Hearst's Eye magazine after a year showed that the establishment itself could not create new media to reach the kids, so squeamish is it about advocating revolution, drugs and sexual liberation. But it is glad to support the media the kids create themselves, and thereby, just as it did with rock, ultimately defang it.

The ramifications of control finally came full circle when Rolling Stone, the leading national rock newspaper, which began 18 months ago on a shoestring, had enough money in the bank to afford a $7000 ad on the back page of the New York Times. Not only was this "hip rock" publication self-consciously taking its place among the communication giants ("NBC was the day before us and Look the day after," said the twenty-two-year-old editor), but the ad's copy made clear the paper's exploitive aim: "If you are a corporate executive trying to understand what is happening to youth today, you cannot afford to be without *Rolling Stone.* If you are a student, a professor, a parent, this is your life because you already know that rock and roll is more than just music; it is the energy center of the new culture and youth revolution." Such a neat reversal of the corporate-to-kids lie into a kids-to-corporate lie is only possible when the kids so believe the lie they have been fed that they want to pass it on.

But rock and roll musicians are in the end artists and entertainers, and were it not for all the talk of the "rock revolution," one would not be led to expect a clear political vision from them. The bitterest irony is that the "rock revolution" hype has come close to fatally limiting the revolutionary potential that rock does contain. So effective has the rock industry been in encouraging the spirit of optimistic youth take-over that rock's truly hard political edge, its constant exploration of the varieties of youthful frustration, has been ignored and softened. Rock musicians, like their followers, have always been torn between the obvious pleasures that America held out and the price paid for them. Rock and roll is not revolutionary music because it has never gotten beyond articulation of this paradox. At best it has offered the defiance of withdrawal; its violence never amounted to more than a cry of, "Don't bother me."

"Leave me alone; anyway, I'm almost grown"; "Don't step on my blue suede shoes"; "There ain't no cure for the summertime blues"; "I can't get no satisfaction": the rock refrains that express despair could be strung out forever. But at least rock has offered an honest appraisal of where its makers and listeners are at, and that radical, if bitterly defeatist, honesty is a touchstone, a starting point. If the companies, as representatives of the corporate structure, can convince the rock world that their revolution is won or almost won, that the walls of the playground are crumbling, not only will the constituents of rock seal their fate by that fatal self-deception, but their music, one of the few things they actually do have going for them, will have been successfully corrupted and truly emasculated.

POINTS TO CONSIDER

Michael Lydon: Rock for Sale

1. What does the author mean when he says, "From the start, rock has been commercial in its very essence"? Is this different from other popular arts?

2. How is rock "background music for growing up"? Do popular songs tend to evoke memories and past moods more than movies, popular fiction, and other popular arts? Explain.

3. In what sense did rock and roll become revolutionary, antisquare, and antiestablishment? How did its commerciality support the "revolution"? Why does Lydon feel this revolution is doomed to failure?

4. What does Lydon say about the apparent wealth of most rock stars? Has the situation improved? If so, how? How is it basically the same?

5. What happened to The Doors? Is theirs a typical case?

6. What is the rock revolution? Do you think art has the power to change society? Explain.

7. How are the record companies connected with the underground press? What does the author suggest will happen as a result of this relationship?

8. Do you feel that the recent deaths of Jimi Hendrix and Janis Joplin support Lydon's ideas about being a rock star? If so, how?

9. What sort of magazine is *Ramparts,* the publication in which this article first appeared? How does the nature of the magazine tie in with the general political attitude of this article?

"His last request is 'Honeysuckle Rose,' by Fats Waller."

Ideas for Investigation, Discussion, and Writing

Popular Music

1. What are some of the major varieties of popular music today? To what different kinds of listeners do they appeal? Which varieties seem to have the widest appeal and which the most limited? Why?

2. What contributions have the following sources made to our current popular music:

   a. baroque and classical music
   b. Spanish and Portugese dance music
   c. African music
   d. Oriental music
   e. folk music and ballads from the United States and other countries
   f. U.S. jazz and blues
   g. U.S. popular music of the 1920s–1950s
   h. electronics and computers
   i. psychedelic and "drug" art

   Can you think of other influences? How do you account for this synthesis of such a variety of sources?

3. How have the lyrics of popular songs changed significantly since the 1940s and the early 1950s? What influences do you think have helped to bring about this change? What relationship do you see between this change and the steady growth of interest in poetry by young people since 1955?

4. How have the styles in rock music changed from the mid-1950s (Bill Haley and early Elvis Presley) to the rock music of today? How has the music of the Beatles changed from "I Want to Hold Your Hand" to "A Day in the Life" or "Revolution #9"? How has the public taste changed during this time?

5. How has the instrumentation of popular music changed in the past fifteen or twenty years to suit the changing nature of the music? What once popular instruments are seldom used now, and what different and new instruments have become popular? What do you make of the fact that much of today's popular music is affected in some way by electronics?

6. Why do you think that much of today's popular music is meant to be heard very loud? What is the function or importance of this loudness? Is this a new phenomenon in popular music?

7. To what extent have musical shows lagged behind or kept pace with the trends in popular music? Compare Broadway and film musicals to "off-Broadway" musicals and try to determine what accounts for the differences between them.

8. How has popular music in the past fifteen or twenty years become increasingly significant as a social force or influence? What changes in our culture does this development reveal?

PART EIGHT

PUBLIC EDUCATION

The subject of public education may seem, at first, inappropriate to the study of mass media and the popular arts. But if we apply our definition of mass media —the tools, instruments, or materials which allow the sender of information to contact large numbers of receivers simultaneously—to public education, we see that it fits. Every day, the public schools in our country—kindergarten through high school—inform millions of young people at the same time, and inform them of practically the same things. Like the other mass media, our system of public education reflects the values and actions of our society while it actively influences them. Like the other mass media, our system of public education sometimes makes it difficult for the receivers of information to communicate with the senders; but, fortunately, increasing numbers of schools are currently trying to correct this weakness.

Public education has long used the mass medium of print to record and transmit information. Now it is using many more different media—photography, motion pictures, sound and video tapes, television, and others—to do these jobs more effectively and interestingly. As more schools become increasingly aware of the effects that the many mass media have upon our lives, both as technology and as conveyors and shapers of the popular arts, they devote increasingly more time and attention to studying them.

The Mass Media in Education

The Challenge of Quality in Education, 1968

. . . I am fully aware that anyone who attempts to apply to education certain concepts from business and industry is automatically suspect.

He is as wide open to criticism as the alleged teacher here in the Detroit area who placed an ad in one of the local newspapers. The ad read: "If you are not satisfied with your child's progress in school, why not have *he* or *she* tutored by an experienced teacher."

Critics are quick to claim that the fellow who tries to translate education into dollars-and-cents terms really wants to cheapen it. They take the position that while automation in office and factory may be beneficial, automation in the classroom simply will not work.

They seem to forget that the biggest forward surge in the history of education was brought about by automation—in the form of the printing press. Then, for the first time, outstandingly gifted teachers were able to set down their ideas in books that spread their wisdom and influence far beyond the narrow reach of their personal contacts. It is well to remember that the book is one of the most important products of automation in the history of man.

The fact is that education has now become our biggest business. It has an annual budget of $20 billion, and more employees and a larger "plant" than either the steel or auto industry.

In industry, over the past half century, output per man-hour has shown a steady increase. This increase has been due basically to our skill in working out constantly better methods, and providing more and better tools to back up each worker.

Experience suggests that we can multiply the effectiveness of the good teacher with improved methods and appropriate tools, just as we have multiplied the effectiveness of the factory worker, the office worker—everybody right up to and including top management. In fact, just as the printing press did.

There are now available a wide variety of new tools and techniques for improving the quality of our educational system. Foremost among them, of course, is television.

Closed-circuit installations are extending the influence of talented teachers from one to several classrooms.

The noncommercial educational stations are carrying their lessons and lectures into the home, as well as the classroom, to a potential listening audience 50 per cent larger than the nation's total school enrollment.

The commercial stations and networks are offering an ever increasing fare of educational and cultural programs to entire regions, and, in the case of NBC's *Continental Classroom,* to the whole nation. Incidentally, *Continental Classroom's* course in Modern Chemistry points up sharply the great value of color television in education. Those early risers among you, who have seen Dr. John Baxter's laboratory demonstrations, can appreciate color TV's amazing capacity for enlivening educational presentations.

I envisage the day when all the nation's schools will be linked in one comprehensive educational television network. Such a network, far from imposing uniformity on local curricula, could help to provide richness and variety.

As interest in educational television grows, TV-set manufacturers are working hard to improve the style and utility of their products for the classroom. For example, RCA is displaying . . . a new television receiver designed specifically for classroom use. This model . . . features greater picture brightness, higher audio levels, precision tuning, ability to be locked, greater mobility, and a special stand that can raise the set to a height of six feet.

This new model was designed on the basis of suggestions offered by educators and educational broadcasters themselves. . . .

Great as its potential is, however, television is not the only new tool available to improve educational quality.

The school of tomorrow will have electronic teaching machines that will free the instructor from routine tasks and give him more time for personal counseling. The teacher's desk will be equipped with a tiny electronic scanning device linked with the library and the records office so that references can be checked quickly. A small-size electronic computer will correct many types of examinations, process student records, survey performance, and determine areas of difficulty.

Magnetic tape, which is even now finding use in the schools as well as in your own educational stations, will extend its usefulness in the years ahead. In fact, schools might well start on a program of automation today with a relatively inexpensive magnetic tape sound system, and build up from there.

Now under development at the RCA Laboratories is a magnetic tape player capable of reproducing pictures as well as sound. It works through a standard television receiver.

This video-tape player will eventually be a natural complement to a school television system. It will permit the flexible use of a library of pre-recorded programs.

By comparison with present professional video-tape recorders used in television stations, the new apparatus will be low in cost. It may be set up to supply a pre-recorded program to one classroom, a group of classrooms, an entire school, or a whole school system.

When these exciting new educational tools are in general use throughout our schools and colleges, their effect on quality in education can be tremendous. Just consider the advantages of closed-circuit television alone.

1. It can help bring about a higher level of instruction. It can extend the great influence of the best teachers far beyond the confines of their own class-rooms, and give them a dramatic medium for projecting their ideas. As one student in Hagerstown, Maryland, put it: "In class, the teacher talks to *us*. On television, she talks to *me*."

Closed-circuit television enables schools to call upon men of specialized talents for occasional lectures. By drawing on a central video-tape library, the closed-circuit system could present lectures by the greatest minds of our times. By linking up with commercial and educational stations, it could take students to the missile range at Cape Canaveral or inside the nuclear submarine *Nautilus,* to the halls of Congress or the Chamber of the Supreme Court.

2. Closed-circuit television can help raise the level of instructors. The big need is to relieve the teacher of all repetitive tasks through automation and give him more time for working with individual students.

Closed-circuit TV can greatly ease the burden on teachers by giving each one a chance to do the thing he is best suited for. One teacher may be best suited for lecturing to a group of several thousand students simultaneously. Another may be able to do an outstanding job of conducting a follow-up classroom session with a handful of students. Through the more effective use of teaching talent, television can make higher salaries a reality throughout the teaching profession.

With many schools and colleges participating in a program and sharing the cost, the salary of a particularly gifted television teacher might well be in the six-figure realm of the highest paid businessmen or other professionals. The entire salary scale could be raised, at lower cost per student. With higher salaries would come increased stature for the teacher in his own community. These factors would, in turn, keep able men and women in the teaching ranks, and attract new teachers of the highest caliber.

Since our nationwide requirements for teachers can never be met by present methods, television certainly poses no problem of unemployment for teachers.

3. Closed-circuit TV can make it possible for the teacher to give greater attention to the individual student. Once the classroom instructor has been freed from many of the chores he now performs, he will be able to devote far more time to personal counseling. Indeed, this opportunity for individualized instruction is one of the great advantages of television, magnetic tape, and other electronic aids to education.

They permit the teacher to reach the student on a highly personal basis. They enable each student, in effect, to set his own pace. The fast-learner in a particular subject is challenged to work up to his full capacity. The average-learner is encouraged to develop what gift he possesses. The slow-learner is encouraged to develop what gift he possesses. The slow-learner is assured of the kind of attention that will prevent his falling hopelessly behind.

A student might be in the third grade in spelling, the second grade in arithmetic, and the fourth grade in history. We do not have equal abilities.

Every pupil has potential talent of some kind, and his value in our democratic society lies in the extent to which he is helped to use his special talent for the common good.

Former President James A. Garfield once said: "A pine bench, with Mark Hopkins at one end of it and me at the other, is a good enough college for me!"

This one-to-one teacher-student ratio has become impossible under modern classroom conditions. But with television and other electronic devices, teachers can have both the time and the means to reach the pupil once more on a person-to-person basis.

POINTS TO CONSIDER

John L. Burns: The Mass Media in Education

1. What parallels does Burns draw between industry and education? Do you feel that these parallels are valid?

2. What electronic media are now being employed in education, and what are the particular benefits which they can provide?

3. What are some of the special educational advantages of closed-circuit television?

4. What does Burns imply is the particular responsibility of education in a democratic society? Do you feel that most public schools are meeting this responsibility?

Drawing by D. Reilly. © 1970, *The New Yorker Magazine, Inc.*

Immediate Experience versus a College Education

Eric Sevareid

Not So Wild a Dream, 1946

If a young man goes directly from secondary school to the university, and completes the study of his profession in theory and principle before entering his first office, everything is quite different. The faces, the titles, the very arrangement of the desks and departments he sees as a functional pattern. He has his mind on the end product of the concern; he knows how and why his product came about in modern society; he knows its present status in terms of history, and he no doubt understands the relationship of himself and his work to the times in which he lives. It must be a great advantage to begin that way, but it also means missing a brief period of complete enchantment. The old Minneapolis *Journal,* no longer extant, was an imposing and venerable institution in that northwest country, identified with the permanent structures of the landscape— the original buildings of Fort Snelling, the first dam on the upper Mississippi, the first roadbed laid by Jim Hill, the Empire Builder. It spoke with authority in the land, if not with wisdom, and it was an interconnecting cog in the social machinery of a widely scattered civilization. I was unaware that its directors were in, hand and glove, with the potentates of railroad, timber, and milling who for a very long time dictated, as if by kingly right, the political and economic affairs of this civilization. I was unaware that the men who wrote its pages *were* aware, bitterly so, of the paper's true function. To me at eighteen it was that most remarkable, most fascinating of all human institutions, a daily newspaper, peopled with those glamorous, incomparable men known as reporters and editors, actually there, alive, touchable, knowable. The ceremony of the "ghost walking" with the pay envelopes on Saturday afternoon was merely one of the more delightful moments of the week, a necessary bit of the engrossing ritual that preceded the ceremony of drinking beer down below at the "Greasy Spoon." The pay check of course was not really essential, these superhuman creatures being above anything so prosaic as the need for food, but was merely a kind of token and badge to signify that one Belonged. There was a positive sensual pleasure when one hurried from below-zero weather, so early it was scarcely light, into the warmth and smells of the city room where the telegraph editor was already waiting for the first yellow strips from the press association machines, into the warmer, noisier, greasier composing room upstairs where the limp, moist galley proofs of overset matter were piled and waiting for distribution below. The movement and noise built up with every hour, with the ordered cacophony of improvised symphony to the thundering finale by the great presses below the street, followed by the quiet aftermath of triumph when I would stagger into the city room with fifty fresh, pungent copies in my arms for the relaxing virtuosi who waited there, feet upon their instruments, gifted fingers lighting cigarettes.

This was my entry into the world of private enterprise in which most Americans pass their earthly existence. Surely, this was the best of all possible systems of life, where one simply chose the thing he most wanted to do, and, because he loved it, worked as hard as he could, and, because he worked hard, steadily rose from position to position, until he had "arrived," when the world would hold no more secrets or problems, and life gracefully leveled out on a plane of confidence, security, and happiness. I was convinced of the truth of this when after only six weeks as a copy runner I was made a reporter, with a desk of my own, admission to the Saturday night poker game around the copy desk, and fifteen dollars a week. Up to that time I had never made an enemy, never known anyone to feel that I was a threat to him, nor felt that anyone else was a threat to me. When I broke the news that I was to become a reporter, to a rewrite man I worshipped, I received the first shock and hurt and began to learn. I expected warm congratulations and perhaps admiring predictions of future greatness. Instead, the Godlike journalist looked at me coldly and said: "For Christ's sake. The bastards." It was some time before I realized that experienced reporters, family men who required more than fifteen dollars a week, were being rebuffed each day in their search for employment.

My one regular chore on the paper, the inescapable heritage of the newest and rawest cub, was to spend each Friday as "religious editor," which meant putting together a page of copy with a summed-up story of Sunday's events, followed by several columns of "church notices" in six-point type. It meant interviewing a few visiting clerics of distinction, who never turned down the request. One of these was Billy Sunday, the evangelist, then in his last days. In his case, no questions were needed. He bounded about the hotel room, now peering intently out the window with one foot on the sill, now grasping the dressing table firmly in both hands while lecturing his reflection in the mirror. I never opened my mouth after introducing myself and scarcely remembered a word of what he said. Suddenly he ceased talking and darted out of the room, whereupon "Ma" Sunday unhooked a half-dozen typewritten sheets from a loose-leaf folder and handed them to me. This was the interview, all prepared, his emphasis marked by capitalized words and phrases in red ink with many exclamation marks. When I first took over this task on the paper I mentioned it one day to a Protestant pastor I happened to know rather well. He clasped his hands together, cast a brief glance upwards, and said: "Thank God for that! I have been grieving over the lack of publicity for our little church." He gripped my shoulder in a brotherly manner and said: "I hope this will be the answer to my prayers." I was quickly to learn that of all the citizens who rang the newspaper or came to the lobby seeking publicity, the men of the church were the most demanding and insatiable. I was frequently embroiled in controversy with pastors who would demand why I had not run the photographs of themselves which they had just sent in, whereas

Pastor X had had *his* picture in the paper twice in the last three months. The rabbis were equally desirous, but generally more clever about it, while the important Catholic priests simply let their assistants handle the publicity question and rarely entered the negotiations in person. I learned that the newspaper was frightened of the preachers. The city desk could tell a vaudeville press agent to go to hell when his demands overreached the decent limit, but nobody ever spoke anything but soft words to the press agent of a church. I could see why nobody else wanted my task, but no doubt it was good training in basic diplomacy.

I was firmly convinced that a newspaper reporter "saw life" as did no one else in current society. (He sees no more of life than the iceman does, but he is compelled to note down and comment and thus acquires some habit of observation, if not reflection. That's all the difference there is.) I wanted to observe "human nature" and for some reason did not believe preachers exhibited any manifestations of human nature. So I seized any other kind of assignment anybody else was too lazy or too wise to want: interviews with the drinkers of canned heat who lived, and often died, in the caves and shacks along the riverbed, with movie stars of more majestic condescension than any bishop. Once I dressed as a waiter and served Katharine Hepburn her breakfast in bed after she had kept the reporters waiting in bitter cold for two hours at the station, then refused to see them. I have a vivid memory of knocking at apartment doors in the dead of night, to inform a young wife that her husband had just been killed in an accident or a police shooting, and did she have a photograph of him? Usually she turned white and ran to grab up the baby from its crib. These experiences left me limp and shaking. But somehow these wretched people—if they were poor, with poor people's belief that the newspapers were powerful things with unquestioned rights—would find a photograph, would, between sobs, answer my questions. It was a surprise to find that the rich did not react the same way. When I went to ask questions of the wife of a manufacturer who had killed a man in disgraceful circumstances, she waited until I had spoken, then coolly requested me to leave the premises before she called the police. I spent three weeks in police headquarters, in Washington Avenue saloons, in the parlors of innumerable citizens, trying to solve the celebrated local mystery of the missing baby, stolen from the bed of its fifteen-year-old "unwed mother" in the city hospital. I worked morning, noon, and night, uncovered various bits of evidence, and finally located a youthful suspect who the police were convinced was the kidnapper, but whom they were unable to convict. I had always had the normal citizen's respect for the police, but during this experience discovered to my surprise that we reporters were frequently hours and days ahead of them unraveling the mystery.

One became, at that age, aware of social structures but not of social forces. One knew that certain individuals represented certain levels of the structure, in the city and inside the office, but one was scarcely aware that these individuals themselves were pushed and pulled by invisible pressures of a class allegiance, in society and business. It took me a long time to understand that the publisher had far more in common with, far more loyalty to, the bankers or grain merchants with whom he lunched at the Minneapolis Club than to the editors and reporters who worked with him to produce the paper. I began work with an idealistic view of the newspaper as the mounted knight of society, pure in heart, its strength as the strength of ten, owing no favor, fearing no man. I did not know that, while many great organs had begun that way (a few retained their integrity) with rugged, incorruptible founders, they had been handed down to sons and grandsons who were less interested in the true social function of the institution than its money-making capacities which secured their position in the luxury class to which they, unlike their fathers and grandfathers, were born. You learned. You learned by listening to the servile voices of the women who wrote the society pages as they asked the great ladies of Lowry Hill to be so very kind as to give them the names of their reception guests. You learned by discovering that if you became involved in controversy with an important businessman about the handling of a given story, you were always wrong and the businessman was always right. You learned by finding that if a picture were published of a Negro, however distinguished, and one of the great ladies, who happened to be from Georgia, telephoned to protest that she was offended, profuse apologies would be offered the sensitive creature.

With this general discovery of the structure of community life came the simultaneous discovery that nearly all men, working in a large American concern, did their daily work under the tyranny of fear. It varied in intensity from man to man, from prosperity to depression, but it was always there. The reporters were afraid of the city editor, the assistant city editor was afraid of the city editor, and the city editor, worried about his job, was afraid of his assistant. All were afraid of the managing editor, who in turn was afraid of the publisher. None of them wanted to feel that way, few were really "after" another's position, but each understood the pressures on the other which might at any moment cause the latter in self-protection to bear down upon the former. I might have learned all this much earlier, as most boys do from their fathers, who come home at night and relate to their wives at dinner the latest move in their "office politics." But my father had been an independent operator most of his life, and even when he did join a large establishment his sense of personal dignity and honor forbade him to discuss his superiors or inferiors, even with his family. And so I had begun working life in the simple faith that one's rise or fall was a matter solely of one's own capacities.

There was a charming old man who lived like an office hermit in a musty room in the interior labyrinths of the *Journal.* He was a scholar of some distinction, in love with the history of the northwest country, and he wrote graceful essays and homilies for the Sunday edition. I was charmed by his style and occasionally would take my portable lunch and bottle of milk at noon to eat with him. I assumed that with his literary attainments he was an important and respected person in the establishment. Once I stayed longer than usual; we were both spellbound with his own fascinating account of a vanished village. He looked suddenly at his watch. He became extremely agitated, grabbed up his copy in trembling fingers, and said: "Excuse me, excuse me. The editors. They will be very rough with me. I am very late." His bent figure shuffled rapidly from the room. He had spent his life on that newspaper.

The financial editor worked at a desk directly behind my own. One night when I was working exceptionally late, he came in slightly unsteady from drinking. He emptied into a suitcase the contents of his locker, a few books, a batch of clippings, a pair of golf shoes. I asked in surprise if he was leaving. He said: "I've been on this paper eighteen years, son. I've just been fired by a guy I used to teach where to put commas." He staggered out, leaving me with a sick, hollow feeling in the pit of my stomach and a dark light dawning in my head. Innocence departed. Life, it seemed, was a relentless, never-ending battle; one never "arrived"; loyalty, achievement, could be forgotten in a moment; a single man's whim could ruin one. I began to take stock of the situation and discovered that the men who got to the top, no matter how long they stayed there, were nearly all men who had studied in universities, who knew something besides the routine of their own desks. It was fear as much as anything else that drove me to college, purely personal ambition as much as curiosity about the world I lived in and what had made it the way I found it to be.

 POINTS TO CONSIDER

Eric Sevareid: Immediate Experience versus a College Education

1. What advantages does Sevareid see in going to college before beginning a profession? What disadvantages does he point out? Can you think of other advantages and disadvantages?

2. What was Sevareid's initial conception of how and why one rose in his chosen profession? What incident forced him to alter that conception?

3. Why do you think "the men of the church" were so "insatiable" in their demands for publicity? Why do you think the newspaper was "frightened of the preachers"?

4. Does Sevareid believe a newspaper reporter "sees life" as no one else does? What advantage does he feel the newspaper reporter has in perceiving the world around him?

5. What do you think accounts for what Sevareid calls "poor people's belief that the newspapers were powerful things with unquestioned rights"? Why aren't the rich as likely to share this belief?

6. According to Sevareid, how do independent, crusading newspapers often become corrupted? Can you cite specific examples of this process?

7. What does Sevareid mean by a "tyranny of fear"? Judging from your own experience, would you say that Sevareid's description applies to most jobs today?

8. Why does Sevareid leave his job to go to college? What did he hope to gain from college? Does he seem to feel that this is the best reason to go to college? Explain.

The Student and Society

Jerry Farber

The Student as Nigger, 1969

The Student and Society: An Annotated Manifesto

School is where you let the dying society put its trip on you. Our schools may seem useful: to make children into doctors, sociologists, engineers—to discover things. But they're poisonous as well. They exploit and enslave students; they petrify society; they make democracy unlikely. And it's not *what* you're taught that does the harm but *how* you're taught. Our schools teach you by pushing you around, by stealing your will and your sense of power, by making timid square apathetic slaves out of you—authority addicts.

Schooling doesn't have to be this destructive. If it weren't compulsory, if schools were autonomous and were run by the people in them, then we could learn without being subdued and stupefied in the process. And, perhaps, we could regain control of our own society.

Students can change things if they want to because they have the power to say "no." When you go to school, you're doing society a favor. And when you say "no," you withhold much more than your attendance. You deny continuity to the dying society; you put the future on strike. Students can have the kind of school they want—or even something else entirely if they want—because there isn't going to be any school at all without them.

. . .

Note 3: "They Exploit and Enslave Students; They Petrify Society . . ."

Let me not be accused of ignoring "what's right with" our schools—to use the patriotic jargon. Schools are where you learn to read, write sort of, and do long division. Everyone knows about that. In college you learn about Pavlov, mitosis, Java Man and why we fought the Civil War. You may forget about Java Man but you get to keep your degree just the same, and it gets you a job. College is also where they discover new medicines, new kinds of plastic and new herbicides to use in Asia. But everybody knows all that. I want to return to the exploit-enslave-and-petrify part.

It's ironic. Radicals dream midnight police raids, or sit around over coffee and talk with glittering eyes about Repression—about those internment camps that are waiting empty. And all the time Miss Jones does her quiet thing with the kids in third grade.

People like to chat about the fascist threat or the communist threat. But their visions of repression are for the most part romantic and self indulgent: massacres, machine guns drowning out La Marseilleise. And in the meantime someone stops another tenth grader for a hall-pass check and notices that his T-shirt doesn't have a pocket on it. In the meantime the Bank of America hands out another round of high-school achievement awards. In the meantime I grade another set of quizzes.

God knows the real massacres continue. But the machine gun isn't really what is to be feared most in our civilized Western world. It just isn't needed all that much. The kids leave Miss Jones' class. And they go on to junior high and high school and college. And most of them will never need to be put in an internment camp. Because they're already there. Do you think I'm overstating it? That's what's so frightening: we have the illusion that we're free.

In school we learn to be good little Americans—or Frenchmen—or Russians. We learn how to take the crap that's going to be shoveled on us all our lives. In school the state wraps up people's minds so tight that it can afford to leave their bodies alone.

Repression? You want to see victims of repression? Come look at most of the students at San Diego State College, where I work. They *want* to be told what to do. They don't know how to be free. They've given their will to this institution just as they'll continue to give their will to the institutions that engulf them in the future.

Schools exploit you because they tap your power and use it to perpetuate society's trip, while they teach you not to respect your own. They turn you away from yourself and toward the institutions around you. Schools petrify society because their method, characterized by coercion from the top down, works against any substantial social change. Students are coerced by teachers, who take orders from administrators, who do the bidding of those stalwarts of the status quo on the board of education or the board of trustees. Schools petrify society because students, through them, learn how to adjust unquestioningly to institutions and how to exercise their critical thought only within narrow limits prescribed by the authorities. In fact, as long as a heavy preponderance of a nation's citizens are "good students" and are in some way rewarded for their performance, then dissenters and radical thinkers are no threat and can be permitted to express their opinions relatively unmolested. In the United States, free expression, to the extent that we have it, is a luxury commodity made available by the high standard of living and by the efficient functioning of such disguised forms of repression as schooling.

Schools preserve the status quo in two complementary ways: by molding the young and by screening them. Today almost all of the positions of relative power in the United States are reserved for those who have completed the full sixteen-year treatment, and perhaps a little more. Persons who are unwilling to have their minds and bodies pushed around incessantly are less likely to get through and therefore tend to be screened out of the power centers; the persons who do get through are more likely to accept things as they are and to make their own contributions in "safe" areas. Thus corporations and government agencies insist that executive trainees have a bachelor's degree, often without specifying any particular major. The degree, therefore, doesn't represent any particular body of knowledge. What *does* it represent? A certain mentality.

It is true, though, that an increasing number of rebels and freaks are getting through (as well as a much larger number of essentially adjusted students who try to have the best of two worlds by pretending that they are rebels and freaks). The small but noisy student rebellion of recent years has had the effect of bringing to campus a number of drop-ins—dissidents who would not otherwise be there. One friend of mine is an excellent example. He belonged to a Trotskyist youth group as a teenager but threw that over in 1963 because the civil rights movement seemed to be accomplishing more than his youth group was. He had made a few futile attempts at college but realized that he had absolutely no interest in it and furthermore had no time for it. After a couple of years in Los Angeles, he disappeared into the Southern movement: Alabama, Mississippi, Georgia. For a while I lost track of him. Then, last year, I heard from him again; he had just enrolled in San Francisco State College—where the action is. He is typical of a growing minority of students; he may do more or less what's needed to stay in school but he is more than willing to risk being expelled or failed out (two years ago he was risking his life). It is unlikely that college will disarm him.

As the tensions in our society work their way up to the surface, some overt rebellion appears in many settings; certainly it appears in schools, which offer at least a meeting place and staging ground for young middle-class rebels. May it grow in good health. But, as our college presidents are fond of pointing out, the great majority—the great silent majority—are there "not to make trouble but to get an education" (for "education," read "degree").

What about this majority? What is the mentality which employers depend upon our school system to deliver? What is most likely to emerge from the sixteen-year molding and screening process?

Well, a "good citizen" of sorts—isn't that the way they put it on report cards? Thoroughly schooled and ready for GE or IBM or the State Department, the graduate is a skilled, neat, disciplined worker with just enough initiative to carry out fairly complicated assignments but not so much initiative that he will seriously question the assignment itself. He is affably but fiercely competitive with his peers and he is submissive to his superiors. In fact, as long as he has some respect from his peers and subordinates, he is willing to be almost naked of dignity in the eyes of his superiors; there is very little shit he will not eat if there is something to be gained by it. In asserting himself he is moderate, even timid—except when he exercises the power of a great institution, when he himself is the superior, when he puts on some kind of real or figurative uniform. At that point he is likely to assume the sacerdotal mask[1] that his teachers wore. At that point—when he becomes official—his jaw hardens.

This college graduate is positively addicted to rules of all sorts at every level. In fact, should he help to form some club or group, it will probably have by-laws and officers and will follow parliamentary procedure. Even in games—cards, Monopoly, whatever—he is likely to have a passionate respect for the rules and to get bent out of shape if their sanctity is violated.

Ever since his gold-and-silver star days he has been hooked on status and achievement symbol systems. He has a hunter's eye for the nuances of such systems in his work, in his leisure life and in the society at large. He carries a series of grade-point averages in his head and they rise or fall with an invitation to lunch, the purchase of a Triumph TR-2, a friendly punch on the arm from his ski instructor or the disrespectful attitude of a bank teller.

Since grade school, also, he has known how to become mildly enthusiastic about narrow choices without ever being tempted to venture rebelliously out of the field of choice assigned to him. His political world, for example, is peopled with Nixons and Humphreys; its frontiers are guarded by McCarthys and Reagans. He himself has had a taste of politics: he was elected sophomore class president in college on a platform that advocated extending snack-bar hours in the evening. Like Auden's "Unknown Citizen" when there is peace, he is for peace; when there is war, he goes. He doesn't expect a wide range to choose from in politics. His chief arena of choice is the marketplace, where he can choose enthusiastically among forty or fifty varieties of cigarette, without, incidentally, ever being tempted to choose the one variety that will turn him on. His drugs are still likely to be the orthodox ones, the consciousness-contractors: liquor, tranquilizers, a little TV.

---

[1] Sacerdotal here means that the person wearing the mask believes he has assumed divine authority.

He yearns for more free time but finds himself uncomfortable with very much of it. His vacations tend to be well structured. From time to time he feels oppressed and would like to "break out" but he isn't sure what that means. Leaving his family? Starting his own business? Buying a boat? He's not sure.

Let me stop at this point. There is, thank God, a limit to the meaningfulness of such a stereotyped characterization. It hits home in those areas where the college graduate has literally been stereotyped by his upbringing and by the rigid matrix of his schools. But it leaves out what makes him one individual, what makes him real. Doesn't he have a self beyond the stereotype? Isn't he unique— splendid—a center of existence? Isn't he, to use Timothy Leary's phrase, a two-billion-year-old carrier of the Light? Of course. But who sees it? His self has been scared into hiding. The stereotype that has been made of him hides his uniqueness, his inner life, his majesty from our eyes and, to a great extent from his own as well. He's got a sure A in Citizenship but he's failing in self-realization (a subject not too likely to appear in the curriculum).

Let's understand, when we consider this college graduate, that harm has been done not only to him but to society as well. There may, after all, be some of us who assume that dehumanization and standardization are no more than the price that an individual pays in return for a smoothly functioning society. But is that true? Is this man really what's good for society?

Social change is not just the radical's hang-up. It's a means of adaptation, of self preservation. Now, as our technology and our environment change with increasing rapidity, as we acquire ever more awesome resources and more bewildering problems, we need the capacity to recreate our society continually rather than be victimized by it. This, of course, is the sort of thing that gets said a great deal nowadays, but what doesn't get said is that we will not meet this need for rebirth without giving up what we now call schooling. A crisis in civilization—and we are in the midst of several—*demands* the radical thought, the radical will and the profound self-confidence which have been schooled out of our college-educated institutional man. His narrow vision and his submissive conformity aren't good for society; they paralyze it. They are a curse on it.

◤ POINTS TO CONSIDER ◥

Jerry Farber: The Student and Society

1. Why does Farber feel that what is taught in schools is relatively unimportant compared with the ways that schools teach?

2. How does Farber feel that schools are preserving the status quo and petrifying society? Do you agree with him or do you think he is exaggerating the problem?

3. If schools are as repressive as Farber claims, why, according to Farber, are they not changed?

4. What does Farber describe as the characteristics of the "good citizen" turned out by our school system? Do you agree with his description? Do you think it applies to any people you know?

5. Compare the last eight paragraphs of Farber's essay to Fromm's "Personality Packages" (p. 5). What are the similarities?

Drawing by Shirvanian. Copyright, Look Magazine.

Freedom and Learning: The Need for Choice

Paul Goodman
Saturday Review, May 18, 1968

The belief that a highly industrialized society requires twelve to twenty years of prior processing of the young is an illusion or a hoax. The evidence is strong that there is no correlation between school performance and life achievement in any of the professions, whether medicine, law, engineering, journalism, or business. Moreover, recent research shows that for more modest clerical, technological, or semiskilled factory jobs there is no advantage in years of schooling or the possession of diplomas. We were not exactly savages in 1900 when only 6 per cent of adolescents graduated from high school.

Whatever the deliberate intention, schooling today serves mainly for policing and for taking up the slack in youth unemployment. It is not surprising that the young are finally rebelling against it, especially since they cannot identify with the goals of so much social engineering—for instance, that 86 per cent of the federal budget for research and development is for military purposes.

We can, I believe, educate the young entirely in terms of their free choice, with no processing whatever. Nothing can be efficiently learned, or, indeed, learned at all—other than through parroting or brute training, when acquired knowledge is promptly forgotten after the examination—unless it meets need, desire, curiosity, or fantasy. Unless there is a reaching from within, the learning cannot become "second nature," as Aristotle called true learning. It seems stupid to decide a priori[1] what the young ought to know and then to try to motivate them, instead of letting the initiative come from them and putting information and relevant equipment at their service. It is false to assert that this kind of freedom will not serve society's needs—at least those needs that should humanly be served; freedom is the only way toward authentic citizenship and real, rather than verbal, philosophy. Free choice is not random but responsive to real situations; both youth and adults live in a nature of things, a polity, an ongoing society, and it is these, in fact, that attract interest and channel need. If the young, as they mature, can follow their bent and choose their topics, times, and teachers, and if teachers teach what they themselves consider important—which is all they can skillfully teach anyway—the needs of society will be adequately met; there will be more lively, independent, and inventive people; and in the fairly short run there will be a more sensible and efficient society.

It is not necessary to argue for free choice as a metaphysical proposition;[2]

[1] A priori means beforehand.

[2] A metaphysical proposition here is a philosophical abstraction.

it is what is indicated by present conditions. Increasingly, the best young people resolutely resist authority, and we will let them have a say or lose them. And more important, since the conditions of modern social and technological organization are so pervasively and rigidly conforming, it is necessary, in order to maintain human initiative, to put our emphasis on protecting the young from top-down direction. The monkish and academic methods which were civilizing for wild shepherds create robots in a period of high technology. The public schools which did a good job of socializing immigrants in an open society now regiment individuals and rigidify class stratification.

Up to age twelve, there is no point to formal subjects or a prearranged curriculum. With guidance, whatever a child experiences is educational. Dewey's idea is a good one: It makes no difference *what* is learned at this age, so long as the child goes on wanting to learn something further. Teachers for this age are those who like children, pay attention to them, answer their questions, enjoy taking them around the city and helping them explore, imitate, try out, and who sing songs with them and teach them games. Any benevolent grownup—literate or illiterate—has plenty to teach an eight-year-old; the only profitable training for teachers is a group therapy and, perhaps, a course in child development.

We see that infants learn to speak in their own way in an environment where there is speaking and where they are addressed and take part. If we tried to teach children to speak according to our own theories and methods and schedules, as we try to teach reading, there would be as many stammerers as there are bad readers. Besides, it has been shown that whatever is useful in the present eight-year elementary curriculum can be learned in four months by a normal child of twelve. If let alone, in fact, he will have learned most of it by himself.

Since we have communities where people do not attend to the children as a matter of course, and since children must be rescued from their homes, for most of these children there should be some kind of school. In a proposal for mini-schools in New York City, I suggested an elementary group of twenty-eight children with four grownups: a licensed teacher, a housewife who can cook, a college senior, and a teen-age school dropout. Such a group can meet in any store front, church basement, settlement house, or housing project; more important, it can often go about the city, as is possible when the student-teacher ratio is 7 to 1. Experience at the First Street School in New York has shown that the cost for such a little school is less than for the public school with a student-teacher ratio of 30 to 1. (In the public system, most of the money goes for administration and for specialists to remedy the lack of contact in the classroom.) As A. S. Neill[3] has shown, attendance need not be compulsory. The school should be located near home so the children can escape from it to home, and from home to

---

[3] A. S. Neill has been for the past fifty years the director of an English private school called Summerhill which allows children to learn in an atmosphere of freedom and honesty.

it. The school should be supported by public money but administered entirely by its own children, teachers, and parents.

In the adolescent and college years, the present mania is to keep students at their lessons for another four to ten years as the only way of their growing up in the world. The correct policy would be to open as many diverse paths as possible, with plenty of opportunity to backtrack and change. It is said by James Conant that about 15 per cent learn well by books and study in an academic setting, and these can opt for high school. Most, including most of the bright students, do better either on their own or as apprentices in activities that are for keeps, rather than through lessons. If their previous eight years had been spent in exploring their own bents and interests, rather than being continually interrupted to do others' assignments on others' schedules, most adolescents would have a clearer notion of what they are after, and many would have found their vocations.

For the 15 per cent of adolescents who learn well in schools and are interested in subjects that are essentially academic, the present catch-all high schools are wasteful. We would do better to return to the small preparatory academy, with perhaps sixty students and three teachers—one in physical sciences, one in social sciences, one in humanities—to prepare for college board examinations. An academy could be located in, and administered by, a university and staffed by graduate students who like to teach and in this way might earn stipends while they write their theses. In such a setting, without dilution by nonacademic subjects and a mass of uninterested fellow students, an academic adolescent can, by spending three hours a day in the classroom, easily be prepared in three or four years for college.

Forcing the nonacademic to attend school breaks the spirit of most and foments alienation in the best. Kept in tutelage, young people, who are necessarily economically dependent, cannot pursue the sexual, adventurous, and political activities congenial to them. Since lively youngsters insist on these anyway, the effect of what we do is to create a gap between them and the oppressive adult world, with a youth subculture and an arrested development.

School methods are simply not competent to teach all the arts, sciences, professions, and skills the school establishment pretends to teach. For some professions—e.g., social work, architecture, pedagogy—trying to earn academic credits is probably harmful because it is an irrelevant and discouraging obstacle course. Most technological know-how has to be learned in actual practice in offices and factories, and this often involves unlearning what has been laboriously crammed for exams. The technical competence required by skilled and semiskilled workmen and average technicians can be acquired in three weeks to a year on the job, with no previous schooling. The importance of even "functional literacy" is much exaggerated; it is the attitude, and not the reading ability, that counts. Those who are creative in the arts and sciences almost invariably go their own course and are usually hampered by schools. Modern languages are best learned by travel. It is pointless to teach social sciences, literary criticism, and philosophy to youngsters who have had no responsible experience in life and society.

Most of the money now spent for high schools and colleges should be devoted to the support of apprenticeships; travel; subsidized browsing in libraries and self-directed study and research; programs such as VISTA, the Peace Corps, Students for a Democratic Society, or the Student Nonviolent Coordinating Committee; rural reconstruction; and work camps for projects in conservation and urban renewal. It is a vast sum of money—but it costs almost $1,500 a year to keep a youth in a blackboard jungle in New York; the schools have become one of our major industries. Consider one kind of opportunity. Since it is important for the very existence of the republic to countervail the now overwhelming national corporate style of information, entertainment, and research, we need scores of thousands of small independent television stations, community radio stations, local newspapers that are more than gossip notes and ads, community theaters, high-brow or dissenting magazines, small design offices for neighborhood renewal that is not bureaucratized, small laboratories for science and invention that are not centrally directed. Such enterprises could present admirable opportunities for bright but unacademic young people to serve as apprentices.

Ideally, the polis[4] itself is the educational environment; a good community consists of worthwhile, attractive, and fulfilling callings and things to do, to grow up into. The policy I am proposing tends in this direction rather than away from it. By multiplying options, it should be possible to find an interesting course for each individual youth, as we now do for only some of the emotionally disturbed and the troublemakers. Voluntary adolescent choices are often random and foolish and usually transitory; but they are the likeliest ways of growing up reasonably. What is most essential is for the youth to see that he is taken seriously as a person, rather than fitted into an institutional system. I don't know if this tailor-made approach would be harder or easier to administer than standardization that in fact fits nobody and results in an increasing number of recalcitrants. On the other hand, as the Civilian Conservation Corps showed in the Thirties, the products of willing youth labor can be valuable even economically, whereas accumulating Regents blue-books is worth nothing except to the school itself.

(By and large, it is not in the adolescent years but in later years that, in all walks of life, there is need for academic withdrawal, periods of study and reflection, synoptic review[5] of the texts. The Greeks understood this and regarded most of our present college curricula as appropriate for only those over the age

---

[4] The polis here means the community; originally it was the city-state of ancient Greece in which all citizens could speak or act directly to influence the governing of the state.

[5] A synoptic review is an overview or summary.

of thirty or thirty-five. To some extent, the churches used to provide a studious environment. We do these things miserably in hurried conferences.)

We have similar problems in the universities. We cram the young with what they do not want at the time and what most of them will never use; but by requiring graded diplomas we make it hard for older people to get what they want and can use. Now, paradoxically, when so many are going to school, the training of authentic learned professionals is proving to be a failure, with dire effects on our ecology, urbanism, polity, communications, and even the direction of science. Doing others' lessons under compulsion for twenty years does not tend to produce professionals who are autonomous, principled, and ethically responsible to client and community. Broken by processing, professionals degenerate to mere professional-personnel. Professional peer groups have become economic lobbies. The licensing and maintenance of standards have been increasingly relinquished to the state, which has no competence.

In licensing professionals, we have to look more realistically at functions, drop mandarin requirements of academic diplomas that are irrelevant, and rid ourselves of the ridiculous fad of awarding diplomas for every skill and trade whatever. In most professions and arts there are important abstract parts that can best be learned academically. The natural procedure is for those actually engaged in a professional activity to go to school to learn what they now know they need; re-entry into the academic track, therefore, should be made easy for those with a strong motive.

Universities are primarily schools of learned professions, and the faculty should be composed primarily not of academics but of working professionals who feel duty-bound and attracted to pass on their tradition to apprentices of a new generation. Being combined in a community of scholars, such professionals teach a noble apprenticeship, humane and with vision toward a more ideal future. It is humane because the disciplines communicate with one another; it is ideal because the young are free and questioning. A good professional school can be tiny. In *The Community of Scholars* I suggest that 150 students and ten professionals—the size of the usual medieval university—are enough. At current faculty salaries, the cost per student would be a fourth of that of our huge administrative machines. And, of course, on such a small scale contact between faculty and students is sought for and easy.

Today, because of the proved incompetence of our adult institutions and the hypocrisy of most professionals, university students have a right to a large say in what goes on. (But this, too, is medieval.) Professors will, of course, teach what they please. My advice to students is that given by Prince Kropotkin, in "A Letter to the Young": "Ask what kind of world do you want to live in? What are you good at and want to work at to build that world? What do you need to know? Demand that your teachers teach you that." Serious teachers would be delighted by this approach.

The idea of the liberal arts college is a beautiful one: to teach the common culture and refine character and citizenship. But it does not happen; the evidence is that the college curriculum has little effect on underlying attitudes, and most cultivated folk do not become so by this route. School friendships and the community of youth do have lasting effects, but these do not require ivied clubhouses. Young men learn more about the theory and practice of government by resisting the draft than they ever learned in Political Science 412.

Much of the present university expansion, needless to say, consists in federal- and corporation-contracted research and other research and has nothing to do with teaching. Surely such expansion can be better carried on in the Government's and corporations' own institutes, which would be unencumbered by the young, except those who are hired or attach themselves as apprentices.

Every part of education can be open to need, desire, choice, and trying out. Nothing needs to be compelled or extrinsically motivated by prizes and threats. I do not know if the procedure here outlined would cost more than our present system—though it is hard to conceive of a need for more money than the school establishment now spends. What would be saved is the pitiful waste of youthful years—caged, daydreaming, sabotaging, and cheating—and the degrading and insulting misuse of teachers.

It has been estimated by James Coleman that the average youth in high school is really "there" about ten minutes a day. Since the growing-up of the young into society to be useful to themselves and others, and to do God's work, is one of the three or four most important functions of any society, no doubt we ought to spend even more on the education of the young than we do; but I would not give a penny to the present administrators, and I would largely dismantle the present school machinery.

⚔ POINTS TO CONSIDER ⚔

Paul Goodman: Freedom and Learning: The Need for Choice

1. What does Goodman believe about the "need" for education? What arguments does he advance to support his position?

2. What does Goodman say is the main function of education today? Do you agree? Explain.

3. What does Goodman mean when he says, "We can, I believe, educate the young entirely in terms of their free choice . . ."? Why does he feel that this is the best way to learn? Do you agree? Explain.

4. According to James Conant, what percentage of students learn well from books and academic study? What does Goodman think should be done with these students? What does he propose for the other students? What justi-

fication does he give for his proposal? What problems do you think might arise if Goodman's suggestions were put into effect?

5. How does Goodman relate the educational system to the much talked about generation gap?

6. What arts, skills, and professions does Goodman feel schools are particularly ill-suited to teach? What remedies does he suggest? Do you see objections to these suggestions? Explain.

7. What does Goodman mean when he says, "Ideally the polis itself is the educational environment"? Why do you think he chose the word "polis" rather than "city" or "community"?

8. Goodman states, ". . . the evidence is that the college curriculum has little effect on underlying attitudes, and most cultivated folk do not become so by this route." Do you think this statement is accurate? What things affect underlying attitudes? What things "cultivate" people?

9. Do you see your years in school as largely wasted—"caged, daydreaming, sabotaging, and cheating"? What things do you remember happening in school that were truly important to your life? Does this suggest any conclusions as to the necessity of formal schooling?

Science, Education and the Enjoyment of Living

Norman Cousins

Saturday Review, April 20, 1968

Let me show my hand at once. I contend that science tends to lengthen life, and education to shorten it; that science has the effect of freeing man for leisure, and that education has the effect of deflecting him from the enjoyment of living.

What seems to me most significant about the gap between the two cultures, starkly lamented by C. P. Snow, is not so much a difference in background or ambience[1] as the fact of paradoxical effect. The dominant tendency in contemporary education is to teach man how to do things rather than how to exercise creative options. The dominant tendency of science is to emancipate man from doing things, enabling him to preside over more open time then he has known since ancient Greece. The combined result is that man has wondrous new options he is not prepared to recognize or enjoy.

Putting it differently, education trains men to perform. It doesn't put nearly so much effort or imagination into the process of self-discovery and creative development, without which freedom tends to be somewhat circumscribed, even brittle. What we have on parallel tracks, then, is science carrying man in the direction of greater freedom—or at least in a direction that gives him access to options he has never known before—while education carries him in a direction that enables him to be functional rather than resourceful. Thus is produced the most poignant of all questions: What happens to a man when he chronically lives under his productive capacity?

The most costly disease in America is not cancer or coronaries. The most costly disease is boredom—costly for both individual and society. The dominant types of boredom in modern civilization, of course, are directly related to shorter work weeks, shorter work days, earlier retirement, and increased life expectancy. The cause is surging technology, rodent control, conquest of microbes, muscular unionism, and adroit politics.

Leisure time in the contemporary world is potentially man's greatest gift to himself; actually, it is a problem of ghastly dimensions. It has thrown man out of joint. People have more time on their hands than their knowledge, interests, or aptitudes can accommodate. Few things are more terrifying in this world for some persons than an open hour if the TV set is out of order. Their relaxation reflexes have been conditioned by the turning of knobs. If the knob does not produce an image, the result is akin to personal disaster.

Even without respect to the pacifying characteristics of the TV screen, how-

[1] Ambience is cultural environment.

ever, a whole new world of potential leisure has sprung up for which people are unprepared. The shorter work week may produce premature retirement symptoms rather than a condition of creative liberation. That is, available new hours are more likely to lead to helplessness and floundering than to active discovery of exciting new options. Retirement, supposed to be a chance to join the winner's circle, has turned out to be more dangerous than automobiles or LSD. Retirement for most people is literal consignment to no-man's land. It is the chance to do everything that leads to nothing. It is the gleaming brass ring that unhorses the rider.

My concern about education, to repeat, is that it tends to shy away from the requirements of the creative process and therefore from the enjoyment of living. In this sense, it is somewhat indifferent to the possibilities inherent in the prolongation of life. It has yet to develop the techniques that can make it richly relevant to new opportunities for leisure. It is not sufficiently enthralled by the mysteries of the inner universe of the individual and therefore it has little to say to him about the essential encounter with the abstract or the uses of the abstract in giving him an enlarged sense of what is joyously fulfilling. It tends to allow difficulties in defining purpose to obstruct the pursuit of purpose. Such a pursuit may not always be either informed or successful, but it is occasionally exhilarating. It may also lead to a greater sense of what is integral; it can provide nourishment for the subconscious.

There is no objective way of determining whether it is good or bad to have increased leisure time during those years when one is not required or even permitted to be part of the accredited community of producers. My judgment—and, if I am lucky, it will have some basis in abstract thought and not just in observation—is that leisure is an option in freedom and that freedom is good, and that there is no impassable distance between the option of freedom and the full exercise of it.

I do not regard the school as the sole means for making man aware of these options or enabling him to use them. Education transcends the school—or should, if the school is any good. But the school must not become an illusion. It must never assume that the world stands ready to do everything it does not. And one of the most important jobs before the school is to educate for a fuller life and a larger one.

Consider the school's introverted attitude toward nonschool hours. It doesn't adequately use these hours to prepare the individual for doing things productively and enjoyably. The student should be encouraged to turn to leisure-time pursuits that need careful cultivation in a world in which the dominant part of an individual's life will consist of free time.

The school's business, quite properly, consists largely of problem-solving. But the school makes a mistake in chasing the student with problem-solving right into his home. Homework ought to be the means for educating a student in the enjoyment of living, not for hammering home the day's lessons. And the place to begin is early in grade school.

There are intimations of Calvinism[2] in the reluctance of many schools to encourage the student to develop creative leisure-time interests. I see nothing subversive or shattering about giving a student an evening assignment to attend a good motion picture or concert, or read a good novel, or see something worthwhile on TV, or listen to some recordings in classical music, pop, or jazz. This kind of homework can lead to exciting classroom discussion. Good talk is one of the most stimulating and rarest experiences on this planet. The school has an opportunity to make it somewhat less rare. Going even further: the community could do worse than to subsidize a boy of modest means to an evening date with his girl friend on the town, including a visit to the theater and perhaps even some after-theater entertainment.

What I am suggesting is that education can be just as relevant in preparing a person for creative and joyous living and for increased life expectancy as it is in preparing him to be an income-producer and a solid citizen. The will to live and everything that goes with it are indigenous[3] parts of the liberal arts. It is in this direction that education may find its greatest energy and widest area of service. The relationship between the good life and the good society remains the most insistent item on the joint agenda of education and the nation.

POINTS TO CONSIDER

Norman Cousins: Science, Education and the Enjoyment of Living

1. How does science lengthen life? According to Cousins, how does education turn man from the enjoyment of life? How does this "shorten life"?

2. In what way is leisure in our present society like LSD or "the brass ring that unhorses the rider"?

3. What does Cousins mean when he says that education "tends to allow difficulties in defining purposes to obstruct the pursuit of purpose"?

4. How does Cousins think a school should deal with the problem of utilizing leisure time?

5. What is Cousins's attitude toward homework? How does homework conflict with educating people in ways to employ their leisure time? What alternative to homework does he offer?

6. To what extent is Cousins's feeling about the "disease" of boredom in our society similar to Fromm's feeling in "Personality Packages," page 5, about man's transformation into a commodity?

[2] Calvinism is the puritanical religious philosophy which embodies the outlook that toil is good for the soul and that leisure leads to spiritual corruption.

[3] Indigenous means natural and inborn.

Courtesy of Publishers-Hall Syndicate, Inc.

"NO COMMENT."

Courtesy of Publishers-Hall Syndicate, Inc.

Ideas for Investigation, Discussion, and Writing

Education

1. In what sense can public education be considered a mass communication medium like the movies, newspapers, magazines, or television? What do school systems have in common with the other media as means of communication? To what extent are they different? What do these similarities and differences reveal about the function which public education serves in our society? What is your opinion of this function?

2. Write an essay comparing the U.S. education system with that of another country. Do the two systems seem to be attempting to create different kinds of people? How? Which system is the more standardized? Why? What effects, good and bad, does this have on the quality of education? How do fundamental approaches differ? What effects do these differences have?

3. Write an essay discussing the statement: "There is no teaching; there is only learning." To what extent is the statement true? How might this statement be applied to actual teaching situations?

4. Investigate and discuss the problem of student violence. Is there a pattern to events on such campuses as Berkeley, Columbia, San Francisco State? If so, what? What relation does student unrest have to the structure of the modern university? To what extent is the problem linked with specific issues such as the Vietnam war, and to what extent is student unrest only the most visible aspect of a larger problem affecting our entire society?

5. After an investigation of several sources write a summary of what psychology tells us about the process of learning. To what extent are these principles being applied in school today? To what extent are they being ignored? Cite examples in each case. Can you give suggestions as to how they might be put into practice in certain educational situations?

6. Investigate and discuss in a report the principles and applications of programmed learning. To what subjects has the programmed approach been applied? To which subjects does it seem the approach lends itself most readily? To which least readily? What advantages does this method offer? What disadvantages?

7. In an essay describe what you would consider to be the ideal grade school, high school, or college. Give as complete a picture of the school as possible including its enrollment, location, physical structure, courses, rules (if any), and resources. Indicate how many teachers there would be and in what

manner they would teach. As you describe the various facets of your school, explain and justify them where you feel it necessary.

8. Discuss in an essay the following statement by Paul Goodman:

   University education—liberal arts and the principles of the professions—is for adults who know something, who have something to philosophize. Otherwise, as Plato pointed out, it is just verbalization.

   What does this statement imply about the present system of education in this country? Do you agree? Why?

9. Investigate and report on the problems of college admission. To what extent is it true that "only the rich go to college"? What sources of financial aid are available to the student? What are quota systems? Where and how are they used? Does the black student have a harder time getting into college than his white peer? Or, is it easier for him? Why?

10. After consulting several authorities, discuss in an essay the question of what should be the role of a college or university. What role should it play in society? Should it train philosophers or accountants or both? Should it seclude itself from politics and government, or should it serve the government?

A. General Magazines: These popular magazines of news and cultural features regularly contain articles and editorials on the mass media and popular arts and offer reviews of books, films, and television shows as well as good photography, cartoons, and advertising.

Atlantic Monthly, Robert Manning, ed. Atlantic Monthly, Inc., 8 Arlington Street, Boston, Mass. 02116.

Commonweal, James O'Gara, ed. Commonweal Publishing Co, Inc., 23 Madison Avenue, New York, N.Y., 10016.

Ebony, John H. Johnson, ed. 1820 S. Michigan Avenue, Chicago, Ill., 60016.

Esquire, Harold Hayes, ed. Esquire, Inc., 488 Madison Avenue, New York, N.Y., 10022.

Evergreen Review, Barney Rosset, ed. Evergreen Review, Inc., 80 University Place, New York, N.Y., 10003.

Harper's Magazine, Willie Morris, ed. Harper's Magazine, Inc., 2 Park Avenue, New York, N.Y., 10016.

Hudson Review, Frederick Morgan, ed. Hudson Review, Inc., 65 East 55th Street, New York, N.Y., 10022.

Ladies Home Journal, John M. Carter, ed. Downe Publishing Co., 641 Lexington Avenue, New York, N.Y., 10022.

Life, Thomas Griffith, ed. Time-Life, Inc., Rockefeller Center, New York, N.Y., 10020.

Mad Magazine, Albert B. Feldstein, ed. E. C. Publications, Inc., 485 Madison Avenue, New York, N.Y., 10022.

McCalls, Shana Alexander, ed. McCall Corporation, 230 Park Avenue, New York, N.Y., 10017.

Nation, Carey McWilliams, ed. Nation Co., Inc. 333 Sixth Avenue, New York, N.Y., 10014.

New Republic, Gilbert A. Harrison, ed. Robert J. Myers, 1244 19th Street NW, Washington, D.C., 10036.

Newsweek, Osborne Elliott, ed. Newsweek, Inc., 444 Madison Avenue, New York, N.Y., 10022.

New Yorker, William Shawn, ed. New Yorker Magazine, Inc., 25 West 43rd Street, New York, N.Y., 10036.

Playboy, Hugh Heffner, ed. HMH Publishing Co., Inc., 919 North Michigan Avenue, Chicago, Illinois, 60611.

Ramparts, Robert Scheer, ed. Ramparts Magazine, Inc., 495 Beach Street, San Francisco, Calif., 94133.

Redbook Magazine, Sey Chassler, ed. McCall Corporation, 230 Park Avenue, New York, N.Y. 10017.

Saturday Review, Norman Cousins, ed. Saturday Review Inc., 380 Madison Avenue, New York, N.Y., 10017.

Time, Henry A. Grunwald, ed. Time, Inc., 504 North Michigan Avenue, Chicago, Ill., 60611.

B. Special Interest Magazines: The following magazines focus particularly on one of the mass media or popular arts.

American Education, Patricia L. Cahn, ed. U.S. Dept. of H.E.W., U.S. Office of Education, 400 Maryland Avenue SW, Washington, D.C., 20202.

Audio-Visual Communications, Arthur Rosien, ed. United Business Publishers, Inc., 200 Madison Avenue, New York, N.Y., 10016.

A-V Communication Review, Robert Heinich, ed. Association for Educational Communications and Technology, 1201 16th Street NW, Washington, D.C., 20036.

Cineaste: A Magazine for the Film Student, Gary Crowdus, ed. Cineaste Magazine, 27 West 11th Street, New York, N.Y.,

Crawdaddy: A Magazine of Rock, Chester Anderson, ed. Crawdaddy Enterprises, 319 6th Avenue, New York, N.Y., 10014.

Down Beat, Dan Morgenstern, ed. Maher Publishers, Inc. 222 West Adams Street, Chicago, Ill., 60606.

Education Digest, Lawrence W. Prakken, ed. Prakken Publishers, Inc., PO Box 623, 416 Longshore Drive, Ann Arbor, Michigan,

Educational Forum, Harry S. Broudy, ed. J. Richard McElhewy, PO Box A, West Lafayette, Ind., 47906.

Educational Record, Charles G. Dobbins, ed. American Council on Education, 1785 Massachusetts Avenue NW, Washington, D.C., 20036.

Educational Screen and Audio-Visual Guide, Henry C. Ruark, ed. Trade Periodicals, Inc., 434 S. Wabash, Chicago, Ill., 60605.

Educational Television, Henry Urrows, ed. C. S. Tepfer Publishing Co., 140 Main Street, Ridgefield, Conn., 06877.

Films in Review, Harry Hart, ed. National Board of Review of Motion Pictures, Inc., 31 Union Square, New York, N.Y. 10003.

Film Society Review, William A. Starr, ed. American Federation of Film Societies, 144 Bleeker Street, New York, N.Y., 10012.

High Fidelity-Musical America, Leonard Marcis, ed. Billboard Publishing Co., 165 West 46th Street, New York, N.Y., 10036.

Improving College and University Teaching, Delmer M. Goode, ed. 101 Waldo Hall, Oregon State University, Corvallis, Oregon, 97331.

Journalism Quarterly, Edwin Emery, ed. Association for Education in Journalism, School of Journalism, University of Minnesota, Minneapolis, Minn., 55455.

Media and Methods, Frank McLaughlin, ed. Media and Methods Institute, 134 North 13th Street, Philadelphia, Pa., 19107.

Modern Photography, Herbert Keppler, ed. 165 West 46th Street, New York, N.Y., 10036.

P M I (Photo Methods for Industry), Merwin Dembling, ed. Gellert Publishing Corp., 33 West 60th Street, New York, N.Y., 10023.

Schwann Record Catalog. W. Schwann, Inc., 137 Newbury Street, Boston, Mass., 02116.

Sight and Sound, Penelope Houston, ed. 155 West 15th Street, New York, N.Y., 10011.

Stereo Review, William Anderson, ed. Ziff-Davis Publishing Co., 1 Park Avenue, New York, N.Y., 10016.

Television Quarterly, David Manning White, ed. National Academy of Television Arts and Sciences, 54 West 40th Street, New York, N.Y., 10018.

TV Guide, Merrill Panitt, ed. Triangle Publications, Inc., PO Box 400, Radnor, Pa.

TV-Radio Mirror, David Ragan, ed. McFadden-Bartell Corporation, 205 East 42nd Street, New York, N.Y., 10017.

Today's Education (Journal of the N.E.A.), Mildred Sandison Fenner, ed. National Education Association of the United States, 1201 16th Street NW, Washington, D.C., 20036.

II. Books

The following books focus on one or more of the mass media and popular arts. Although a few older volumes are included, the emphasis is on books published in the past fifteen years and particularly on those published in the past five to eight years.

A. The Mass Media and Popular Arts in General

Blum, Eleanor. *Reference Books in the Mass Media.* Urbana, Ill.: University of Illinois Press, 1952.

Carpenter, Edmund S. and H. Marshall McLuhan, eds. *Explorations in Communications: An Anthology.* Boston: Beacon Press, 1960.

Casty, Alan, ed. *Mass Media and Mass Man.* New York: Holt, Rinehart, and Winston, Inc., 1968.

Colby, Venita, ed. *American Culture in the Sixties.* New York: H. W. Wilson Company, 1964.

Deer, Irving and Harriet A. Deer, eds. *The Popular Arts: A Critical Reader.* New York: Charles Scribner's Sons, 1967.

Dexter, James A. and David Manning White. *People, Society and Mass Communications.* New York: The Free Press, 1964.

Emery, Edwin, Philip Ault, and Warren Agee. *Introduction to Mass Communication.* New York: Dodd, Mead and Co., 1960.

Hall, James B. and Barry Ulanov, eds. *Modern Culture and the Arts.* New York: McGraw-Hill, 1967.

Hall, Stuart and Paddy Whannel. *The Popular Arts.* New York: Random House, 1964.

Klapper, Joseph T. *The Effects of Mass Communication.* New York: The Free Press, 1960.

Lacy, Dan. *Freedom and Communications.* Urbana: University of Illinois Press, 1961.

Larsen, Otto N., ed. *Violence and the Mass Media.* New York: Harper and Row, 1968.

McLuhan, H. Marshall. *Counterblast.* New York: Harcourt, Brace, and World, 1969.

————. *The Gutenberg Galaxy: The Making of Typographic Man.* Toronto: University of Toronto Press, 1962.

————. *The Mechanical Bride: Folklore of Industrial Man.* Boston: Beacon Press, 1967.

———— and Quentin Fiore. *The Medium is the Massage: An Inventory of Effects.* New York: Bantam Books, 1967.

————. *Understanding Media: The Extensions of Man.* New York: McGraw-Hill, 1964.

Rivers, William. *The Opinion Makers.* Boston: Beacon Press, 1965.

Rosenberg, Bernard and David Manning White. *Mass Culture: The Popular Arts in America.* New York: The Free Press, 1957.

Schramm, Wilbur. *Communications: A Book of Readings.* Urbana: University of Illinois Press, 1960.

————. *The Process and Effects of Mass Communication.* Urbana: University of Illinois Press, 1954.

————. *Responsibility in Mass Communication.* New York: Harper and Row, 1957.

Stearn, Gerald E., ed. *McLuhan: Hot and Cool.* New York: Dial Press, 1967.

Steinberg, Charles C. *Mass Media and Communication.* New York: Hastings House, 1966.

B. Advertising

Baker, Stephen. *Visual Persuasion.* New York: McGraw-Hill, 1961.

Buzzi, Giancarlo. *Advertising: Its Cultural and Political Effects.* Translated by B. David Garmize. Minneapolis: University of Minnesota Press, 1967.

Foster, G. Allen. *Advertising: Ancient Market Place to Television.* New York: Criterion Books, 1967.

Goulart, Ronald. *Assault on Childhood.* Los Angeles: Shelborne Press, 1969.

Lucas, Darrell Blaine. *Measuring Advertising Effectiveness.* New York: McGraw-Hill, 1963

McGinnis, Joe. *The Selling of the President.* New York: Trident Press, 1968.

Ogilvy, David. *Confessions of an Advertising Man.* New York: Atheneum Press, 1963.

Packard, Vance. *The Hidden Persuaders.* New York: D. McKay Co., 1957.

Seldin, Joseph J. *The Golden Fleece: Selling the Good Life to Americans.* New York: Macmillan, 1963.

Sondage, Charles H. and Vernon Fryburger. *Advertising Theory and Practice.* Homewood, Ill.: Richard D. Irwin, 1958.

Watkins, Julian L. *One Hundred Greatest Ads, Who Wrote Them, and What They Did.* New York: Dover Publications, 1959.

C. Journalism, Cartoons, and Publishing

Agee, Warren K. *The Press and the Public Interest.* Washington, D.C.: Public Affairs Press, 1968.

Alsop, Joseph and Stewart. *The Reporter's Trade.* New York: Reynal and Co., Inc., 1958.

Bailey, Herbert Smith. *The Art and Science of Book Publishing.* New York: Harper and Row, 1970.

Bond, Frank F. *An Introduction to Journalism: A Survey of the Fourth Estate in All Its Forms.* New York: Macmillan, 1961.

Bradley, Duane. *The Newspaper: Its Place in a Democracy.* New York: Van Nostrand-Reinhold Co., 1965.

Casey, Ralph D. *The Press in Perspective.* Baton Rouge, La.: Louisiana State University Press, 1965.

Clor, Harry M. *Obscenity and Public Morality: Censorship in a Liberal Society.* Chicago: University of Chicago Press, 1954.

Couperie, Pierre. *A History of the Comic Strip.* New York: Crown Publishers, 1968.

Dembner, S. Arthur and William E. Massee. *Modern Circulation Methods.* New York: McGraw-Hill, 1968.

Dressel, Paul L. *Liberal Education and Journalism.* New York: Columbia University Press, 1960.

Feiffer, Jules. *The Great Comic Book Heroes.* New York: Dial Press, 1965.

Fisher, Paul. *Race and the News Media.* New York: Praeger, 1967.

Freeman, Gillian. *The Undergrowth of Literature.* London: Nelson, 1967.

Gerald, J. Edward. *The Social Responsibility of the Press.* Minneapolis: University of Minnesota Press, 1963.

Gross, Gerald, ed. *The Responsibility of the Press.* New York: Fleet Publishing Corporation, 1966.

Gunther, Max. *Writing the Modern Magazine Article.* Boston: The Writer, Inc., 1968.

Hacket, Alice Payne. *Sixty Years of Best Sellers: 1895–1955.* New York: Bowker, 1956.

Hohenberg, John. *The New Front Page.* New York: Columbia University Press, 1966.

————. *The News Media: A Journalist Looks at His Profession.* New York: Holt, Rinehart, and Winston, 1968.

Kobre, Sidney. *The Development of American Journalism.* Dubuque, Iowa: W. C. Brown Co., 1969.

Lindstrom, Carl E. *The Fading American Newspaper.* Garden City, N.Y.: Doubleday, 1960.

Lowenthal, Leo. *Literature, Popular Culture, and Society.* Palo Alto, Calif.: Pacific Books, 1968.

MacDougall, Curtis D. *The Press and Its Problems.* Dubuque, Iowa: W. C. Brown Co., 1964.

Madison, Charles Allan. *Book Publishing in America.* New York: McGraw-Hill, 1966.

McGaffin, William and Erwin Knoll. *Anything But the Truth: The Credibility Gap.* New York: Putnam, 1968.

McLean, Ruari. *Magazine Design.* New York: Oxford University Press, 1969.

Merill, John Calhoun. *The Elite Press: Great Newspapers of the World.* New York: Pitman Publishing Corporation, 1968.

Mott, Frank L. *American Journalism.* New York: Macmillan, 1962.

Peterson, Theodore B. *Magazines in the Twentieth Century.* Urbana: University of Illinois Press, 1964.

Rothstein, Arthur. *Photojournalism: Pictures for Magazines and Newspapers.* New York: American Photographic Book Publishing Co., 1965.

Rucker, Frank W. and Herbert Lee Williams. *Newspaper Organization and Management.* Ames, Iowa: Iowa State University Press, 1965.

Schramm, Wilbur. *One Day in the World's Press: Fourteen Great Newspapers on a Day of Crisis—November 2, 1956*. Stanford, Calif.: Stanford University Press, 1959.

Short, Robert L. *The Gospel According to Peanuts*. Richmond: John Knox Press, 1965.

_____. *Parables of Peanuts*. New York: Harper and Row, 1968.

Steinberg, Sigfrid. *Five Hundred Years of Printing*. New York: Criterion Books, 1959.

Tebbel, John. *The Compact History of the American Newspaper*. New York: Hawthorne Books, 1969.

White, David Manning and Robert Abel, eds. *The Funnies: An American Idiom*. New York: The Free Press, 1963.

Wolseley, Roland E. *Understanding Magazines*. Ames, Iowa: Iowa University Press, 1965.

D. Radio and Television

Arlen, Michael J. *The Living Room War*. New York: Viking Press, 1969.

Arons, Leon and Mark A. May. *Television and Human Behavior: Tomorrow's Research in Mass Communication*. New York: Appleton-Century-Crofts, 1963.

Barnouw, Erik. *A History of Broadcasting in the United States*. New York: Oxford University Press, 1966.

Bluem, A. William. *Television in the Public Interest*. New York: Hastings House, 1961.

Blumler, Jay G. *Television in Politics*. Chicago: University of Chicago Press, 1969.

Bogart, Leo. *The Age of Television: A Study of the Viewing Habits and the Impact of Television on American Life*. New York: Friedrich Ungar, 1958.

Carboni, Erberto. *Radio and Television Publicity*. Greenwich, Conn.: New York Graphic Society, 1959.

Carnegie Commission on Educational Television. *The Impact of Educational Television*. Urbana, Ill.: University of Illinois Press, 1960.

CBS. *The Eighth Art*. New York: Holt, Rinehart, and Winston, 1962.

Chester, Edward W. *Radio, Television, and American Politics*. New York: Sheed and Ward, 1969.

Dizard, Wilson P. *Television—A World View*. Syracuse, N.Y.: Syracuse University Press, 1966.

Elliott, William Y., ed. *Television's Impact on American Culture*. East Lansing, Mich.: Michigan State University Press, 1956.

Emery, Walter B. *National and International Systems of Television Broadcasting: Their History, Operation, and Control*. East Lansing: Michigan State University Press, 1969.

Friendly, Fred W. *Due to Circumstances beyond Our Control.* New York: Random House, 1967.

Gattegno, Caleb. *Towards a Visual Culture.* New York: Guterbridge and Diensfrey, 1969.

Green, Maury. *Television News: Anatomy and Process.* Belmont, Calif.: Wadsworth Publishing Co., 1969.

Hilliard, Robert L. *Radio Broadcasting.* New York: Hastings House, 1967.

Hodgkinson, A. W. *Screen Education: Teaching a Critical Approach to Cinema and Television.* Paris: UNESCO, 1964.

Lang, Kurt and Gladys Engel Lang. *Voting and Nonvoting: Implications of Broadcasting Returns Before Polls are Closed.* Waltham, Mass.: Blaisdell Publishing Co., 1968.

McGinniss, Joe. *The Selling of the President.* New York: Trident Press, 1968.

National Educational Television and Radio Center. *Impact of Educational Television.* Urbana, Ill.: University of Illinois Press, 1960.

Roe, Yale. *Television Dilemma: Search for a Solution.* New York: Hastings House, 1962.

Schramm, Wilbur. *People Look at Educational Television.* Stanford, Calif.: Stanford University Press, 1963.

————. *Television in the Lives of Our Children.* Stanford, Calif.: Stanford University Press, 1961.

Skornia, Harry Jay. *Problems and Controversies in Television and Radio.* Palo Alto, Calif.: Pacific Books, 1968.

————. *Television and the News.* Palo Alto, Calif.: Pacific Books, 1968.

————. *Television and Society: An Inquest and Agenda for Improvement.* New York: McGraw-Hill, 1965.

Smead, Elmer E. *Freedom of Speech by Radio and Television.* Washington, D.C.: Public Affairs Press, 1959.

Sopkin, Charles. *Seven Glorious Days, Seven Fun-Filled Nights.* New York: Simon and Schuster, 1968.

Steiner, Gary A. *People Look at Television.* New York: Alfred A. Knopf, 1963.

Summers, Robert E. *Broadcasting and the Public.* Belmont, Calif.: Wadsworth, 1966.

Weinberg, Meyer. *TV in America: The Morality of Hard Cash.* New York: Ballantine Books, 1962.

White, David Manning and Richard Averson. *Sight, Sound, and Society: Motion Pictures and Television in America.* Boston: Beacon Press, 1968.

Wood, William Almon. *Electronic Journalism.* New York: Columbia University Press, 1967.

E. Photography

Boucher, Paul Edward. *Fundamentals of Photography.* Princeton, N.J.: Van Nostrand, 1963.

Braive, Michel F. *The Photograph: A Social History.* New York: McGraw-Hill, 1966.

Brandt, Bill. *Shadow of Light.* New York: Viking Press, 1966.

Capa, Cornell, ed. *The Concerned Photographer.* New York: Grossman, 1968.

Cartier-Bresson, Henri. *The World of Henri Cartier-Bresson.* New York: Viking Press, 1968.

Cousteau, Jacques Yves. *The Living Sea.* New York: Harper and Row, 1963.

Croy, Otto Roman. *Creative Photography.* London: Focal Press, 1965.

Eisenstaedt, Alfred. *Witness to Our Time.* New York: Viking Press, 1966.

Evans, Walker. *American Photographs.* New York: Doubleday for the Museum of Modern Art, 1961.

Feininger, Andreas. *The Complete Photographer.* Englewood Cliffs, N.J.: Prentice-Hall, 1965.

Germar, Herb. *The Student Journalist and Photojournalism.* New York: Richard Rosen Press, 1967.

Gernsheim, Helmut and Alison Gernsheim. *A Concise History of Photography.* New York: Grosset and Dunlap, 1966.

Hillson, Peter J. *Photography: A Study in Versatility.* Garden City, N.Y.: Doubleday, 1969.

Hymers, Robert P. *The Professional Photographer in Practice.* London: Fountain Press, 1964.

Karsh, Yousuf. *Karsh Portfolio.* London: Nelson, 1967.

Langford, Michael J. *Basic Photography.* New York: Focal Press, 1965.

Larmore, Lewis. *Introduction to Photographic Principles.* New York: Dover Publications, 1965.

Lyons, Nathan, ed. *Photographers on Photography.* Englewood Cliffs, N.J.: Prentice-Hall, 1966.

———. *Toward a Social Landscape.* New York: Horizon Press, 1967.

Miller, Thomas H. and Wyatt Brummitt. *This Is Photography, Its Means and Its Ends.* Rochester, N.Y.: The Case-Hoyt Corporation for Doubleday, 1963.

Newhall, Beaumont. *The History of Photography from 1839 to the Present Day.* New York: Doubleday for the Museum of Modern Art, 1964.

Rhode, Robert Bartlett. *Introduction to Photography.* New York: Macmillan, 1965.

Steichen, Edward, ed. *The Family of Man.* New York: MACO Magazine for the Museum of Modern Art, 1955.

F. Motion Pictures

Agee, James. *Agee on Film.* New York: Ivan Oblensky, 1958.

Arnheim, Rudolph. *Film As Art.* Berkeley, Calif.: University of California Press, 1957.

Battock, Gregory, comp. *The New American Cinema.* New York: E. P. Dutton, 1967.

Bazin, André. *What Is Cinema?* Berkeley, Calif.: University of California Press, 1967.

Bobker, Lee R. *Elements of Film.* New York: Harcourt, Brace, and World, 1969.

Carmen, Ira H. *Movies, Censorship, and the Law.* Ann Arbor, Mich.: University of Michigan Press, 1966.

Carvie, Peter. *Seventy Years of Cinema.* South Brunswick, N.J.: A. S. Barnes, 1969.

Crowther, Bosley. *The Great Films: Fifty Golden Years of Motion Pictures.* New York: Putnam, 1967.

Fenin, George N. and William K. Everson. *The Western Film: From Silents to Cinerama.* New York: Grossman Publishers, Inc., 1962.

Ferguson, Robert. *Group Film-Making.* London: Studio Vista, 1969.

Fulton, Albert R. *Motion Pictures: The Development of an Art from Silent Films to the Age of Television.* Norman, Okla: University of Oklahoma Press, 1960.

Geduld, Harry M., comp. *Film Makers on Film Making.* Bloomington, Ind.: Indiana University Press, 1967.

Houston, Penelope. *The Contemporary Cinema.* Baltimore: Penguin Books, Inc., 1963.

Jacobs, Lewis. *The Emergence of Film Art.* New York: Hopkinson and Blake, 1969.

————. *An Introduction to the Art of Movies.* New York: The Noonday Press, 1960.

Kael, Pauline. *I Lost It at the Movies.* Boston: Little, Brown, and Co., 1965.

————. *Kiss, Kiss, Bang, Bang.* Boston: Atlantic, Little, Brown, and Co., 1968.

Kauffmann, Stanley. *A World on Film.* New York: Harper and Row, 1966.

Knight, Arthur. *The Liveliest Art.* New York: Macmillan, 1957.

Knight, Derrick. *A Long Look at Short Films.* Oxford, N.Y.: Pergamon Press, 1968.

Kuhns, William and Robert Stanley. *Exploring the Film.* Dayton, Ohio: G. F. Pflaumm, 1968.

Lawson, John H. *Film: The Creative Process.* New York: Hill and Wang, 1960.

Lindgren, Ernest. *The Art of the Film.* New York: Macmillan, 1963.

MacCann, Richard Dyer. *Film: A Montage of Theories.* New York: E. P. Dutton, 1966.

Macgowan, Kenneth. *Behind the Screen: The History and Techniques of the Motion Picture.* New York: Delacorte Press, 1965.

Mallery, David. *The School and the Art of Motion Pictures.* Boston: National Association of Independent Schools, 1966.

Mascelli, Joseph U. *The Five C's of Cinematography: Motion Picture Filming Techniques Simplified.* Hollywood, Calif.: Cine/Grafic Publications, 1965.

Montagu, Ivor. *Film World: A Guide to Cinema.* Baltimore: Pelican Books, 1968.

Peters, J. M. L. *Teaching About the Film.* New York: UNESCO Publications, 1961.

Randall, Richard. *Censorship of the Movies*. Madison, Wis.: University of Wisconsin Press, 1968.

Renan, Sheldon. *An Introduction to the American Underground Film*. New York: E. P. Dutton and Co., 1967.

Sarris, Andrew. *Film*. Indianapolis: Bobbs Merrill, 1968.

Spottiswoode, Raymond. *Film and Its Technique*. Berkeley, Calif.: University of California Press, 1967.

Stephenson, Ralph and J. R. Debrix. *Cinema as Art*. Baltimore: Penguin Books, 1966.

Stewart, David, ed. *Film Study in Higher Education*. Washington, D.C.: American Council on Education, 1966.

Talbot, Daniel. *Film*. New York: Simon and Schuster, Inc., 1960.

Taylor, John Russell. *Cinema Eye, Cinema Ear: Some Key Film Makers of the Sixties*. New York: Hill and Wang, 1964.

White, David Manning, ed. *Sight, Sound, and Society*. Boston: Beacon Press, 1968.

G. Popular Music

Baez, Joan. *Daybreak*. New York: Dial Press, 1968.

Cohn, Nik. *Rock from the Beginning*. New York: Stein and Day, 1969.

Courlander, Harold. *Negro Folk Music*. New York: Columbia University Press, 1963.

Eisen, Jonathan, comp. *The Age of Rock: Sounds of the American Cultural Revolution*. New York: Random House, 1969.

Engel, Lehman. *American Theatre Music*. New York: Macmillan, 1967.

Ewen, David W., ed. *American Popular Songs from the Revolutionary War to the Present*. New York: Random House, 1966.

————. *The Story of America's Musical Theatre*. Philadelphia: Chilton Book Co., 1968.

Gahr, David and Robert Shelton. *The Face of Folk*. New York: Citadel Press, 1968.

Garland, Phyl. *The Sound of Soul*. Chicago: H. Regnery Co., 1969.

Jones, Leroi. *Black Music*. New York: W. Morrow, 1967.

————. *Blues People: Negro Music in White America*. New York: W. Morrow, 1963.

Kiel, Charles. *Urban Blues*. Chicago: University of Chicago Press, 1966.

Malone, Bill C. *Country Music*. Austin: University of Texas Press, 1968.

Marks, J. *Rock and Other Four Letter Words: Music of the Electric Generation*. New York: Bantam Books, 1968.

Patterson, Lindsay, comp. *The Negro in Music and Art*. New York: Publishers Company, 1967.

Peck, Ira. *The New Sound, Yes.* New York: Four Winds Press, 1966.

Rublowsky, John. *Popular Music.* New York: Basic Books, 1967.

Shapiro, Nat, ed. *Popular Music.* New York: Adrian Press, 1964.

Shemel, Sidney. *More About This Business of Music.* New York: Billboard Publishing Co., 1967.

————. *This Business of Music.* New York: Billboard Publishing Co., 1964.

Stambler, Irwin. *Encyclopedia of Popular Music.* New York: St. Martin's Press, 1965.

Swanwick, Kieth. *Popular Music and the Teacher.* Oxford, N.Y.: Pergamon Press, 1968.

Ulanov, Barry. *A History of Jazz in America.* New York: Viking Press, 1952.

H. Education

Fallon, Berlie J., ed. *Educational Innovation in the United States.* Bloomington, Ind.: Phi Delta Kappa, 1966.

Farber, Jerry. *The Student as Nigger.* North Hollywood, Calif.: Contact Books, 1969.

Goodman, Paul. *Compulsory Miseducation and The Community of Scholars.* New York: Vintage Books, 1966.

Harris, Seymour E., ed. *Challenge and Change in American Education.* New York: Wiley, 1965.

Keats, John. *The Sheepskin Psychosis.* Philadelphia: Lippincott, 1965.

Leonard, George B. *Education and Ecstasy.* New York: Delacorte Press, 1968.

Mayhew, Lewis B. *Higher Education in the Revolutionary Decades.* Berkeley, Calif.: McCutchan Publishing Co., 1967.

Martin, Warren B. *Alternative to Irrelevance.* Nashville: Abingdon Press, 1968.

Martin, William T., ed. *Curriculum Improvement and Innovation.* Cambridge, Mass.: R. Bentley, 1966.

Miles, Matthew B., ed. *Innovation in Education.* New York: Columbia University Press, 1964.

Neill, A. S. *Freedom—Not License!* New York: Hart Publishing Co., 1966.

————. *Summerhill: A Radical Approach to Child Rearing.* New York: Hart Publishing Co., 1960.

Postman, Neil and Charles Weingartner. *Teaching As a Subversive Activity.* New York: Delacorte Press, 1969.

Schrag, Peter. *Voices in the Classroom.* Boston: Beacon Press, 1965.

Silberman, Charles E. *Crisis in the Classroom.* New York: Random House, 1970.

Taylor, Harold. *Students without Teachers.* New York: McGraw-Hill, 1969.

Thornton, James W. *New Media and College Teaching.* Washington, D.C.: National Education Association, 1968.

Woodring, Paul. *Higher Learning in America.* New York: McGraw-Hill, 1968.

Index of Names, Subjects, and Sources

Names in this index are cited as subjects and not as authors. Page numbers in *italic* following names of publications indicate selections from these publications; other citations represent the publications as subjects.

Index of Names, Subjects, and Sources